Praise for Growing Out Loud

Rashid Nuri's story is one of life, liberty and the pursuit of something greater than happiness – a civic agricultural system for all. From a pioneering Black man at Harvard in 1960s with an endless thirst for knowledge and meaning, to a globetrotting farmer across the planet, Nuri's Growing Out Loud takes us on his journey and reshapes our thoughts on the scale and importance of urban food systems. Through the chapters of his life, we cheer him on during perennial blooms of prosperity and root for his resilience through cultural and ecological firestorms that attempt to besiege his course, time after time.

At the confluence of the book's major themes lies a garden, Truly Living Well Center for Natural Urban Agriculture, where the only forbidden fruit is that which is neither eaten nor shared. Standing tall as a lighthouse of nutrition, Truly Living Well serves as Atlanta's vanguard urban agricultural institution.

Mario Cambardella
City of Atlanta Urban Agriculture Director

Growing Out Loud is a book that everyone who cares about our collective future should read and learn from. It's a fun book to read, not only documenting a highly accomplished life, but also taking an unflinching look at what is wrong with our global system of food production. As a teacher, agitator, mentor and friend, Rashid Nuri has demonstrated how to serve the higher good for humanity. As a leader in urban agriculture, he has pointed the way for all of us living in urban areas to grow, distribute, and consume locally grown food. He put all those lessons to work in an urban farm known affectionately as Truly Living Well, a slice of paradise in southwest Atlanta that serves as a living example for the world.

Bill Bolling
Founder, Atlanta Community Food Bank & Food Well Alliance

Rashid Nuri has, by any measure, led a remarkable life. His life has paralleled the struggles of Black and Brown people globally to break free from the physical and mental bondage of colonialism and to grapple with the difficult task of feeding their populations. His journey is unique. It crosses decades and national boundaries. He has journeyed through academia, the corporate world, temples, jazz clubs and grassroots communities. His journey has helped him to develop a profound understanding of agriculture and the many lessons it holds for humanity.

Baba Rashid is multi-dimensional. *Growing Out Loud* chronicles his struggle for identity, his love of family, his desire for fundamental social change and his deep appreciation for jazz and other Black art forms. It is the holism that comes from having lived such a rich life that informs his views of spirituality, liberation and agriculture.

Growing Out Loud comes at a critical time when there is a rising interest in sustainable, regenerative agriculture as a way of nurturing greater food sovereignty, repairing our fragile social fabric and protecting the environment. In many ways, our very survival as a species depends on doing agriculture differently.

Rashid Nuri is a guide, a shining light and a builder. He can legitimately be called a wise elder. As such, he has embraced his responsibility of summing up his life experiences and the wisdom that has derived from those experiences, and sharing them with those of us who will continue the work of growing healthy food, reconnecting people with the earth and making freedom. *Growing Out Loud* makes an important contribution towards equipping us for the work ahead.

Malik Yakini
Executive Director, Detroit Black Community Food Security Network

This is a beautiful book. So open. So vulnerable. Raw with the truth of who you are and how you have become. It is an honor to call you Brother.

This is the story of how a Black Baby Boomer grew himself up to become Baba Rashid, father of many and much. He tells how he has grown people and communities and provides a blueprint for eating well, living well, and growing what is needed to make a world that is a healthy place for all people. Politics, Economics, Agriculture and Love. A powerful recipe for us all.

Kikanza Nuri-Robins
Organization Development Consultant

Growing Out Loud is a highly engaging account of one man's innate desire to make a meaningful contribution during his time on this planet. Nuri has given a beautiful testament to the power of education to open eyes, change lives and reclaim our responsibility to the Earth. An Indian saying states that we do not inherit the planet, but rather we borrow it from our children and generations to come. When we consider that civilization as we know it is 6,000 years old, the detrimental consequences of industrialization over only 200 years cannot be overstated. Rashid Nuri reminds us that our time on this planet is short. Humans need shelter, water and food for survival. The monocropping practices instilled by the industrial food production complex have had a devastating effect on the very environment that sustains humankind. Rashid's story inspires us to use that time to create powerful change that impacts our communities and our Earth home as a whole.

Dhiru Thadani
Architect & Urbanist

The book [Rashid] has written about his life is so appreciated. In it he shares how his passion for a healthier food system evolved over time. This includes the lessons he learned from his experiences in all realms of the food system: from local food production to corporate agribusiness; to the government's role in agriculture; to the infrastructure of organizations and outlets that support and teach youth and adults about healthy organic food production and, importantly, digging your hands in the soil. As Rashid says, by "digging your hands in the soil" you become "grounded."

Heather Gray
Former Director of Communications, Federation of Southern

What a refreshing classic! Growing Out Loud: Journey of a Food Revolutionary is an autobiographical journey of Baba K. Rashid Nuri, an African American agricultural icon. The book begins with a young man entering full manhood who seeks a purpose-driven life by sheer will, determination and faith. As he matriculates through college and street life, he faces multiple ordeals, opportunities and situations. We, the readers, get a glimpse of the world through the eyes of an intelligent Black man, trying to make a difference. From Massachusetts, to San Diego, India, Nigeria and several places in between, K. Rashid Nuri witnesses agriculture, as it is the basis of freedom around the world.

After realizing that he can make a greater impact in America, K. Rashid Nuri returns to the States to create Truly Living Well, a community farm and educational institution for agriculture. As lifelong friendships aid in its progression, TLW faces its own ordeals and growing pains. As the journey comes to an end, the story doesn't, as TLW has taken flight within the community, giving life to youth and adults looking to agriculture as a life-altering love affair that started with the vision of a revolutionary icon, K. Rashid Nuri.

Peace and happy reading,
Bryan R. Ingram

Growing Out Loud

Journey of a Food Revolutionary

K. Rashid Nuri

The Nuri Group, LLC
Atlanta

Acknowledgments

———————

This manuscript is written for my grandchildren: Troy Horton, Sofia Nuri, Kadin Nuri, Nylah Nuri, Kai Nuri, Trevor Horton, Koa Nuri, and all who may show up in years to come. There are so many questions I did not ask my ancestors that I wish I had. Perhaps this book will provide my children and grandchildren answers when they figure out the questions they could have asked. As Luther Vandross sang, "I'd love to dance with my father again!"

Njemile Z. Ali is an intellectual giant. She has served as researcher, editor and essentially been a partner in this endeavor. Thank you very much.

My family, siblings, wives and mothers of my children are the thread that binds these stories together. They have given me the life that this book describes.

Too many people to mention have asked to read these tales. Thanks go to all for the inspiration.

Peace.

Table of Contents

—ↄ/ʕ/ɔ—

Foreword

—⚏⚏⚏—

Growing Out Loud: Journey of a Food Revolutionary
is an amazing work of history, science, business, politics, philosophy and faith, intermingled, juxtaposed and extrapolat-
ed throughout one extraordinarily well-lived life. I've known
Rashid Nuri for 50 years now, and thought I had a pretty good
grasp of his background, experience and philosophical underpinnings—until I read this truly engaging and enlightening autobiographical work. Rashid has lived a life of discovery and
even intrigue that most of us can only imagine or read about,
and this book allows us to do both.

Rashid shares his multi-layered life story, which is captivating
by itself, but he also unfolds a wealth of political and economic
historical background that gives context to "exclusive food
industry insider information." He addresses a myriad of
contemporary issues and pressing concerns, i.e. monopolies,
minimum wage, disease, neo-colonialism, Africa, eugenics,
White Nationalism and urbanism, just to name a few. Yet he
never strays too far from food, its production, distribution,
accessibility and quality.

We all should know Rashid Nuri as the go-to Guru of the urban organic agricultural movement, and this book clarifies how and why he earned and deserves that status. What Growing Out Loud also does though, is it captures the depth, breadth, height of a life that has loved and pursued knowledge, understanding, purpose, application and service for the benefit of all and for the fulfillment of his God-given calling. This Food Revolutionary has *truly lived well*.

Imam Plemon T. El-Amin
Atlanta Masjid of Al-Islam

Growing Out Loud

Journey of a Food Revolutionary

Prologue

——⟨⟨∅∅⟩⟩——

God. There is no God but He, the Living, the Self-subsisting, Eternal. No slumber can seize Him nor sleep. His are all things in the heavens and on earth. Who is there can intercede in His presence except as He permits? He knows what (appears to His creatures as) before or after or behind them. Nor shall they compass anything of His knowledge except as He wills. His Throne does extend over the heavens and the earth, and He feels no fatigue in guarding and preserving them for He is the Most High, the Supreme (in glory).

Quran Sura II:255 - Ayatu'l-Kursi

It is simply service that measures success.

George Washington Carver

INTRODUCTION
The Revolutionary's Backpack

There is a food uprising happening in America. We live under a commercial food system that is broken and beyond repair. It demands replacement. Urban agriculture is a solution. A paradigm shift has already taken place.

True revolution is evolving from the urban rebellions of the 1960s. Social and community structures that were destroyed in urban centers fifty years ago are being replaced with systems that address the essential needs of the people. Fundamentally, communities need control over their own food, clothing, shelter and education.

Catalyzing the new paradigm of community control is the New Food Movement. In order to have a viable community, you must be able to feed, clothe and shelter your people. All health, all wealth, all life comes from the soil. The New Food Movement takes on the imperative of local control by bringing the production of naturally grown, nutritious food close to where people live. 82% of Americans live in urban centers, according to 2018 data from the Population Reference Bureau. The United Nations 2018 data project predicts that 68% of the global population will be urban by 2050.

Across the nation, urban food revolutionaries are growing crops wherever they can find a patch of soil. Vacant lots, abandoned fields, balconies and prison yards are just a few of the places being transformed into oases and community gathering spaces. Urban dwellers are being reacquainted with the land and the growth cycles of the planet. Likewise, homesteaders, women and small farmers are transforming the rural landscape. Thousand-acre monocropping, with no actual food for miles around, is being replaced with naturally grown vegetable gardens, organic farms and humane ranches. Culinary artists are growing herbs and vegetables in farm-to-table operations that provide a holistic experience for workers and patrons alike.

This book describes the life and times of one food revolutionary, whose food odyssey began during the turbulent 1960s and continued through the innovation-driven new millennium. As an elder revolutionary, I am offering my journey in the context of a set of principles and practices that marked my growth, and the growth of the food revolution.

These principles and practices both summarize the spirit of the revolutionary and serve as reminders and course correctors when the going gets tough. My work has always been risky, both personally and professionally. I had to travel with both a compass and a safety net. Self-awareness, surveillance, strategy and skills, sustenance, structure, synergy and service filled my backpack and served me well. I hope and trust my younger and newer comrades will also find them useful.

Of all my experiences on four of Earth's seven continents, I have found service to be supremely rewarding. The conscious action of working toward the future that I envision has been a healing balm for my inner struggles and a place maker in my search for community. The sense of making a contribution has shaped the track of my fervent race from birth toward its inevitable twin. Along the track, the work of many who gave their service and passed the baton showed me a way out of the dark and into the light of my own soul.

What is the opposite of death? Most people say life. I say it is birth. We are born into this life, and each of us eventually dies. What we have is the surprisingly short period between birth and death to actually make a contribution.

It is not good enough to stand around waiting for someone else to do the work. Having benefited from the service of titans who came before, I will not accept less than the best of myself and those with whom I work. As soon as I hear somebody say, "That's good enough," I know they have not done the best that they can do, all they could do. Service—especially diligent service—gives meaning to today's actions. We must be of service. We must make a contribution. We must create the world that we want the future to be. It is important that we all strive with our innate talents and learned skills, to do the best that we can, to be the best people that we can possibly be and create the future in which we want to live.

Life has taught me in my 70 years to stay focused, to stay in the moment. I'm still learning that. If I spend too much time thinking about outcomes, I get lost. Does the end justify the means? Not on my track. I believe the means, the process, is what's most important, the integrity that we bring to the moment. Tomorrow is the now, which heralds its approach, but never ever arrives. Constantly thinking about what's going to happen tomorrow sets you up to miss what's right in front of you. Staying focused and in the moment is essential. The expression, think globally and act locally, encompasses time, space, policies and people.

Growing Out Loud is an uncompromising, unapologetic polemic that offers solutions as well as arguments. It is also a how-to for community builders and food growers, woven around the memoir of my career in agriculture. Beyond discussing the 360° of food production, the book is also about personal growth, intellectually and spiritually.

I began writing six years ago, but could not finish the book until I had created an ending for the stories. I am a builder. One of the greatest stories of my life is birthing and growing the Truly Living Well Center for Natural Urban Agriculture in Atlanta. I have committed my life to growing food, growing people and growing community. This work brought many of the tributaries of my search for service into a single rushing river. Relinquishing leadership of Truly Living Well provided an opportunity to create a first ending for the stories. Another birth is in progress.

K. Rashid Nuri
Atlanta 2019

Part I

SELF-AWARENESS

―――∽∾∾∽―――

Pouring libation as homage to the ancestors is the opening act of meetings in many communities around the world. Respect is given to the people who have preceded us in history and on whose shoulders we stand as we make our way through this life. Knowing where you come from is an important part of self-awareness. Knowledge of ancestors often shapes and sharpens our worldview.

Being honest with oneself is both the main door and central corridor of self-awareness. Conscious knowledge of one's own character, feelings, motives and desires requires paying attention to what's going on inside us. The ongoing process of self-awareness requires introspection and the ability to recognize oneself as an individual, separate from the environment.

As we come into consciousness as children, we begin to know that we are separate from our parents, caregivers and experiences. It can be difficult to realize that our conscious observations—what we see with our own eyes—may be in conflict with what we have been taught. Even more difficult is the recognition that our behavior may be in conflict with what we think we believe. The process of coming to know yourself can be painful, as we take an honest look at the good, the bad and the ugly within. Introspection involves inspection—turning over thoughts, feelings, attitudes and behaviors to explore their origins and choose whether we want to keep them or let them go. Our health and success depend on those choices.

The rewards for this inner work are magnificent. We come to know the essential being, the Inner One who connects with God and Creation. Self-acceptance, clarity and the ability to engage in synergistic relationships are enabled. An understanding and appreciation of self can power empathy, curiosity, analytics, belief, passion, optimism and adaptability.

Re-living my life and work through this narrative forces me to examine every nook and cranny of my existence, hopefully in an open and honest manner. Writing furthers my inner work, helping me process my thoughts, feel connected and be more at peace with myself. With any luck, you—the reader—will gain points of insight that will help to power your revolutionary journey.

I observe myself, and so I come to know others.

Lao Tzu

Chapter 1

Beginnings

What is more revolutionary than a seed? Once buried, the seed bursts through clay, sand, rock, concrete—whatever it takes, to fulfill the purpose imprinted in its DNA. While it takes the shape designated by the markings of heredity, the taste and nutritional balance in the growing plant are greatly influenced by the source of its nourishment, the soil in which it was planted. Nature and nurture conspire to create change.

Are revolutionaries born? Or are they molded from the very clay of family and social conditions in which they were planted? I was planted in soil nourished by the fire of global liberation movements in Africa, Asia and Latin America.

I was also born with the blood of Jamaican Maroons pounding through my heart, urging me to push every boundary, to go all out for full freedom—now. First, I found the inner freedom to break some of the bonds of my home environment. It was an environment that first, held my Maroon roots in secret, and second, seemed—to my young mind—bound and determined to tie me to a stifling non-acceptance of who I was.

I broke away. I lived my life away from home by day and returned to the watering hole at the latest hour permitted to prepare for another day of outside adventures.

Each of us is born with a nature and nurture that, often unwittingly, prepares us for a particular mission in life. Our pains and challenges become our passions and driving forces. Our self-awareness grows in concentric circles. The hope is that we come to see that even actions and non-actions inspired by the worst of motives have given us the fuel to create the change that is imprinted on our souls. No one said it was going to be easy.

"You're not from around here, are you?"

You'd think the pain of that question would diminish after hearing it over and over again. It did not. The incessant travels of my youth began at the tender age of 4 or 5; they took me to 14 schools and many states before I graduated from high school in beautiful San Diego, California. At each port of call, I struggled to find my place among the locals. Although I was curious and outgoing, I never gained the treasured status of "one of us." As it turned out, those travels were not just the standard luggage of being a Navy brat. There was more. But it was only after high school graduation and the dawning of manhood that a partial truth was revealed.

John Wesley Woodard was the sailor that my mom married after she and my father divorced. The many places that my family landed, courtesy of the U.S. Navy, were not as random as they seemed at the time. I found out that my stepfather had some choice in the matter. I believe he chose so many years on the West Coast because he and my mother wanted to get me as far away as possible from my father in New York. I was 19 before I found my father again.

Not only did my mother and stepfather separate me from my father, they also robbed me of an early connection with my name. Names are very important. They give off vibrations that affect people's behavior. I was born Keith Freeman Robins at City Hospital in Boston, Massachusetts. I can only imagine the person that I might have become if I had known my paternal family history and the significance of the name Freeman.

The focusing power of time allows me to look back on my early experiences and see how they influenced the revolutionary spirit that grew as I did.

Mary Freeman was my paternal grandmother's maiden name. She married William Robins, my paternal grandfather, and became Mary Freeman Robins. My grandmother was a Maroon from Mandeville in the parish of Manchester in the county of Middlesex, Jamaica. The Maroons (Spanish: Cimarron, "fierce" or "unruly") were runaway slaves who established free settlements throughout Spanish-conquered territories in Latin America and the Caribbean. In Jamaica, the Maroons settled in the mountains in 1655, taking advantage of the British takeover from the Spanish at that time. Fierce fighters and excellent tacticians, the outnumbered Maroons successfully defended their settlement against two rounds of open warfare against British armed forces. The first peace agreement in 1739 brought about some years of peace between the Maroons and the colonists. In 1795, the new governor of Jamaica, Balcarres, chose to fight the Maroons again, against the advice of local British settlers.

Once more, the Maroons held out against a larger contingent of British soldiers, and a peace agreement was reached. Balcarres immediately violated the agreement. When the Maroons laid down their arms, the governor had many of them arrested and transported to Nova Scotia and later, to Sierra Leone. My grandmother was a descendant of those who managed to avoid capture and continued to build a free economy.

I learned none of this when I was gathering family history from my mother to complete an 8th-grade genealogy paper. Neither she nor my stepfather wanted to acknowledge my grandmother's name. Instead, they told the story of the name being taken by freed slaves, conveniently leaving out the most relevant personal details: that I carried the name of my grandmother's paternal line, who were born and raised in

Jamaica. I did not learn the Jamaican Maroon connection until much later.

Grandfather William Robins was a merchant marine born in Kingston, Jamaica. My grandmother was from a prominent family from Mandeville, in the Jamaican mountains. My grandfather traveled a lot and was very fortunate to marry a woman of my grandmother's stature. They migrated from Jamaica through Ellis Island in the early 1900s and settled in Queens, New York. My father, Winston Hersley Robins, was born in Corona, Queens on 2 May 1925. Except for his time at Boston University and the Army, Pop spent his entire life in the New York area.

My mother's family, on the other hand, is proud to be pure New England Yankee as far back as I can trace those roots. The only exception was my great-great-grandfather, a Native American from North Dakota named John Reesby. He had traveled through Canada down into New England and lived in Chelsea, Massachusetts. The extended family disparagingly referred to Grandpa Reesby as "The Indian."

Mom was born Barbara Estelle Latimer in Lynn, Massachusetts on Boston's north shore. She grew up in a three-generation household, headed by her grandmother, Beatrice Cornelia Reesby Harris, whom we called Nana. Nana, the daughter of "The Indian," was the matriarch who lovingly spoiled everyone, so much so that her daughter (my Grandmother, Gogo) never left home, despite having five children of her own. Of her five children, my mother was Gogo's only daughter. Gogo wanted to be called Grandmother, but as a baby, Gogo was the best I could pronounce. The name stuck for multiple generations. We learned years later that "Gogo" means "grandmother" in many Southern African languages, such as Shona.

My parents gifted me a love for music, which would later both drive and accompany my search for community. They were studying music when they met, Pop at Boston University and my mother at the Duncanberry School of Music. In the late 1940s, it was unusual for Black folk to attend either of these institutions;

it was quite special for both my parents. Their shared love for music is still alive in me. To this day, I constantly hear music in my head. People tell me I'm humming when I don't even know it. The first thing I do when I get home is turn on some music. Music entered my soul and has never left. It's not a far stretch to imagine that my career might have turned toward the music industry at some level. In fact, when I wrote the "what I want to be when I grow up" paper in the 8th grade, I chose to be a musician.

My Maroon bloodline had other plans.

Based on family stories and legends, I concluded early in life that I was a Thanksgiving surprise for my young parents. My birthdate on 31 August 1948 certainly makes the math work for backdating my conception. They brought me home to a place on West Springfield Street in the South End, just down the street from City Hospital. We later moved to the Lenox Street projects in Roxbury. I've been back to Boston trying to find those landmarks, and they are just not there. The sensation of having parts of my personal history vanish feels a lot like the words that I heard so often over the years. Although they were not meant to be hurtful, the words continued to sting deeply: "You're not from around here, are you?" Those words and losses have helped to feed my drive to make a lasting contribution, to build communities that will not vanish without a word or a trace.

Apparently, my parents' capacity to be together vanished, along with many of the places that marked their union. Their separation created the first void in my chest, one that I have yet to fill completely. Divorce is a pathology that runs throughout my entire family history, and it has not left me untouched. The marriages of my great-grandparents, grandparents and parents all ended in divorce. Mine too. Three times!

I never met Nana's husband, Will Harris, with whom she had two children. Although Nana and Mr. Harris never divorced, they lived separately for decades. The principal reason my grandmother Gogo and her husband Frances E. Latimer divorced is likely because my grandfather pursued women and fathered at least 14 other children. He was a distant nephew of Lewis H. Latimer, the man who invented the filament that made electric lights possible. I have no idea what he did for a living, but he socialized with musicians and entertainers throughout New England. Perhaps we have him to thank for my mother's love of music.

The family pattern of divorce resulted in my having only one sibling with whom I share both parents, my sister Kikanza. I am the eldest of a clan of nine siblings from six parents. My mother bore six children: me, Kikanza, Hodari, Shirin, Michelle and Jim, in that order. My sister Grace was named after her mother, who was of Barbados descent and my father's second wife.

Mom, God rest her soul, truly believed in marriage. She did it often enough. After I had gone to college, she married her third husband, Virgil David Johnson. The mother of his two children had died, so DJ and Julie came into the family and were raised by my mother when they were very young. I did not grow up with DJ and Julie, but my younger siblings did.

Kikanza and I are 16 months apart in age. She has these vivid memories of what happened inside our house that I really don't have. Most of my memories are outside of the house. Obviously, there was discord that I have blocked out of memory. I did not get along with my stepfather, that's for sure. John Woodard was born in Mississippi and raised in Indianapolis. He retired from the Navy as an E-7 Chief Radioman, considered by many as near top of the profession for an enlisted man. I know he did the best he could, but he died a very troubled man. Still, he was the one who started the travels that showed me a lot of this country. In many ways, I credit those experiences with preparing me for my life's work.

I remember leaving the house as often as possible looking for different adventures, and I always seemed to find them. I joined the Cub Scout and Boy Scout troops, played intramural sports and participated with many school clubs. It was likely my insatiable curiosity that urged me to join after-school clubs, or perhaps just not wanting to return to a crowded, but somehow empty household. When junior high school and high school came along, I got involved in student government and politics. By that time my nascent cultural identity and desire for social change were seeking pathways for expression.

I would leave the house early in the morning for 7:00 a.m. classes, come home at suppertime, do homework, go to bed, then get up and do it all over again. I can remember playing some board games when we were younger, particularly Monopoly, but I don't have really strong memories of family in that sense. One of my scant family memories was the year we cut down our own Christmas tree from the beautiful old growth forest surrounding our neighborhood in Whidby Island, Washington. A lot of families sit down and have grand discussions at dinner; I don't remember doing that as a child. Despite so many people around, I remember my youth with a sense of aloneness.

A theme of aloneness has run through my life. My sense of being the outsider is part of my baggage, part of the stuff that I carry while trying to find a sense of place. The flip side is that, because I have an interest in people and I look to find areas of commonality rather than difference, I've been able to get along with people wherever I went. They appreciated the fact that I would demonstrate an interest, rather than a disdain for them and their culture. I've spent a lot of my life trying to fit in, trying to be accepted, while at the same time being a revolutionary and a pioneer. I realize that I was often overcompensating, overachieving in an attempt to be accepted. That yearning for acceptance walked hand-in-hand with a genuine commitment to excellence. The difficulty came when trying to distinguish one from the other.

My family was upper lower class at best. We were fortunate to have military housing, commissary privileges and good medical care, courtesy of the U.S. Navy. Those amenities did give my family a leg up, compared to some of my classmates and others in the community. At the same time, there was no weekly allowance for me. If I wanted to have spending money, I had to earn it. And I did. I have been working hard all my life. The practical work ethic that I established early has lasted a lifetime. I used to tell my children I began working at 8 years old, when I sold TV Guides door-to-door. That was not quite accurate.

Many years ago, my mother sent me a stack of memorabilia. Among the greeting cards, report cards and event programs, I found a letter that I wrote to my great grandmother Nana. Taped across the top of the letter were two dimes and a nickel. I wrote, "I'm sending you the money that I borrowed. I earned it doing yard work." The date of the letter proves that I was actually 7 years old, so my children can never say it was just one of those stories parents like to tell. I used to get up early and go to the commissary to carry out groceries and fetch carts for change. Other times I sold newspapers and earned three cents of a ten-cent paper.

Of all the places that I have traveled, I have to admit that my favorite is the San Diego of my youth, even though it now only exists as a memory. It was the place I lived the longest during my formative years. I finished Montgomery Junior and Kearny Senior High School there. I primarily lived in Linda Vista, which means "beautiful view" in Spanish. The area lived up to its name. We lived ten minutes from the beach and thirty minutes from the mountains.

The city is built right on the Pacific Ocean. White sand beaches with 3 to 6-foot rolling waves abound. We could go to Imperial Beach, Point Loma, Ocean Beach, Dog Beach, Mission Beach, Mission Bay, Pacific Beach, Black's Beach, La Jolla, Torrey Pines. I spent many summer days on those beaches, primarily Mission Beach. The summer before 10th grade, I missed only three days of body surfing on the beach, despite attending two sessions of summer school and having a job. You could go the world's finest zoo in Balboa Park and to the Tamale Factory in Old Town, where we made our own rolled tacos, or visit Tijuana with all of its many splendors. San Diego was an idyllic place to grow up.

It was a blue-collar, highly integrated military transient

community. At that time, San Diego had 27 military bases, clearly making it a military town. Black, Mexican and White families lived together in relative harmony. I felt safe. I enjoyed being young. I enjoyed the city. We were in walking distance from our schools. Of all the Black folk who went to school with me, only one person was actually born in San Diego. Everybody else came from someplace else. People migrated from Texas and Louisiana for jobs in construction and defense manufacturing. California back in the fifties and sixties was a place where people came to start a new life, to create a new identity, just like Atlanta is today.

I liked school. I loved to read books about people and places. I began reading the comic page of the newspaper at age three. I cannot remember a time when I wasn't reading. My mother and grandparents kept reading material in front of me, and I loved libraries. When the library had contests in the summer to see who would read the most books, I always won. Looking back, I realize I was not competing against other children.

I had a rich inner life into which I could escape through my books. The challenge for me was to see how many books I could complete in the time frame allotted. It was an internal competition. I particularly enjoyed reading biographies and histories. I remember a series of blue hard-covered books that were biographies, primarily of Americans, written for young people. Challenging myself to read books and encountering the lives of great men and women through biography inspired and motivated me all my life to be and do my best.

The first inkling that I would take a path toward social change happened in high school. Rev. Martin Luther King said, "The arc of the universe bends toward justice." Even the shortest line contains an arc with seeds of justice. Ultimately, these seeds will blossom throughout the whole. One indicator of this is humanity's incessant push for fairness and equity. The arc of my life bent toward building strong communities by establishing sustainable systems of nourishment.

When I ran for Kearney High School student body president in 1965, I prepared a platform of ten things that I wanted to accomplish while I was in office. I think my platform was unique. Most school campaigns were popularity contests, yet I strove to provide substance over rhetoric. One of the things on my list was to have a fresh fruit and juice machine installed on campus as an alternative to all the soda and candy that was available to students. Looking back, that was pretty revolutionary. Schools today still don't have fresh fruit and real juice available on a widespread basis. I certainly did not know it was a portent of things to come and the beginning of my work in agriculture and community building.

I did very well in high school academically and was very much involved in school politics. Running for Student Body President, my campaign slogan was the double entendre, "Put a little color in your life." I was also president of the San Diego Association of Student Councils, and Representative to the Board of Education. I was the President of all the presidents and would go to Board of Education meetings representing the interests of all the students. I took that responsibility very seriously. Rev. George Smith was Chairman of the School Board at that time. I saw him many years later, and he told me how much of a pain in the ass I was. I said, "Yes, sir, that was true."

High school volunteering and other extracurricular activities wound up informing my career choices. Nature, nutrition and work were consistent themes. One summer, I helped build dioramas as an assistant to an elder artist at the Board of Education. Our dioramas were three-dimensional nature scenes that were placed on display in the Board of Education building. I had a very lucrative job working as a bag boy at Safeway grocery store in Linda Vista. I began asking for that job when I was 14, and they said I couldn't work until I was 16. As soon as I was 16, they gave me the job. I belonged to the Retail Clerks' Union. We made a whopping $1.65 an hour, which was good money back in the early 60s. At that time, Coke-a-Colas were a nickel, Hershey bars were five cents, and gasoline was probably thirty-five cents a gallon. So, a dollar sixty-five cents an hour was good money for a high school boy back in those days—a good, solid job. The first year I had the job, I was happy to be able to buy gifts for my family. I was most excited to present a small television to my mother for Christmas.

Travel and change are motifs that started at age three or four and continued to run throughout my adult life. I've always gone to new places and would build and construct organizations and activities. I like taking an idea, a concept, and making it practical—organizing it, building it, putting it together. Whether it was in high school, making a list of things that I wanted to accomplish during my senior year as the student body president, or working with the poverty program and building the Roxbury, Massachusetts Businessmen's Association. There has always been something that I was putting together, building, constructing and creating.

I am convinced that there is a discernable pattern in the lives of each one of us, especially those of us who have a penchant for pushing the boundaries of the status quo. Following those patterns leads to a clearing in the woods of daily experience. In this clearing, the light of purpose is unshaded by the surrounding foliage. Moments of certainty activate previously dormant genes in revolutionaries, and they begin to express those innate tendencies through conscious action.

Self-awareness continued to unfold for me in concentric circles. It would be years before I understood how and why I ran into brick walls in my work of creating change. For me, the need for a new way was as clear as sunshine in the meadow. The need was not so clear for the powers that were. Often—most times, I would say—I did not manage the projects I developed and built. I would pass the work on to the next set of creative individuals for ongoing management. Frequently, I was forced to pass it on. Those in control wanted me out.

Obstacles can provide psychic fuel in the same way that nutrition provides biological food. The wild ride of my youth had been a deliberate attempt to separate me from half of my roots. It was a sinister motive that would help prepare me for a divine purpose. I had no idea where all those travels would eventually take me. In spite of the watered-down version of my family history that Mom and my stepfather represented to me, they could not suppress the fierce determination for freedom that coursed through my veins. I reclaimed that birthright with a name of my own choosing, that ultimately proved to encapsulate my life's work.

My name is Keith Rashid Nuri. Keith is a Scottish name that means, "He comes to the battle." I show up. Rashid is derived from ar-Rashid, one of the 99 names of God found in the Holy Quran, and translates as "the right guide." Nuri is from an-Nur, "the light." Rashid and Nuri are both Arabic names. Together, my name means: "He comes to the battle as a guiding light." My personal Orisha is Ogun, from the West African Yoruba cosmology. Ogun is the builder. Ogun comes and prepares the world for man to live safely and correctly. My field of work has been agricultural development. Agriculture was given to me as a career path, and it is the mode, the means through which I am able to give service and create the world in which I want to live. I continue to build the world in which I want to see my children, grandchildren and progeny live.

I have lived on the lip of insanity,
wanting to know reasons,
knocking on a door. It opens.
I have been knocking from the inside!

Jalāl ad-Dīn Muhammad Rūmi

Chapter 2

Harvard One

One day, I was walking through the campus of Kearny High School, when a teacher called to me and said, "I want you to sign up for my class." David P. Hermanson taught American Government and social studies. I can't say he changed my life, but he was certainly one of the most influential persons during my last two years of high school. Mr. Hermanson challenged me academically during the school year, as well as in the two summer classes I studied under him. Originating from Iowa, Mr. Hermanson was very conservative in his political views, but encouraged me to think outside the box. He helped me to see the world in a broader sense than my narrow youthful perspective.

As my guidance counselor for college admission, Mr. Hermanson wrote the letters of recommendation for me in the fall of 1965. In applying to college, I was either very lucky or very stupid. I submitted applications to only two schools, Harvard and Stanford. Harvard was the only college I wanted to attend. I think it was Gogo who planted that seed in my head. Stanford recruited me for my student political acumen, so I had a backup if Harvard rejected me. But they didn't. I was a National Merit Scholar and received a full academic scholarship to Harvard College.

My application to Harvard was contrary to the wishes of my parents. "It's too far from home…You'll never adjust to the weather…the people…homesick…scared…rejected." An endless tirade of reasons. "Don't go to Harvard. Perhaps Stanford, Berkeley—stay at home." Perhaps they objected because Harvard was near New York and my father.

Whatever their reasons, I was not deterred. I plowed forward with my application, acceptance and preparation. Somehow, in the midst of the hullabaloo, I managed to send a graduation announcement to my father. Needless to say, that did not make things better at home.

When my stepfather found out, he was highly incensed. His angry outburst must have come when Pop's response landed in our mailbox. John Woodard must have thought he and my mother had been successful in causing me to forget about my father. Not a chance. Certainly, the distance and lack of communication had created an emotional detachment. Surprisingly, I had bounced through my youthful adventures without a sense of missing my father. Yet, he was always part of my consciousness. I was not going to forget him. My graduation was a major event in my life. I wanted my father to know about it, at least, even if he wasn't able to be there.

After my acceptance to Harvard was announced in newspapers and on television in San Diego, several White boys came up to me in the hallways at Kearny High School and said, "You don't deserve to be at Harvard; the only reason you got in is because you're Black." Wow. That really hurt. It was the beginning of a major transition that would shed light on how my personal experiences were part of much larger social realities. My self-awareness was expanding to include my place in the world.

The summer after my high school graduation in 1966, I worked at a Peace Corps training facility based at the University of California San Diego. We were preparing volunteers for work in Nigeria. Two men that I met that summer, David Crippens and Sam Carradine, had a profound and lasting influence on my intellectual future. They gave me books to read. The Autobiography of Malcolm X by Alex Haley was my first real exposure to the Nation of Islam.

Two of my classmates at Kearny grew up in the Nation, but they did their best to fit in, so I had not learned much about the teachings. David and Sam spent hours counseling me on how a young Black man should think and act in contemporary society. They raised my consciousness on matters of race, using a surprising array of sources. One source was The Godfather by Mario Puzo. We discussed how the book is an allegory of American history. Puzo's narrative illustrated the interconnection of law and politics, capital and corruption in the building of America. This is the kind of information these two men were putting in my head.

I turned 18 in August. By the time my birthday came, I had taken the Greyhound bus from San Diego to Boston to begin my college career at Harvard. I rode all the way across the country by myself. It felt like second nature—travel was in my blood. There was no fear, just get on the bus and go to school.

Most of my mother's family still lived in New England. In addition to my grandmothers, I had uncles, aunts, cousins and lots of family friends who warmly welcomed me back to the region of my birth. I had not seen most of those folk for many years. It was nice to be reacquainted with that side of the family.

My New England kin were middle class black people who worked as school administrators, teachers, small business owners, etc. My grandmother, Gogo, began her career while working as the elevator operator at the offices of The Lynn Daily Item in 1943 and ultimately became librarian for the paper. She retired in 1975. They were regular community folk, who all still attended the same Bethel African Methodist Episcopal Church in Lynn, Massachusetts, across the street from the house where Mom grew up.

I have described my childhood as being part of an upper lower-class family. In reality, we were poor Black folk, just like the White and Hispanic people living in my neighborhood. At the time, I was somewhat ignorant of class distinctions. Harvard truly changed that.

There were 1200 students in the Harvard freshman class of 1966. About fifty were Black, and this was a major increase. Three years earlier, only ten Black students were admitted, and this included the women of Radcliffe College. It was during the mid-60s that the school began admitting "lower class" Black students, in an effort to make the University look more like the demographics of America. My eldest son attended Harvard a quarter century later. By that time, there were more Black students in his class than we had in the entire school when I was there.

Only two people from San Diego County were accepted at Harvard that year. We were both Black, and became roommates. I soon learned that many of my Black classmates were solid middle- and upper-class folk, whose way of life was totally new to me; it was really a culture shock. I never knew that Jack and Jill, a social organization for upwardly mobile Black children, even existed until I was 19 years old. I had no idea what that organization was about. Later, I learned that it was a social service organization, started by a group of Black mothers in Philadelphia, with chapters across the country. Today, Jack and Jill of America, Inc. counts 40,000 family members under the organization's umbrella of 230 chapters. Their website describes "a membership organization of mothers with children ages 2-19, dedicated to nurturing future African American leaders by strengthening children through leadership development, volunteer service, philanthropic giving and civic duty." I'm certain that young people who passed through their training were much better prepared than I was to enter schools like Harvard.

For me and many other Black students in my class, it was disconcerting to be invited to a sherry sip at four o'clock in the afternoon—what is that? We were asked to wear coats and ties to breakfast, lunch and dinner. Before and after admission, classmates and others challenged me, saying I did not deserve to be admitted into Harvard. Staff and Harvard students told us that certain behaviors, common to young Black folk, were considered unbecoming to a Harvard man. We played loud music on campus, doo-wopped in the Harvard yard under streetlights and dressed casually in the dining hall. Harvard just wasn't used to young Black folk being comfortable in their own skins. Survival at the school demanded the ability for Black students to code-switch, i.e., as Dubois pointed out, live in two realities, one Black and one White.

I lived on campus for only one semester. My youthful aspiration to attend the school had come to seem misguided and uninformed. I didn't like Harvard, particularly at that time in the mid-60s. I did not like the association, what it represented or the expectations that came with being a "Harvard man." Nor did the school administrators like how many of the Black students approached the institution. I remember once a man said to me, "That's not the way a Harvard man is supposed to act."

I said, "What are you talking about? I am a Harvard man."

Many of the classes, however, were intellectually stimulating. It was rewarding to have classes with professors who were world-renowned. I took biology from Nobel Prize winner George Wald, who discovered the benefits of Vitamin A for vision. Wald chose to teach first-level Biology class, so he could help to train the youngest minds on campus. He loved having after-class rap sessions with students on the state of the world. James Watson, who decoded DNA, taught Molecular Biology. He was boring. Martin Kilson was the first tenured Black faculty member at Harvard. He taught my first class in the Government Department on African Politics. Kilson was the fifth generation of his family to graduate from Lincoln University in Pennsylvania. He really knew his stuff, and he was totally irreverent toward his Harvard faculty colleagues.

I had a Black house tutor who used to speak with a clipped, affected British accent. I can remember him saying, "I usually don't have tea with freshman. But we will make an exception in your case." This brother was from Louisiana talking all that pretentious stuff. I didn't like any of that. I soon realized that I was fundamentally uncomfortable at Harvard. There was nobody there who could help me adjust, so I went in search of community. Although I was still enrolled at Harvard, I went out to the streets of Boston and New York to continue my education.

I moved in with my Uncle Kenneth E. Latimer and his family. Uncle Kenneth was eighteen months older than my mother. He and I had great fun together; he was as much a friend as an uncle and remains so today. The family lived on Blue Hill Avenue, next door to the welfare office where the King riots began in 1968.

I was consciously searching for community. My childhood sense of self had been shattered, beginning with the Harvard preview that I received in the hallway at Kearney High. I deeply longed for a sense of belonging. I felt I needed to be in the Black community, and ran from the embourgeoisement process that was Harvard. In hindsight, I was searching for an authentic Negro experience, or so I thought. My search took me deep into layers of the Black community that had been foreign to me. I needed to know who I was. It was self-awareness or bust. I received a tremendous education, in every way you can imagine.

I worked in all the programs associated with President Lyndon Johnson's War on Poverty. We organized a job-training program. When I was with the Area Planning Action Council, we created the Roxbury Businessmen's Association. I would divide up the food we bought collectively with the small corner grocers in Roxbury. During the delivery trips, I had the opportunity to observe how they ran their businesses. The most important thing I learned was the difference between a cash flow statement and a profit and loss statement. Those brothers and sisters had cash in their registers and thought they had money to buy a big car, not understanding that they had more debts than cash. I learned how to make the distinction between their situations and business people who did not have money in the register, but who also did not have any debts. Those were lessons that I've been able to utilize all my life.

I organized a trip from the Boston area to New York. We took 250 people to visit the Rockefeller Center, the United Nations and the Apollo Theatre, and have lunch at a truck stop. Most of them had never been outside their neighborhoods; they didn't even know Boston, never mind New York. The Apollo Theatre did not sell advance tickets; you had to get in line and purchase admission tickets on the spot. I convinced Charles "Honi" Coles, the great tap dancer who worked as production manager at the Apollo, to sell 250 tickets for our group from Boston. Taking on that level of responsibility at the age of 18, I gained a great deal of confidence in my ability to organize and relate to people.

In between all that community organizing, I ran the streets of Boston and New York. I got to hear fabulous music while I explored East Coast nightlife. I created a fake ID so I could get into the jazz clubs. I guess the people on the door thought, if this boy worked that hard to create an ID card to get in, we need to let him hear the music. I was finding and exploring what would become lifelong enthusiasms.

I listened to Miles Davis at Lenny's on the Turnpike; I heard Ahmad Jamal play Poinciana; Carmen McRae at Satch's; Thelonious Monk at the Vanguard in New York. I heard so many of the great jazz musicians. I would go to Slugs and Pee Wee's in the East Village of New York, Connelly's on Tremont Avenue in Boston. I did happy hour at the Rainbow Lounge. I frequented the Sugar Shack, with acts like Funkadelic, Sam and Dave, Peaches and Herb and the Temptations—all those top name groups that were coming through town. I had a ball. I've always loved music. Music is my real passion. To this day, I can sit down and sing the jazz solos from recordings of that music. That's what we were doing when I was young—listening

31

to music. Just loving it.

I had been socially sheltered in high school. Once I got out of San Diego, I fully made up for any socio-cultural deficits. I had a great time. I absorbed a lot that has served me well, just in terms of the "mother wit" that I developed. I was not a street person in any sense when I was in high school, just a nerd, president of everything and academically oriented. I grew to become the social director during my freshman year. Folk came to me to know where to find a party. Getting away from home and exploring the big cities on the East Coast was an invaluable experience for me. I loved it!

In fact, I earned my first degree from the streets. Pimps and hustlers and dope dealers and junkies were some of my instructors. My other teachers included community organizers and working families. Watching street folk and working in the poverty programs was the best education that money could **not** buy. I spent time in the Black community with regular folk— truck drivers, postal workers, clerks, grocery men—and learned about parts of Black life I had never experienced. I walked the same streets that Malcolm X walked, and Farrakhan after him. I could feel the power and presence of that history. That was a real education.

I met Lauren, my first wife, on Mt. Auburn Street, one block over from Harvard Square. It was a Friday night in October 1967. I looked out the window of my car and saw this young woman with a big Afro walking by. "Where y'all going?" I asked Lauren and Patti, her schoolmate, whom I already knew.

"There's a party over at Quincy House [one of the residences for Harvard upperclassmen]," she said. It was love at first sight.

At the party, I invited Lauren to the movies. The next day, we were walking from the theatre near Boston Commons. I told her right then, "You're going to be my woman." Nothing to discuss or argue about, time will prove it out. Her maiden name was Hazel, the same color as her eyes. She came from an upper middle-class family who lived in Lexington, Massachusetts, where there weren't very many Black people at the time. The local police were so unfamiliar with seeing a dark-skinned Black man in the neighborhood, they stopped me every single time I went to visit. Only after six trips did they cease stopping me for driving while Black. Lauren and I eventually made six babies together. She traveled with me all over the world.

It was while I was earning my street degree that I reunited with my father. Pop rarely traveled outside of New York. I had not seen him for 12 years. Although I had sent him a high school graduation announcement, I did not reach out to him for a year after I came east. Years of separation had created a wide gulf between us. What would I say? Would we be able to bridge the time and distance? I suppose I had to grow up just a bit more, become something of my own man, before I was ready to sail those choppy waters.

I traveled to New York for the reunion. I met my Grandfather Bill, Aunt Doris, Pop's wife Grace and my sister Grace, who was nicknamed Tinker, as in Tinkerbell. The re-introductions were somewhat awkward at first and overly formal. Pop did his best to be welcoming, but made it clear he was not going to relate to me out of any sense of guilt. I don't think there were wounds of injury to heal, perhaps just lingering and residual pain from years of loss. We both worked at creating a real relationship.

Pop told me that my grandmother Mary died from the grief of losing contact with my sister and me. That thought gave me a new sense of belonging. Up until that point, I had no knowledge that anyone missed us when we left the East Coast. My father also told me that my Grandfather Bill lived long enough to greet my return to New York. He then died just a few months later. Pop explained the incredible loss he felt when my sister and I disappeared, and he had no idea where we had gone. As we got to know one another, Pop and I developed an honest love and respect. A pure blessing was that my father and I had 30 good years together before he dropped his body in 1996. For that reason alone, my odyssey back East was worth any difficulties that I encountered.

This was the sixties, liberation time—a mind-expanding

period to come of age. Reconnecting with my Pop, meeting Lauren, fleeing Harvard, running the streets—all this happened in the midst of a tumultuous segment of American history. The U.S. Civil Rights Movement was at its height. Beginning with Ghana in 1957 and Nigeria in 1960, African nations were demanding liberation from colonial rule. Students were rebelling in France, England and the United States. China had its cultural revolution. Women demanded liberation and equality while burning bras. Watts and Detroit burned. Protest against the Vietnam War escalated. Muhammad Ali declared, "Ain't no Viet Cong ever call me a nigger," and refused induction into the army. I fully agreed with his position.

The heightened political and social consciousness was reflected in music and the arts. Artists were at the top of their game. In addition to collecting recorded music by Miles Davis, John Coltrane, Bird, Eric Dolphy and other jazz giants, I was reading and writing. Leonard Feather had two volumes: Encyclopedia of Jazz (1955) and The Encyclopedia of Jazz in the Sixties (1966) that I consumed cover-to-cover. Leroi Jones (later and better known as Amiri Baraka) became an intellectual mentor. I learned the origins of contemporary Black music from Baraka's Blues People (1963) and Black Music (1967). My poetic writing style was borrowed from his Preface to a Twenty Volume Suicide Note (1961) and The Dead Lecturer (1964).

Most of the poetry and papers I wrote were angry and focused on class, race and identification. I suppose some of the anger came from realizing the extent of my naivete before I was accepted to Harvard College and stepped onto the campus that felt so foreign to me. I was awakening to the inequities of American society and the people who created the disparities. Ferdinand Lundberg's The Rich and the Super-Rich (1968) informed my awareness of my personal story in the context of larger social forces. I bought two copies from the Harvard Coop. Coming to consciousness in this turbulent era, I did not yet have an answer to the question that began to consume me: What can I do to be part of the solution, rather than a part of the problem? It was at that time that I had my first direct association with the Nation of Islam, just months before the assassination of Dr. Martin Luther King.

I was in the chair at a barbershop named Beau Nubian Brummel, on Humboldt Avenue in Roxbury. The barber, who was an orthodox Muslim named Malik, saw the Saint Christopher medal around my neck and asked what it was. I told him that Christopher was the patron saint of travelers. The barber informed me that the travelers blessed by Christopher were the Crusaders who traveled to the Middle East to kill Black people and Muslims. He said, "You need to go over to Muhammad's Temple of Islam #11 on Intervale Street and get some knowledge." And I did. It was there that I first made Shahada, the Islamic profession of faith: La ilaha illallah. Muhamadan rasulallah. There is no God but God. Muhammad is the Messenger of God.

Led by The Honorable Elijah Muhammad, the Nation taught a theology of racial identification and communal self-sufficiency for Black people. For thirteen years, Malcolm X was the national spokesman for the Nation. I obtained two books at the Temple that became important to my growth, both written by Elijah Muhammad: Message to the Black Man in America (1965) and How to Eat to Live (1967). The Nation of Islam provided both an intellectual and political framework for my life. It was years later when I received my conscious spiritual awakening.

Malik's barber chair continued to be a place of learning for me. One day, he told me about his grandson named Kaamel Nuri, which translates as "My Light is Complete." I felt an immediate resonance with the name. The name Nuri is derived from an-Nur, one of the 99 names of God written in the Quran. It means "The Light," as in "God is the Light." I did not use the name immediately, however. I began to use it formally only after the birth of my first son. His birth enlightened my life.

In 1968, I lived in the middle of Grove Hall, right next to the welfare office building where the King riots began. Grove Hall was an intersection where several main arteries converged.

Warren Street, Washington Street and Geneva Avenue each converged onto Blue Hill Avenue. Seaver Street, which bordered Franklin Park, was the southern boundary of Grove Hall. The intersection creates a wide avenue where a large number of people were able to congregate.

As news of Dr. King's assassination spread, folk gathered in front of the welfare office, screaming and shouting in anger at the murder of the civil rights hero. The crowd swelled and spilled onto neighboring streets. Flags were burned and the tumult of the people morphed into a street rebellion that moved north down Blue Hill Avenue. Storefronts and shops were looted and burned. The National Guard was mobilized to patrol the streets and attempt to neutralize the multitudes of angry Black people.

Very much a part of the angry gathering of black folk, I moved with the crowd down the avenue where I saw a white Guardsman in full combat uniform assaulting a young Black woman, beating her with the butt of his combat rifle. I had no idea why they were attacking her. An unarmed Black woman being beaten in the street by a White man was simply unacceptable. Byron Rushing was a man I knew casually as a former Black Harvard student. He and I simultaneously initiated an intervention, putting ourselves between the woman and her assailant and stopped the beating. We took a few blows before another Guardsmen threw us on the ground, handcuffed and arrested us for defending the Sister against an unwarranted assault by another white Guardsman. My Uncle Kenneth, who knew many of the cops at the Roxbury police station house, came down to the jail and secured my release.

A James Brown concert had been scheduled for that night. Thinking quickly, Mayor Kevin White went to the concert location and ordered that it be broadcast on television. That tactic kept Black folk off the streets to sit home and watch James Brown, instead of burning and looting.

It had become impossible for me to focus on the academics and politics of being a "Harvard man" in the midst of so much personal transformation and social upheaval. After two years, my Harvard education took a forced sabbatical. I was expelled for failing grades, for not going to class and spending so much time away from Cambridge. When they kicked me out of school, I had become indifferent to the concept of being a Harvard man. It was really not that important. A new set of priorities had begun to crystalize in my mind: how to solve the problems of Black people in America. I had become unapologetically BLACK!!

Another year of running the streets landed me in the hospital. One night while walking in downtown Boston, I was almost hit by a motorist making a turn as I was crossing the street. Angry, I loudly protested, and he yelled back at me. I took offense at his response. I ran around the car to the driver's window and started throwing blows at the occupant. The driver opened his door. As he emerged, he seemed to grow larger and larger in stature. He must have been at least 6' 7" and weighed 250 pounds. He bull-rushed and slammed me against the hood of his car. I knew I was in trouble. I may have weighed 150 pounds at that time. A witness said you better get out of here. The cops are coming. And I did, as fast as I could. My spleen was broken as a result of the altercation. I lived with excruciating pain for quite some time and grew increasingly unwell.

One day, Lauren decided enough was enough. She called my father and told him what had been going on. They had me admitted to Flower and Fifth Avenue Hospital in East Harlem. The doctors performed several exploratory operations on my young body, with the justification that I might have had Hodgkin's Lymphoma. In any case, surgery was not a normal diagnostic technique for Hodgkin's disease, and certainly not a treatment. The surgeons opened my guts up, put them on the table, examined them and stuffed everything back inside.

After this major surgery, I woke up surrounded by a gaggle of young people in white coats. Many years later, I realized that the teaching hospital used my body as an instructional tool for students and resident doctors. Here they had this young Black boy, twenty-one years old, whom they used as a living lesson in dissection. I suppose I can count myself lucky they finally said I did not have cancer. Had they deemed me positive for the disease, I'm certain the cure would have been worse. As it is, I have scars all over my body from that experience.

My hospitalization was a watershed moment. I had tired of what was going on in the streets. I thought I was in search of community. In truth, I was in search of myself, looking to find out who I truly was, who I wanted to be in this life. I discovered that the answers were not in the streets. The answers were already inside of me, but remained a mystery for some time. I gained exposure and experience in those three years. Sometimes, the lessons didn't unfold until much later. Just being exposed profoundly changed my awareness and set me up for a new way of perceiving the world and my place in it.

Part II

SURVEILLANCE

———⧿⧿⧿———

There were several years in which I undertook intense study and close observation of people and groups. I was interested in national development: how you build countries. I was interested in the men and women who created the post-colonial world. I was interested in developing practical skills to contribute to Black liberation.

My surveillance was learning all that I could for the sake of proper direction and control of my life. Surveillance is often associated with the careful watching of a person or place, especially by the police or army because of a crime that has happened or is expected. Too many crimes in history have been glossed over or marginalized by those in power. Chattel slavery and colonialism are examples. My surveillance armed me with the knowledge to implement actions to minimize such crimes in the future.

That period of study was motivated by a burning desire to understand the forces of history. It was also important to establish a personal philosophical base. I desired a better understanding of the thought processes of the men and women creating the post-colonial world. I bumped into the outer world as a teen. Conflicts and pure adventures set me off on a quest for self-awareness. I then had to bounce back and learn more about an often-confusing new world, about things that lay beyond my personal experience, until I could establish my own philosophical underpinnings. My surveillance included ravenous reading, which I detail in the following chapters.

Surveillance also included original research—observing behaviors of those who looked like me and those who didn't, looking for patterns that could guide my search for direction. The blessed thing is that as I look back on my life, I am amazed at the consistency of my direction. Advocating for fruit and fruit juices in my high school campus vending machines presaged my desire to bring nutritious foods to urban communities fifty years later.

As you will see in this section, my deepest desires, openness and zeal made a way. I've heard that Michael Jackson (and perhaps Quincy Jones) spoke about "leaving space for God to come in the room." Music well represents that divine space. The spaces between the notes are just as important as the melody and the drumbeats. Surveillance mixes with self-awareness to keep that space open.

What are your deepest desires? To what are you open to learning? What incites your zeal? Find and keep those spaces and carry your revolutionary work to the next level.

The paradox of education is precisely this—that as one begins to become conscious, one begins to examine the society in which he is being educated.

James Baldwin 1963

Chapter 3

Iqraa

I was still recovering from the horrific surgery in New York when I returned to San Diego in late1969. I had scars, both physical and mental, that came from the hard-driving lifestyle I had chosen. I didn't realize the fragility of the human body. It had not dawned on me that your body could actually wear out. I'm paying for that now.

Probably, I would not have done anything different had I known. From childhood through my middle adult years, I had a major trauma every seven years or so of my life. At seven years old, my mother remarried. I suppose her remarriage dashed any hopes I may have harbored about her reuniting with my father. Could that be the original trauma? That is something that I am still contemplating. What I know for sure is what happened in the ensuing years.

When I was fourteen, I went through a growth spurt and developed Osgood-Schlatters, an inflammatory disease of the knees often experienced by growing adolescents. The exploratory surgery in search of Hodgkin's Lymphoma happened when I was twenty-one. At twenty-eight, I broke my jaw in seven places when I passed out doing a yogic breathing exercise. I tore my Achilles tendon playing basketball and went through extensive rehabilitation when I was thirty-five. At forty-two, I had surgery on both knees. Every seven years, there was some serious trauma.

Back in my beloved California, with the backdrop of mountains and ocean, I had the time and space to quietly examine what I was going to do with the rest of my life. Several enthusiasms became abundantly clear. First of all, I loved music. This made sense, since both my parents were involved with music. My attachment to music came early. Pursuing music in Boston and New York had been logical. Music constantly swirls in my head. If I never heard another radio or CD or saw a YouTube video, I would still have plenty of musical memories to replay in my head. Music, in all its manifestations, is the healing force of the universe and an undeniable comfort for me.

I processed the lessons from my East Coast street degree as I considered my future options. I studied aspects of life in Black communities that had been foreign just a short time before. I had taken a deep dive into music that seemed to rise from my bones as much as it wafted into my ears. The workings of power and power relationships were beginning to dawn on me. Through all this, the Maroon in me wanted more. What emerged was a desire—a need—to know more, to understand more.

According to mainstream Islamic tradition, while Prophet Muhammad was in contemplation, the archangel Gabriel appeared before him in the year 609 CE and said, "Read," upon which he replied, "I am unable to read." This happened two more times, after which the angel commanded Muhammad to recite the following verses:

Proclaim! (Or read!) In the name of thy Lord and Cherisher,
Who Created man, out of a clot of congealed blood:

Proclaim! And thy Lord is Most Bountiful—
Who taught by the pen—
Taught man that which he knew not.
Quran 96:1–5

IQRAA: Read!! These were the first words Prophet Muhammad received in his revelation from God. The event took place in a cave called Hira, located on Mt. Jaba an-Nour, near Makah.

In 1969, the command to read awakened inside me in San Diego. And read I did! As intensely as I had thrown myself into the street life of Boston and New York, I plunged into a vast library of books written by thinkers who had found their own answers to my quest: *how shall I serve?*

I wanted to learn, to grow intellectually, to understand the forces responsible for the injustices that my education in the streets had laid bare. As a child of the 1960s, we talked about Black economic and political power, nation building. I wrestled with the question: "Do I want to be a Harvard man?" Despite having been kicked out of Harvard, I was clear that what was most important was getting an education, not necessarily a degree from Harvard. I wanted to study the lives and teachings of the men and women who created the post-colonial world. It was important for me to learn how to build countries.

My focus became the thought and works of the revolutionaries who took on the arduous task of fighting colonialism, imperialism and capitalism. It was important to understand the history and principles that created the political and economic conditions subjugating the majority of the world's population to western domination. That's when I became a Pan-Africanist. Today, Wikipedia defines Pan-Africanism as "a worldwide movement that aims to encourage and strengthen bonds of solidarity between all people of African descent. It is based on the belief that unity is vital to economic, social and political progress. Pan-Africanism aims to "unify and uplift" people of African descent." Without the benefit of the Wikipedia definition, but guided by the revolutionary spirit extant at the time, I began studying the subject deeply.

Kwame Nkrumah of Ghana was one of the freedom fighters that had a leading influence on my thought. Ghana, then known as the Gold Coast, was the first sub-Saharan country in Africa to gain independence from colonial rule. When Britain granted independence to Ghana in 1957, Kwame Nkrumah served as its first Prime Minister and President. Nkrumah literally and figuratively surveyed his home continent, envisioning Ghana as a modern industrialized state, and all of Africa unified as a single economic unit. All of my children have Ghanaian day names, taken from the day of the week they were born, because of my admiration for Osageyfo Kwame Nkrumah.

Nkrumah spent twelve years studying abroad. He attended Lincoln University, the University of Pennsylvania and the London School of Economics. He was an activist student, an influential politician and ardent community organizer. He taught me much, specifically about Africa, and about world politics in general. It was from studying his numerous writings that I developed a worldview with a body of principles, rules and standards that became my personal canon.

One of the first books I read during this period was <u>Neo-Colonialism: The Last Stage of Imperialism</u> (1965). In the introduction, Nkrumah wrote, "The essence of neo-colonialism is that the State which is subject to it is, in theory, independent and has all the outward trappings of international sovereignty. In reality its economic system and thus its political policy is directed from outside." Subsequently, this paradigm became the basis for my analysis of politics and history, both domestic and international. The following books by Nkrumah have a permanent place on my shelves:

<u>Ghana: The Autobiography of Kwame Nkrumah</u> (1957)
<u>Africa Must Unite</u> (1963)
<u>Axioms of Kwame Nkrumah</u> (1967)
<u>African Socialism Revisited</u> (1967)
<u>Dark Days in Ghana</u> (1968)

Handbook of Revolutionary Warfare (1968)
Consciencism: Philosophy and Ideology for De-Colonization (1970)
Class Struggle in Africa (1970)

I read everything I could by and about Malcolm X. Malcolm was a student of the Honorable Elijah Muhammad, leader and teacher of the Nation of Islam. Malcolm joined the Nation while a prisoner in a Massachusetts penitentiary and rose to become the national spokesman for the Nation. It was during his 13 years representing Mr. Muhammad that the Nation grew to prominence in America. His split with the community in 1964 created a division in ideological thought that still resonates in Black intellectual and activist circles to this day. The primary threads of the debate were: integration within American society versus separation and self-sufficient development; and community self-defense versus non-violent protest.

Malcolm was an intellectual and ideological mentor for me. The insights and perspectives that he provided were very important in 1970. Over the years, much research and scholarly dissertations have been written about Malcolm. I continue to read and study his life and work. I had already read The Autobiography of Malcolm X as told to Alex Haley (1965). During my time in San Diego, I read:

Malcolm X Speaks: Selected Speeches and Statements, George Breitman, ed. (1965)
The Speeches of Malcolm X at Harvard, Archie Epps, ed. (1969)
By Any Means Necessary: Speeches, Interviews, and a Letter by Malcolm X, George Breitman, ed. (1970)
The Last Year of Malcolm X, by George Breitman (1967)
From the Dead Level: Malcolm X and Me, by Hakim A. Jamal (1972)

I read African history:
The World and Africa by W.E.B. Dubois (1947) was a primer

on Africa. Basil Davidson published twenty-five books on African history and civilization. I studied:

African Slave Trade: Pre-colonial History 1450-1850 (1961)
Lost Cities of Africa (1959)
The Africans (1969)
The African Past (1964)
The African Genius (1969)
Report on Southern Africa (1952)

I consumed them all.

I read Pedagogy of the Oppressed (1968) by Paulo Friere. C.L.R. James wrote A History of Pan-African Revolt (1938). George Padmore produced Pan-Africanism or Communism (1956). Franz Fanon was a West Indian psychiatrist and social philosopher, known for his theory that some neuroses are socially generated. He wrote in support of the national liberation of colonial peoples. Among his noted works is Black Skin, White Masks (1952), a multidisciplinary analysis of the effect of colonialism on racial consciousness. Fanon's social critiques influenced me, along with subsequent generations of thinkers and activists.

Fanon articulated an expanded view of the psychosocial repercussions of colonialism on colonized people. The publication shortly before his death of The Wretched of the Earth (1961) established Fanon as a leading intellectual in the international decolonization movement. Fanon perceived colonialism as a form of domination whose necessary goal for success was the reordering of the world of indigenous peoples. He saw violence as the defining characteristic of colonialism. Amos Wilson later wrote about the generational mental sickness of Black people in the United States in The Falsification of Afrikan Consciousness (1993). He asserted that this illness resulted from centuries of oppression, manifested in post slave traumatic disorder.

The intense energy of the 60s still brimmed in San Diego. Although my time in the city was brief, I was swept up in political and community development work. For a brief period, I worked at the San Diego Urban League. My task was to integrate the building trades through the unions, who had no interest in allowing Blacks or Chicanos into the occupations. The best we could accomplish was the creation of a pre-apprenticeship training program in San Diego.

The Model Cities Program was an element of President Lyndon Johnson's Great Society and War on Poverty. In 1966, new legislation funded more than 150 five-year-long Model Cities experiments to develop new anti-poverty programs and alternative forms of municipal government. The ambitious federal urban aid program succeeded in fostering a new generation of mostly middle class Black urban leaders. The major flaw in the program was the limited lifespan of only five years.

In 1970 and 1971, Tommy Meshack, Harold Sadikifu and I put together a project as part of San Diego's Model Cities Program. Of the 28 projects in the cohort, ours was the only one designed to be self-sufficient at the end of the five years. What the poverty programs did was create a Black middle class, giving educated Black people enough money to buy a decent house, which intensified class distinctions in the Black community. The workers got a little bit of money, but there was nothing left over. It really didn't help the poor folks—they were never positively impacted.

We created an organization called The Kuumba Foundation. Kuumba is the Swahili word for creativity. As part of the Foundation's work, we started the Southeast San Diego Communications Complex, which had a multifaceted array of programming. To this day, vestiges of our work still exist in the Education Centre located in Southeast San Diego, doing the same work that we did in 1971.

I planted my first garden in 1969, at 21 years old. Brother Randy McFadden turned me on to agriculture. Randy was growing food in the yard at his house. He had been mentored by another remarkable brother named Tim. Tim didn't believe he should have to pay rent for the house he occupied. One day, the Sheriffs came to his abode to evict him, and Tim went after them with a rake. The Sheriffs shot Brother Tim five times, and he survived. Thereafter, he became a legend in the community. An avid survivalist, Tim taught, "We've gotta do for self." He lived his proclamation by growing his own food.

That wonderful food-growing bug infected Randy, and I got it from him. I said, "Wow! I could grow my own food!" I was poor; we were struggling and broke. I was working in the community for practically nothing. Looking back, I can see this period was another time of preparation for my life's work as an agriculturalist. Brother Randy got me started. I love him to this day.

Randy always said that corn tastes best when you boil the water first, go out and harvest the ears and drop them in the boiling water. And it's true. Actually, good, fresh sweet corn does not need any water. It doesn't need to be cooked. One day I saw a silkworm, a corn worm, on one of my plants. I went out and bought some powder that would kill worms. I put so much out there, the whole yard was white. I had white powder all over everything, and me, trying to kill every single worm. I had no idea how poisonous that stuff was. But that's where I got started and began the process of learning about agriculture.

Brother Randy's lasting legacy has been as an exemplar of how to live simply, honestly and with great inner peace. One spring day, we took his MG roadster on a psychedelic trip to the top of Mt. Palomar. Palomar Mountain stands isolated from the rest of the Agua Tibia Mountain Range. Its location is such that it intercepts many storms coming from the coast, making it one of the wettest locations in Southern California. At an elevation of 6126 feet, it is high enough to provide uninterrupted vistas of Mt. Laguna, downtown San Diego and the Pacific Ocean, including San Clemente and Catalina Islands.

The mountain's elevation also gives it a great view of the stars. Mt. Palomar State Park is the home of a major astronomical observation site. Palomar Observatory is owned and operated by the California Institute of Technology. The Observatory supports the scientific research programs of Caltech's faculty and students.

About halfway up the mountain, we drove into what appeared to be one of Southern California's notorious fog banks, wet and dark. Despite the close proximity to where we had grown up, neither of us had ever visited the mountain before. The fog put a real damper on our excitement. Disappointed, we considered turning around. Suddenly, the shroud lifted, and we were awash in the bright sunshine of a cloudless sky. We had actually driven through the clouds and were now high enough to be above them.

Reaching the summit, we parked next to an unassuming VW Kombi, painted with only a flat beige undercoat. At first glance, there was nothing special about the van. When I got out of the car, I began to notice the extensive customizing that the owner had done. Through the window, I could see intricate woodwork, fabricated to fit the contours of the interior. There were pull out drawers and finely finished cabinets. The creativity was impressive. As I was summoning Brother Randy over to admire the work, a man and woman came up the hill and walked toward the bus. After I complimented the man, he proudly showed me the details of his resourcefulness. A fast affinity developed between us. I asked him, "What did you see down there?" referring to his climb up the steep slope. His answer, "The other side of the mountain," hit me like a sledgehammer.

The profundity of that simple statement still moves me, almost 50 years later. The other side of the mountain is what lies beyond. To go beyond, to contribute, to improve the world requires seeing and experiencing the other side of the mountain. People tend to ignore the obvious if it conflicts with the orthodoxy of their early training. Foolish consistency is the hobgoblin of small minds. Knowledge is a precious thing. Wisdom is even more precious than knowledge. You must go beyond knowledge and wisdom to even get near illumination, and illumination can only be found on the other side of the mountain.

However, it is important to know where the clouds end, and the cliff begins. The cloud and the cliff form a borderland, a demarcation between this world and another. A person who climbs the mountains of life, seeking the highest peaks of success, the big gold dream, acclaim or even spiritual perfection, experiences a series of paradigm shifts. The seeker must remain aware of the boundary between cliff and cloud. I know this now. If you do not sense the boundary, you can easily walk off the side of a mountain and somersault into a deep, dark abyss. Staying sensitive to the boundaries opens the doors to inner and outer success.

I did experience a significant paradigm shift in consciousness during this period. The most transformative thing that happened was the birth of my first child, Kwesi Kamal Nuri. I became a very young and very proud father.

He let you hear His voice from heaven to discipline you,
and on earth He showed you His great fire,
and you heard His words out of the fire.

Deuteronomy 4:36

Chapter 4
Harvard Two – The Burning Bush

The Africa Research Group brought me back to the East Coast in late 1971. I was invited by Roy Campanella, Jr. to be a part of the collective, which studied contemporary African Politics. Campanella, a Hollywood documentary film director, was in my graduating class at Harvard. The Africa Research Group analyzed issues concerning African liberation movements. It was interesting work, but internecine issues caused the collective to fall apart in three to four months. I decided to go back to school and continue the studies that I began in San Diego. I remained interested in national development and the leaders who were shaping the post-colonial world.

I explored many schools in the Boston area to continue my studies. It was not important to me where I studied, because I was clear about what I wanted to learn. As it turned out, Harvard was the easiest place for me to enter and receive the most financial assistance. By this time, I had a wife and two sons to support. My second son, Kwabena Koro Nuri, had been born in January 1972. During the re-entrance interview at Harvard, the Dean said, "We're not sure we want you here, because we think you are an infectious agent."

I thought, "Damn! Is this what I have to put up with?" After a moment, I let the comment roll off my back. I realized that, yes, this is what I had to put up with at Harvard. I was clear on my mission this time around, so his posture did not deter me. Today, in hindsight, I realize that he was right. I have spent a lifetime helping to make change and correct the wrongs and disparities of society. The Dean's attitude was not an obstacle; it was both confirmation and inspiration.

When I arrived at Harvard for the first time in the fall of 1966, our class was the second that had a significant number of Black students. "Significant" meant that there were about 50 Black students out of 1200 in my freshman class. This was par for the course in Ivy League circles. My sister-in-law was three years older than me, and there were only 10 Black students in her class when she attended Radcliffe.

Some of my classmates were already very familiar with the Harvard environment and culture, like Ernie Wilson, who was a third generation Harvard man. His father and his uncle had all gone there before. I don't think he had any problem adjusting. But there were a whole lot of us that came out of the hood and underserved communities, who had never been in the rarified, gentrified atmosphere that enveloped the Harvard community, nor any environment like it. Some made it, some didn't, and some faced more struggles than others. But I came back. This time, I was very focused, very intense.

The disciplines I was practicing at the time have served me well. I was very intentional about what and when I ate. I was eating once a day and fasting three days a month, as taught by the Honorable Elijah Muhammad. I was doing yoga, running, practicing martial arts, playing basketball. I was in incredible physical condition, which enabled me to make good babies. I am sure one of the reasons my children have all turned out very well is because my wife Lauren and I were in such good physical shape then. Any day of the week, I could tell you exactly where I'd be. If you said 7:30 p.m. on Tuesday, I would be at the laundromat washing clothes for the family while I read books for a class. We lived in Mattapan, directly south of Roxbury/Dorchester. It took about 45-60 minutes for me to commute to class via public transportation. I used that time to read course work.

The house system at Harvard groups students in eating and living arrangements that create a level of intimacy. I was assigned to Dudley House, which was for students who lived off-campus. We had our own small, private library, where my work-study job was located. I would sit there and check out patrons' books while I studied. Instead of taking the standard four classes per semester, I took six. I was very, very intent on my studies and consistently busy during that time. I used to carry half a bundle of Muhammad Speaks newspapers to school every week and sell them on campus. Everybody came to get his or her Muhammad Speaks from me. Oh, it was deep. It was an intensely purposeful period of time. I loved it.

One of my goals during those years was to sit in the yoga lotus position. I also had a goal to travel to Africa. It took 8 years of practice to coax my hips into accepting the lotus position and 18 years to position myself to get to Africa. I still carry memory implants from the disciplines I learned. The training helped me focus on attaining the goals that I set in my life. I was able to discover and explore the depths of my personal human potential, which helped inform much of the work that I've done since then.

It was during this period that I had what I call my "burning bush" experience. This moment of clarity came while sitting in the Dudley House library writing a paper on theory and practice, comparing the work of Julius Nyerere in Tanzania and Jomo Kenyatta in Kenya. These two leaders had very contrasting approaches to national development; Nyerere advocated African socialism. He apologized many years later, because his concept of African socialism, Ujamaa, did not work in Tanzania. Jomo Kenyatta was a pure capitalist.

In the library, I was reading a book by a man named Tom Mboya, the former Finance Minister in Kenya under Kenyatta. He was subsequently assassinated. Mboya wrote that with all of the technology available in the world today, there is no reason we could not chemically synthesize enough food to feed all the people. Part of my study was health and nutrition. I had learned that the chemicals used in agriculture and industry wound up being served to people. Those chemicals were killing folk. When I read Mboya's statement, it was like a bolt of lightning came out of the sky. This was the spiritual experience that set the direction for the rest of my life.

Right there, in the quiet confines of Harvard's Dudley House Library, I heard the voice of God come through to me. It sounded strange, but somehow, familiar. The voice was loud and expansive. The experience was multisensory, coming through as a feeling, a vision and even an object, all at once. It seemed particularly strange in a library, of all places. Maybe not so strange, though, considering I was there to learn. I felt as though a suit of clothes had dropped onto me, dressing me for a new adventure—complete with a world map in the inside pocket. Life changed for me in a single moment, and I could see the odd contours of my previous path take shape as preparation for what was to come. Past as prologue. That was the seminal moment that gave focus and direction to the rest of my life.

God said, "Learn everything you can about food, from the seed to the table, and do it experientially." If one engages in inner space exploration, as I had been doing, then messages from God must be heard and obeyed. And so it began: a food odyssey that would take me around the globe. The journey would identify food production as the seed of every human society and the keeper of our connection with the Earth. There is no culture without agriculture.

It was a shining moment. I had been thinking about what career path to follow. I wasn't interested in any of the occupations that most of my classmates pursued—doctors, lawyers, dentists and all those types of professions. I was engrossed in health and nutrition. I was in pursuit of nation building. To build a nation, you have to feed, clothe and shelter your people. Did I want to be a carpenter and build houses? Did I want to be a printer of magazines and newspapers to facilitate communication amongst folk?

Suddenly, I found myself with the Most High speaking in my ear, telling me what I'm supposed to do with my life: "Learn everything about food from the seed to the table…" The pursuit of agricultural knowledge became the focus. Receiving a call from The Most High, being given instructions on what to do, created great freedom for me. I no longer dwelled on what I was going to do with my life. The path has been clear and straight since that afternoon, and there has been no choice, no deviation. Within that framework is great freedom.

I finished three years of coursework in a year and a half, to earn my A.B. in Government from Harvard. I knew what I was to do with my life, but very little about agriculture. It was clear I needed to continue my formal education. I searched in every department and career service at Harvard that I could think of, and none of them could tell me anything about how to select a school for agricultural studies. I didn't know where to go.

The University of Massachusetts was the closest place that offered an agriculture program. It was down the road from Boston in Amherst, Massachusetts. I decided to pursue a Master of Science Degree in Plant and Soil Science at UMass.

Throughout my children's education, I always insisted that they take some form of math and science courses each year. I did that as well and could easily have attended medical school had that been my choice. That preparation enabled me to be accepted into a graduate program in the sciences, even though my undergraduate degree was in government. I would have to learn about the politics of agriculture on my own.

Mad world! Mad kings! Mad composition!

King John, Act II, Sc.1

═══════════

Chapter 5
UMASS

The early 1970s was a remarkable time for the University of Massachusetts. It was a hub for Black intellectual and artistic talent. Bill Strickland, Michael Thelwell, Sonia Sanchez, Max Roach, Archie Shepp, Yusef Lateef, among others, were all in residence. I was elected president of the New Africa House at the University. The building housed students, offices and activities for Black students. It was really an exciting time and place. The feeling of unity and familial community is the memory that sticks.

UMass is located in the Connecticut River Valley, a beautiful place that was once the breadbasket for New York City. Fresh fruits and vegetables were abundant and could be purchased at the many produce stands in the community. A number of excellent tertiary educational institutions are there: Amherst College, Smith College, Mt. Holyoke College and Hampshire College. Five people in my family were educated in that valley.

The first academic work at UMass was to learn the basic language of agriculture, because I certainly didn't know anything about the science of it. The program provided a basic grounding in ag science, and I intended to build on those fundamentals. The fundamental elements of agriculture are plants and soil, so that's what I chose. I registered to earn a Master of Science degree in Plant and Soil Science.

I took basic classes in soil geology, plant biology, botany, world soils, etc. The department gave me a choice of writing a master's thesis or giving a lecture to the faculty. I chose the lecture. All of the classes I took at UMass were geared towards the seminar that I had to present. I knew early on that my thesis topic was the Factors of National Development, how to build a country. Even though I was in the Plant and Soil Science Department, I wanted to integrate what I'd learned in my three previous undergraduate degrees (Government, Street Life and Community Development) about national development. For example, in the Statistics class, I did regression analyses. I factored in education, wealth, health, land—all the elements that are part of national development. The regression analyses showed that the most important things determining the level of development of a country are land, labor and capital.

In 2016, I read a book called The Empire of Cotton, written by Harvard professor, Sven Beckert. The book codifies the thinking I had come to embrace by the end of my formal education. Beckert uses land, labor and capital to explain the role that cotton has played in industrial development. Reading the book was a tremendous confirmation, because I have been talking about this for years. My background in government at Harvard, coupled with the intense independent study curriculum that I pursued at UMass, had helped me form the theoretical framework that Beckert describes.

Beckert explained how the aristocrats of Britain felt the feudal system was good for the vassals, the working peasants, because they had a place to live; they were taken care of and were even buried on the same property. The slaves should be grateful. Essentially, there have been slaves throughout history. The upper classes have believed they were doing the slaves a favor by providing them with consistent labor opportunities. Capitalism has solidified the position of the aristocracy, and modern industry created new classes of capitalists, bankers and industrialists. The cycle continues.

America is the richest empire in the entire history of the world. The country achieved empire status because the land and all the resources it contained were stolen from the Native Americans. Labor was coerced from captured people, Black like me, to work the land. Capital investments came from Europe. The triangular trade that began with slaves and sugar financed the Industrial Revolution in Europe.

Barbados was the first slave colony. Toward the end of the 1700s and the beginning of the 1800s, cotton became the fuel for industrial development. In order to build the cotton economy, labor was needed. That labor was provided by the chattel captivity and enslavement of Black people. As history is examined, it becomes unequivocally clear that over the millennia, land, labor and capital form the basis of all empires, big or small.

I had a revelation one day, years after my time at UMass, while speaking to a man in Macon, Georgia about plantation society. We were discussing confined animal feedlot operations, which demand that pigs, cows and chickens be raised in crowded spaces. Farm operators give the animals drugs and chemicals to keep them alive and reasonably healthy. Then it occurred to me. That is exactly the same thing that was done with captive Africans. My ancestors were stacked into boats, as many as slave traders could fit. Captives had to live in their own filth, just like the cows and pigs. Feedlots produce animals that are sick. The food that comes from the flesh of animals raised in unhealthy environments is sick. Black people remain sick because of the continuing impacts of the tormented legacy of chattel captivity.

In one calendar year at UMass, I met all departmental requirements to obtain the M.S. degree. My seminar presentation was successful; I was able to address and answer all challenges from professors and other grad students. The professor who was my advisor commented that he did not understand how I could get a master's degree in such a short period of time. He remarked that I only knew as much as an undergraduate. I reminded him that he provided the rules at the beginning of our association, and I just followed them. I got what I came for and left with an academic ticket.

When I finished grad school, one of my classmates gave me a great compliment. He said, "You've been serious a long time, haven't you?" He had observed how intently I did my work. My routine was school, work, exercise, gardening and taking care of my family of five. My third child and first daughter, Ama Aliyah Nuri, was born while I was in grad school. I tell people that I flunked recess in kindergarten because I don't play. Even today, I can walk into my office and pull out my third-grade report card that says I flunked recess and aced everything else. So, yes, I've been serious for a long time. At UMass, I was serious about learning agriculture.

Part III

STRATEGY

———❧❧❧———

Strategy was not always upfront in my mind as I repeatedly did the unprecedented, pushed the envelope and pioneered new approaches.

Strategy is the science and art of employing the political, economic and psychological forces to afford the maximum support to adopted policies. The strategic planning process generally involves setting goals, determining actions to achieve the goals and mobilizing resources to execute the actions that bring about a desired future. A strategy describes how the ends (goals) will be achieved by the means (resources) available.

Building an effective and healthy food system requires strategic planning that includes the big picture and local initiatives. Strategies require knowledge of the current state of affairs, as well as a willingness to act in one's own community. The nature of the next level of development of our food system is local control. My observations of the food industry, along with the political and economic systems that support it, coalesced to produce a framework for action. The following set of essays describes the framework that evolved over my 50 years of work in agriculture.

The Politics of Food addresses the policies that have created the most productive agricultural system in the history of the known world, here in the U.S.A. It also explains the role government has played in developing the business interests that make this production capability possible, and the support systems that undergird the entire process.

Industrial Agriculture and Its Impact explores the modalities of Big Ag and tracks their interest in spreading the theology of Big Ag internationally.

Urban Agriculture discusses the transformative power of the local food economy and its ability to sustain community vitality.

A new vision emerged from my global, hands-on study of agricultural strategies in many forms, from community gardens to commercial agribusiness. The strategy that unfolded is focused on returning the power of land, labor and capital to the people from whom those resources were amassed. Food revolutionaries across the country and around the globe are creatively strategizing natural, healthy and sustainable ways to live in harmony with the Earth and each other. Have you found your strategies?

In the land of the blind, the one-eyed man is king.
The masses buy the lie, and swallow everything.

Desiderius Erasmus/P.O.D.

Chapter 6

The Politics of Food

We all need to eat. We need to grow food naturally, as close to our family tables as possible, so that we can get the best food possible. The only reason to make these very simple truths complicated, is to make money, not health; and certainly not community wealth. After thousands of years of growing food, humanity basically has the hang of it. Seeds, soil, water, sunshine. Pull weeds. Harvest. It's like: *Wash. Rinse. Repeat.*

So, why is much of our food inadequate for producing good health? Why is so much of our food downright dangerous for our health? And why are so many people hungry or have limited access to fresh, nutritious food?

It's a power thing.

Modern civilization was built on our capacity to deliberately cultivate food—as I say so often, there is no culture without agriculture. As societies advanced beyond the hunter-gatherer stage, they quickly moved into the division of labor. Thus, overall productivity was increased, and there was more time to further develop technology. Enter politics—the process of deciding how the expanding resources of the community would be distributed. Somewhere along the way, in spite of economic expansion, the deceptive philosophy of scarcity arose, and with it, the desire to control those so-called scarce resources. Today, that desire to control resources has evolved into a super-powered techno-elite with an insatiable appetite.

Another simple truth is: whoever controls your food, controls you. The politics of agriculture is about how you get food to the people. The modern division of labor is so extreme that many individuals in recent generations think the grocery store is the original source of food. They simply have no thought about how the food arrives in the store or its origin. They have never been required to connect to that process. That level of disconnect is simply unhealthy and leaves individuals and communities vulnerable to the power-based decisions of others. How can such technologically oriented individuals be expected to steward the Earth? They lack a fundamental understanding of growth and life cycles—understanding that is essential for self-protection, survival and sustainability.

The politics is this: there's plenty of food in the world. There is plenty of capacity to grow nutritious food, using local resources in most cases. We have vast pockets of poverty, where people are starving, or not able to get quality food or the amount of food that's necessary. There's always a political element to it. Somebody controls the means of distribution and exchange of that food. According to the U.S. Department of Agriculture, 17 million Americans do not have access to "fresh" food in grocery stores. It's easier to get food stamps than to get support for a small farm. Food stamps do not change the power relationships that exist. Putting land, knowledge and resources into the lives of people produces change.

All this leads to our capacity as human beings to create an equitable distribution of power and resources. Communities must have the knowledge, power and resources to grow their own food. Local control is one of the fundamental tenets of democracy, enshrined in the U.S. Constitution. In order to progress, we must go back to the future of American liberty and back to the future of agriculture. It is essential that people realize our power to grow food close to urban areas, where 81 percent of us live. It is also vital that we return power to smaller rural farms. We are all better off when agriculture uses more manpower and less chemical power, whether in urban or rural areas.

Food self-sufficiency was the foundation of the U.S. economy when the country was founded. By 1785, a clear system for distributing government land had been developed, which was already skewed to ownership by the richest citizens. At that time, only a few people could afford the minimum purchase of one square mile of land, or 640 acres, at $1 per acre. Over the next 50 years, the growth of the homesteading movement led to a reduction in the required number of acres that an individual had to purchase, and ultimately led to the passage of the Homestead Act of 1862 and the Land Grant College Acts of 1862 and 1890.

A good example of infrastructure supports is what happened after the Homestead Act of 1862 was passed. Millions of White American homesteaders were invited to settle and farm in the Midwest and West, at no cost for the land. Six months after the law was activated, Congress passed the Railroad Act, which opened up homesteading regions to the Transcontinental Railroad. This provided White settlers with faster transportation and access to the manufactured goods that they would need to ease life on the frontier.

Under the Homestead Act of 1862, enterprising Americans were granted 160 acres of land to settle and farm in the West and Midwest. In the same year, the Land Grant Act gave states land to sell, with the money earned going to support agricultural colleges. This early, full-circle subsidizing of agriculture developed into the current system of commodity subsidies that keep Big Ag big, and keep the numbers of family farms dropping each year.

Dr. Martin Luther King, Jr. said it best on the eve of his trip to Memphis, Tennessee in 1968, where he was assassinated. He said:

> *At the very same time that America refused to give the Negro any land, through an act of Congress, our government was giving away millions of acres of land in the West and the Midwest. Which meant that it was willing to undergird its White peasants from Europe with an economic floor. But not only did they give the land, they built land grant colleges with government money to teach them how to farm. Not only that: they provided county agents to further their expertise in farming. Not only that: they provided low interest rates in order that they could mechanize their farms. Not only that: today many of these people are receiving millions of dollars in federal subsidies, not to farm. And they are the very people telling the Black man that he oughta lift himself by his own bootstraps. Now this is what we are faced with, and this is the reality. Now when we come to Washington in this campaign, we are coming to get our check.*

Today, Black farmers and poor White farmers still have checks to pick up, from a very big payroll. USDA subsidies between 1995 and 2014 totaled $322.7 billion dollars. A handful of Big Ag growers of only five commodities receive the bulk of those subsidies: corn, soybeans, wheat, cotton, and rice. As F. William Engdahl describes in his book, <u>Seeds of Destruction</u>, these commodities are used on the world market to control prices and the flow of capital. More insidiously, they are used to control the economies of developing nations in the name of "international aid."

Peanuts, sorghum and mohair receive subsidies also, at a much smaller rate than the big five commodities. Dairy and sugar producers are supported by other programs. Producers of meat, fruits and vegetables can generally access only two subsidy programs: subsidized crop insurance and federal disaster payments. This structure leaves out almost all small to medium farmers, lending support to a handful of Big Ag companies. It's interesting to note that eight out of the ten states receiving the largest subsidies are in the Midwest, where much of the lands granted under the Homestead Act are located.

Farming is increasingly concentrated, with many fewer growers occupying much larger acreage. The number of farms in the U.S. peaked in 1935, at 6.8 million. By 2016, there were only 2.1 million farms, occupying the same number of acres. Large farms "eat up" smaller ones by having greater access to land, equipment and markets. The small farmers that have weathered the onslaught of commercial farming are finding it difficult to survive. According to a 2016 USDA report, 59 to 78 percent of small farms, those with gross incomes up to $349,999, were operating in the red in 2015. On the other hand, farms with incomes of $1-5 million and above were more likely to bring in profits averaging 25 percent.

The widespread hybridization of agricultural crops and mechanized production are known as the Green Revolution, which was seeded by research that began in the 1930s. The work of plant geneticists, including Henry A. Wallace and Norman Borlaug, in combination with industrial innovations, set the stage for a technological takeover of farming, food processing and food distribution on a global scale. Norman Borlaug is credited with being the "Father of the Green Revolution", for which he received the Nobel Peace Prize in 1970. Borlaug's hybrid varieties of wheat, rice and corn produced large yields, enhanced by their resistance to disease and ability to utilize chemical fertilizers. Evidence has shown that the quality of the food has suffered. After a few years of planting these hybrids, the increase in production tends to fall, and more and more chemical and technological inputs—fertilizers, herbicides and pesticides—are required to maintain the high level of output.

Statistician and geneticist, Henry A. Wallace, served two terms as Secretary of Agriculture, from 1933-1940. He was one of the first to apply econometrics to agriculture. Born to an Iowa farming family, Wallace's early horticultural training began with his mother teaching him to crossbreed pansies in her garden. He grew up to design the first successfully marketed variety of hybrid corn. He continued to develop and market hybrid varieties through his highly profitable Hi-Bred ("Hybrid") Seed Company. Wallace's son eventually sold the company to DuPont for an estimated $10 billion.

Wallace's story is something of a study in contradictions and a demonstration of the harsh realities of unintended consequences. An advocate for farmers, the poor and racial equality, Wallace's work as Secretary of Agriculture was pivotal in changing lives and instituting iconic agricultural programs. He almost single-handedly reversed the devastation that farmers endured during the Great Depression, through policies such as: paying farmers to let their fields lie fallow in order to conserve the soil and increase prices for farm output; introducing food stamps and school lunches for the poor; and developing drought and disease-resistant corn varieties.

Ultimately, however, huge growers became the primary beneficiaries of no-planting and commodity farm subsidies. Food stamps, while they provide great nutritional benefits to the poor, do not change the status quo of food insecurity that derives from poor people being alienated from food production. Hybrid seed varieties set the stage for the frankenfoods that permeate today's food supply. GMOs (Genetically Modified Organisms), for example, wreak havoc on human health, the environment and the livelihoods of small farmers, both here and abroad.

The fatal flaw is the mindset to control nature, rather than to cooperate and communicate with the life principles that support us. Genetic changes that occur in nature require that new species prove themselves within the context of a complex ecosystem that can balance those changes over time. Producing genetic varieties in a laboratory, then unleashing them on unsuspecting human and environmental biospheres is simply reckless and irresponsible. Just as the medical profession invents more drugs to cure the adverse effects of "miracle cures," commercial agriculture seeks more and more technologies to cover the errors of previous "breakthroughs."

Meanwhile, the Earth's environments—forests, meadows, waterways and even deserts—demonstrate the processes of sustainable growth. System-wide interactions keep all the elements in a perpetual flow that is, generally, maintained for millennia. Trees drop leaves on the forest floor. The leaves become food for microorganisms that break down the leaves to become soil. The microorganisms are food for larger organisms that move through the system, carrying pollen and nutrients to other inhabitants and to the water, where other life is fed.

Although agriculture is not a part of the natural environment, it can be made to emulate nature and fit synergistically within ecosystems. Smaller agricultural footprints reduce the impact on the environment, promote biodiversity and human contact with other humans in a life-giving context. Small farms help maintain social and economic balance by requiring more hands-on labor. The more we move away from the Earth, the more technologies we need to fix our ailments. For example, more mechanization means less physical labor, so now we need artificial exercise environments to keep our bodies functional. The more timesaving technologies we invent, the less time we have to be human. We need a bridge back to our humanity. Food production can be that bridge, utilizing the land right under our feet.

Control the food and you control the people.
Control the oil and you control the nation.
Control the money and you control the world.

Henry Kissinger

Chapter 7

Industrial Agriculture and Its Impact

Some humans prefer to dominate and control, rather than be in harmony with the natural order of things. Chemicals kill everything that is in the soil. Chemicals support a system of agricultural production that is killing the Earth and her inhabitants.

Once upon a time, humankind had a much closer relationship with nature than we do today. In Western developed nations, we have lost that closeness to nature. Unfortunately, citizens of developing nations are aspiring to live as we do in America. We have changed the way we think about ourselves and the way we think about our relation to the material world around us. Let me take a minute and explain.

Isaac Newton (1643-1727) created a new way of thinking. For 200 years, science progressed along the track of Newtonian physics, Newtonian mechanics and Newtonian cosmology.

Thomas Kuhn, in <u>The Structure of Scientific Revolutions</u>, explains how science does not progress in a linear and continuous way. Rather, we undergo periodic paradigm shifts that open new ways of thinking and approaching life. The next major paradigm shift came with Albert Einstein and his <u>Relativity: The Special and the General Theory</u> in the early 20th century. Now our thinking has expanded to quantum mechanics and wave theory.

Rather than looking for ways to be in tune with nature and the core of nature, science moved to the point where man thought he could control and dominate nature. Scientists were able to look at the universe, apply mathematics to their observations and predict what was going to happen...to a certain extent. This thought process became the way to approach all of agriculture and all of life. Scientists today feel as though they can take nature apart and put it back together better than nature can do so itself.

One metaphor is this. A clock is broken. You are able to take the clock apart and see where all the parts fit. As you find the one part that is broken, you can fix it and put it back into the clock and make it work again. But nature doesn't work quite like that. The narrow focus on a few key minerals to encourage plant growth is an example of the inefficacy of this "plug and play" approach to agriculture.

The use of compost to grow food was commonplace until the mid-1800s. It was then that Justus von Liebig, a German scientist, discovered that plants needed certain nutrients at a minimum in order to be able to grow. He narrowed the requirements down to nitrogen, phosphorus and potassium as the key elements. Having isolated those elements as necessary, he formed a theory called the Law of the Minimum. Whichever nutrients are available to the plants at the minimum amount will determine that plant's ability to grow.

Liebig's Law of the Minimum led to the invention of nitrogen-based fertilizers and the propagation of plants utilizing these synthetic chemicals. This concept determines the amount of fertilizer to apply in modern agriculture. Plant growth in conventional commercial agriculture is controlled, not by the total resources available, but by the scarcest resource. Minimal plant nutrient requirements are chemically synthesized and added to the dirt. In Liebig's paradigm, the soil is no longer the source of plant nutrition. It is used only as a receptacle for holding plant roots.

With that perspective on plant growth, agriculturalists began to use fertilizer on the plants at the minimum required levels—not thinking about the soil, not thinking about the life in the soil and isolating the plants from the soil. In effect, they were saying, "We know more than God does." The thinking was, if we just add nitrogen, phosphorus and potassium to these plants, then we will be able to grow things.

The Law of the Minimum does not work on a long-term basis, because there are many elements that have been left out. Soil microorganisms and micronutrients in combination with each other create a symbiosis that helps plants to grow naturally. Plant and soil scientists, rather than farmers, now lead agricultural production. Farmers have relinquished their capacity to see what nature has provided and emulate how all of nature works together.

The Liebig perspective found proponents and allies in many researchers of the 1930s. The work of plant geneticists, including Henry A. Wallace and Norman Borlaug, in combination with industrial innovations, set the stage for a technological takeover of farming, food processing and food distribution on a global scale. I have a hero and an anti-hero in agriculture. George Washington Carver is my hero, and Norman Borlaug is my anti-hero. Borlaug is credited with saving over a billion people from starvation through the development of high-yielding varieties of cereal grains, expansion of irrigation infrastructure and modernization of management techniques, as well as distribution of hybridized seeds, synthetic fertilizers and pesticides to farmers.

Borlaug's work in plant genetics was greatly advanced when

Agricultural Secretary Henry A. Wallace sent the scientist to Mexico for agricultural and genetic research. Borlaug's hybrid varieties of wheat, rice and corn produced large yields, enhanced by their resistance to disease and ability to withstand chemical fertilizers. Evidence has shown, however, that the quality of the food has suffered.

Hybridization is the process of crossing two genetically different individuals to result in a third genotype with a different, often preferred, set of traits. Plants of the same species cross easily in the field and produce fertile progeny. Such plants are referred to as cross-pollinated plants. Seed companies create hybridized seeds such as corn, soy, wheat and rice in laboratories. It is not possible to replant these synthetically hybridized seeds. The problem with hybridization is that the seeds cannot be put back in the ground. Rather than saving seed for next year's crop, as farmers have always done, farmers must return to the seed companies to purchase the seeds for the new crop. In the 20th century this represented a major power shift, from the individual farmer's control over production, to corporate control.

Wallace and Borlaug were likely well-intentioned. However, the results of their thought processes and the paradigms in which they worked led to many of the problems we are working to solve today. There's an assumption that we can dominate nature and we're finding out every day that you cannot. The many natural disasters we have witnessed in this century alone should let people know that you can't dominate nature. It is so important to be in harmony with, and in tune with nature. This is the essence of natural agriculture.

The Second World War came on the heels of the Great Depression. Generally, war is an extraordinarily profitable enterprise. America's involvement in Iraq and Afghanistan mark the first time in history that recession and war occurred at the same time. Generally, people make money, and countries do very well when they're dominating and winning wars. After WWII ended, there were surplus chemicals that had been used in the war effort. Chemical and munitions manufacturers wanted to keep making money.

Ammonium nitrate had been used for manufacturing gunpowder during WWII. Varying forms of ammonia are principal elements in fertilizers. Ammonia provides nitrogen, which plants easily absorb. What were the munitions industries going to do with the surplus? In a shortsighted epiphany, they decided, "Wow! Let's sell it to the farmers." The farmers were able to grow more crops, but the chemicals also killed everything that's in the soil. Manufacturers like Dow, DuPont and Monsanto continued to make money.

Raj Patel, author of <u>Stuffed and Starved</u>, discusses the hidden battle for the world's food system. Western thought processes about agriculture have been exported all over the world. Now, a rush is underway for Westerners to acquire land in Africa. The continent of Africa has an abundance of natural resources that have been exploited by the West for centuries. World powers are attracted to these resources now, more than ever. The Chinese built a railway in Kenya, taking the port of Mombasa as collateral. The American military founded an Africa Command to establish a warning to the rest of the world of its hegemony. Arabs are buying land so that they, too, can export commercial agriculture and continue to dominate the populations. There's a global rush on the part of powerful political economies to re-colonize Africa. And that's a problem for the poor and impoverished.

After World War II, U.S. agricultural surpluses were used to dominate world politics by using food as a weapon rather than guns. The interesting parallel here is that food is grown from ammonium nitrate, a war material. Corn becomes bullets— ammunition for global economic dominance.

What do I mean? How does 'food as a weapon' work?

Many countries were devastated after WWII. People needed food. They had to eat. The American government told poorer nations, "We will give you food if you let us invest in your country and if you follow our rules." They instituted "Food for

Peace," the Public Law 480 program that came to fruition in the late 40s and early 50s. In essence, "You give us the political agreement that we ask for, and we'll ship you tons of food." National economies have been destroyed with these tactics.

Meanwhile, American players became entrenched in all aspects of global food production and distribution. Shipping companies make money by moving commodities around the world; large farmers make money through subsidized pricing; grain companies make money through storage and brokering. Everybody makes money except the folk in the countries who are receiving the food. In addition, there is an inequitable exchange for the raw materials obtained from the countries receiving the food. The essence of neo-colonialism is the exploitation and expropriation of raw materials for the benefit of Western civilization. Raw materials such as cocoa, shea nuts, rubber and strategic metals are brought back to the United States or Europe for added value processing, leaving the poor countries even poorer.

Along with the use of chemicals in food production, the U.S. government subsidized breeding programs to hybridize commodities and standardized them such that they all grow to the same height, making harvesting easier and more efficient. The principal grains around the world are corn, wheat, rice and soybeans; cotton is the other major crop. These five commodities stand out as the prime commercial crops around the world.

The Green Revolution has created a loss of food self-sufficiency around the world, rather than equitable growth. Commercial agriculture has become more concentrated, removing small farmers from the land. Those who remain are increasingly indebted because of the chemical-laden seeds and fertilizers that the Green Revolution brought into vogue. The only folks who have become rich are the grain companies and chemical companies that provide the agricultural inputs. The farmers themselves are not doing nearly as well.

Since civilization began, farmers have saved their seed for next year's crop. That's where the concept of tithing comes from. Historically, you plant a crop and every 10 seeds you get back, you save one and eat the other nine. You will find tithing all through the Bible. This is what happened in Egypt with David, Joseph and Pharaoh. That's why churches tithe now. It makes good sense. With hybridization, you cannot tithe. You have to return to the seed company. Then you have to purchase expensive inputs—petrochemicals like fertilizers and pesticides—for the seeds to produce effectively.

Monocrop culture and hybridized food are the antithesis of what you find in nature. In the woods, you see biodiversity—ecological diversity. There are many varieties of tall plants, short plants, trees and forests. Both tall and short grasses thrive in the savannahs. The specific grasses change over the course of a season, similar to how fruit progresses through the season. In the summer, you start with berries and cherries, peaches, apricots and nectarines. As the season progresses into fall, you get apples, persimmons and pears. The same thing happens out in the plains and the prairies, where the grasses grow. Buffalo followed the seasonal changes in grass variety as they roamed the prairies.

Go to any country practicing commercial agriculture, and you will see one commodity in the field, and that's it—a monocrop. One of the major problems with this form of production is, if you get a "dis-ease" or an insect infestation, it will eat up everything in the field, and your crop is gone. The insects are saying, "Here's lunch, let's eat!" In these circumstances, the whole field is the insects' favorite meal, the same crop with none of the protections provided by diversity.

A diverse biosphere brings good insects and bad insects. The good insects will ward off the bad ones. Certain plants growing next to each other help to repel insects and disease. Farmers who emulate nature's example utilize companion planting. The natural approach to agriculture creates a balance that produces sustainable harmony. You're always going to lose some, but you don't want to put yourself in a position of losing it all. The easiest way to lose it all is to have one crop growing in your fields. The old nursery warning applies here: "Don't put all your eggs in one basket." This is what we have done in commercial agriculture—we've put all our eggs in one basket, creating a need to keep administering chemical fertilizers and lots of water. It all becomes very precarious.

That brings us to genetically modified seeds, GMOs. Rather than hybridizing or cross-breeding plants, since the early 90s scientists have been taking genes and splicing them into seeds to produce the characteristics the chemical company wants. An important hybrid is Bt Cotton. Bt, Bacillus thuringiensis, is a bacterium that kills boll weevils and other bugs. I will use Bt, but I don't want a seed that has it spliced into its DNA. The bacteria are natural; I have used them occasionally to kill soft worms. I don't have to use it very often because our soil is healthy, and the plants are resistant to infestation.

Another significant use of GMO technology is Roundup. It is a broad-spectrum systemic herbicide and crop desiccant. The generic name is Glyphosate, and it is used to kill weeds, especially annual broad leaf weeds and grasses that compete with crops. Roundup kills all broad leaf plants. Companies spray Roundup from airplanes, they spray it with tractors, they spray by hand. Monsanto, now owned by Bayer of Germany, is a very large chemical company. Bayer, with annual revenues of US$40 billion, and DuPont, with annual revenues in excess of US$25 billion, are two of the biggest companies that make these agriculture chemicals.

Monsanto has created Roundup-Ready corn, cotton and soybeans. These GMOs are resistant to Roundup. Farmers can spray without fear that the Roundup will kill their crops. Scientists have inserted a gene into the seed itself so that it will resist the herbicide that kills the broad leaf weeds that emerge on the farm or in the garden. The only things that will grow are the corn, cotton and soybeans. No weeds—until super weeds evolve, that are immune to Roundup. Every year you plant, the plants and the insects become more and more resistant to all these chemicals. This demonstrates how nature will resist this science-based agriculture. You can't dominate nature.

While regulatory bodies worldwide have approved glyphosate and formulations such as Roundup, concerns about their effects on humans and the environment persist. Roundup adds more chemicals to the soil, to the food that we're eating and to the environment. Studies by the National Institute of Health (NIH) and the World Health Organization (WHO) indicate that human consumption of pesticides increases the incidence of chronic diseases, including diabetes, cancer, Alzheimer and Parkinson, as well as acute poisonings. Poor farming practices, including non-compliance with usage of masks and over-usage of chemicals, compound this situation. In 1989, WHO and the United Nations Environment Programme (UNEP) estimated that there were around 1 million human pesticide poisonings annually. Some 20,000 (mostly in developing countries) ended in death, as a result of poor labeling and loose safety standards.

What is Roundup doing to us, to the soil, to the people, to global climate change? It is supporting a system of agricultural production that is killing the earth. Those chemicals kill everything that's in the soil and leach into our groundwater. Often, before farmers even plant seeds, they will go into the fields with chemicals to kill all the weeds that are there. Then they spray Roundup to kill the weeds as they emerge from the soil. Farming this way requires chemical fertilizers, tremendous amounts of irrigation and pesticides.

Worldwide, farmers are convinced to use this new technology that makes money for corporations here in the West. To employ this new technology, farmers borrow the money to start their crops and, instead of making money, they become further and further in debt. This is sharecropping on a global scale. Most of these farmers, as in India, have never had to borrow money like this before. They were historically self-sufficient in that sense. It takes a tremendous amount of capital to grow industrial crops. Large-scale farming can be profitable by earning a small margin on a very large volume of production.

Early in my career I read two great books about organic

agriculture by Sir Albert Howard, one of the pioneers of the organic movement. His earliest publication, An Agricultural Testament (1940), is a classic organic farming text. He emphasizes the importance of maintaining humus, keeping water in the soil, and the role of soil mycorrhiza. Howard's other book that became part of my reference library is The Soil and Health: A Study of Organic Agriculture (1947). Howard spent many years in India and used elephant dung and other agricultural waste products to make humus and compost for growing food. Howard advocated studying the forest in order to farm like the forest. He tried to emulate nature, not conquer it. And it was very effective.

The natural approach is focused on creating biological life in the soil. The soil is a living thing, a part of Mother Earth. You have to feed the soil. Out in the woods, you can see humus all around. In it, you will find a multitude of life—centipedes, roly-polies, millipedes, earthworms, spiders—all kinds of insects, bacteria and fungus that make the soil a living, breathing thing.

The key indicator of soil quality is the number of earthworms that live in it. Earthworms can thrive only in healthy soil. If no earthworms are present, the soil is dead. If you start adding organic material like compost to the soil, the worms will suddenly appear. I don't know if they come out of the air or not, but they will appear.

In many places around the world, people collect dung from animals on the farm and use it as fertilizer. They use cows, horses, mules, goats, chickens and they even use human manure to feed the soil. All over the world, people use their own waste to put back in the ground and feed the soil. But I wouldn't do that in America. Think about what goes into the toilet in your home and decide if you would want some of the chemicals in your diet, prescription drugs and house cleaning products going back into your foods. No, I don't think so.

More water is needed with high technology agriculture, because water provides the transport system that underlies it all. The water is not just for the roots. Tons of water are required to get the chemicals down in the soil, to hold them down and to help them uptake to the plants. It takes more water to suction the chemicals up into all parts of the plants.

A great question is why does the Food and Drug Administration (FDA) allow these chemicals to be ingested if they are so dangerous to humans and the planet? It really is quite simple. The chemical companies, particularly Monsanto and DuPont, own the FDA. You can buy a politician. With all due respect to my political colleagues, the American political system is for sale. He who gives big bucks gets what he wants.

The Food and Drug Administration will not test to see if something is healthy. They will say that, based upon the information they have received from the manufacturer, who has agreed that they have tested these things, we feel that this product is safe. There's no safety there. Just like an audit that you get from an accountant, it is based upon the information that has been provided to the accountant, not forensic work. The FDA authorizes the use of Roundup as a chemical good to use on food because Monsanto said it is safe to be sold to the public.

These companies send their agents to Washington to represent their interests by lobbying the government or taking seats within the government. U.S. Trade Representatives and many high-level administrators at USDA, FDA and EPA often come out of the agricultural chemical industry. Michael Taylor, who worked as a lawyer for Monsanto, is a good example of this interconnection. From 1991-1994, he was Deputy Commissioner for Policy at the U.S. Food and Drug Administration. From 1994-1996, Taylor served as the Administrator of the Food Safety & Inspection Service at the United States Department of Agriculture. He went back to Monsanto from 1996-2000 as Vice President for Public Policy. Then he returned to the FDA from 2009-2016 as Deputy Commissioner for Foods. He is not the only example.

Familiar names working for Monsanto include:

Anne Veneman, U.S. Secretary of Agriculture 2001-2005

Monsanto Board of Directors
Veneman previously served on the Board of Calgene. In 1994, Calgene was the first company to bring genetically engineered food, the Flavr Savr tomato, to supermarket shelves. Monsanto bought out Calgene in 1997.

Donald Rumsfeld, Former U.S. Secretary of Defense 2001-2006
Monsanto Board of Directors
From 1977 to 1985, Rumsfeld served as Chief Executive Officer, President, and then Chairman of G. D. Searle & Company, a worldwide pharmaceutical company. In 1985, Searle was sold to the Monsanto Company.

Mickey Kantor, U.S. Trade Representative 1993-1996; U.S. Secretary of Commerce 1996 & 1997
Monsanto Board of Directors

Hillary Clinton, U.S. Secretary of State 2009-2013
Monsanto Board of Directors; Monsanto Lawyer
Clinton hired Monsanto lobbyist, Jerry Crawford, as the lobbyist for her campaign in 2015.

Clarence Thomas, U.S. Supreme Court Justice 1992-present
Corporate lawyer for Monsanto in the 1970s

Roger Beachy, Director, USDA National Institute of Food & Agriculture 2009-11
President (1999-2009) of Monsanto's de facto nonprofit research arm, the Danforth Plant Science Center.

This list is far from exhaustive. Interlocking associations can be found throughout U.S. government agencies. The very companies that are polluting and destroying the planet have their representatives helping to make the decisions in Congress and in the executive branch of the U.S. government.

A lot of political machinations occur, with individuals and companies trying to control and dominate, not only the world of nature, but also the people in the world. If I give a major campaign contribution directly or through a political action committee to a member of Congress and the member gets re-elected, they already know my point of view on a subject. The member is going to listen to me because they want to keep those contributions flowing. In 2010, the Supreme Court determined that corporations are people and can make campaign contributions. It's an insidious system, but it's the one we have.

We can rail against this, but I decided that I have to be part of creating an alternative. We educate people and help them to have a better understanding of these paradigms and how they affect us. The most effective remedy comes from the real actions that we take. Organizations like Truly Living Well Center for Natural Urban Agriculture, which grows food naturally, are creating the alternative.

The question is, what are you going to do about it?

If you come to me and say, "I have 10 acres of land," I would say take half of it and plant fruits trees. That's the first thing one should do, and then start growing vegetables. Get your long-term food, fruit trees, in the ground first. It is called edible landscaping. If you want to sit in some shade, why not plant a fruit tree so you can eat fruit while you enjoy the shade. An apple could hit you in the head and you could eat it for lunch. You don't have to stay in the hammock all day. Let that land be productive. Grow your own food naturally.

The USDA organic standard is a patented phrase. It's something that agricultural producers buy. There are many U.S. commercial farmers growing organic food as a market niche, not as a way of life. There are problems with organic terminology; too many loopholes in the rules allow commercial growers to circumvent organic regulations. For example, if organic seed is not readily available, a farmer can use commercial seed, as long as the seed is untreated, i.e. not sprayed with any chemicals.

Many biologic chemicals can be used that are toxic to insects and fungi, and likely toxic to people, and the food can still be labeled organic—for example, copper-based pesticides, which are used as fungicides in both organic and conventional fruit production. Further, synthetic pesticides on the national organic standards list may be used as a last resort if organic products are not adequate to control the problems.

It's oxymoronic to me to have food that was produced in China travel 12,000 miles and sold at Wal-Mart with an organic stamp on it. A current debate is whether hydroponic production, which has no connection to soil, can be certified organic.

The only way you're really going to know what you're getting in your food is to grow it yourself, or go to someone you know, who is growing the food for you. People can attain horticultural literacy. It is extremely important for people to know who grows their food, the quality of their food and where their food comes from. Just because it's labeled organic does not mean it's healthful and safe. You have to know what it is. The best place to buy fresh food is at a local farmer's market, where you can know the farmers' sources and growing practices.

Urban agriculture transforms both people and places.
It is a powerful catalyst for sustainable community vitality.
Our work builds self-sufficiency through food production
and education.

K. Rashid Nuri

Chapter 8

Urban Agriculture

The power and promise of urban agriculture became crystal clear to me over time. Urban agriculture is the wave of the future. The food paradigm we live in is broken. With most Americans living in urban areas, we need to produce food where we live. Historically, people lived within walking distance of their source of food. Today, that's no longer true. Food travels thousands of miles to get to our tables, creates a huge carbon footprint, uses up fossil fuel and becomes nutrient-depleted before it gets to our tables. Urban agriculture is not only about repairing the food system, but also our way of life. It's a way of restoring communities, transforming both people and places.

The American agricultural system is broken. It is not growing food that is healthy and accessible to all the people. There are too many blockages in the system, and too many people being left out of the process. The agricultural wealth of the country is concentrated in the hands of a few producers, distributors and processors. I saw that concentration of wealth and power up close and personal at Cargill. Travels throughout the lower 48 showed me how the people suffer under our industrial-based food system.

Many people in this country—children in this country—go to bed hungry. And many of the people who have plenty of food to eat are being fed substances that are not suitable for human consumption—petroleum-based fertilizers, pesticides and herbicides. Food has been out of the ground so long by the time it gets to the consumer that the nutritional value has long been depleted. Many nutrients are destroyed, along with the soil, which has been subjected to a host of chemical additives.

Food production is like an hourglass, with the farmers who are producing on top, the people who eat the food on the bottom and food brokers squeezed in the middle. Food brokers include the processors, transporters, distributors and grocery stores. The players in the middle choke the system, blocking the way of producers and consumers. The local food economy that we are creating skips unnecessary brokers in the middle, getting the food directly from the folks who are producing it to the people who are consuming it. That is one of the principal benefits of a local food economy.

The good news is, hunger among consumers for living, healthy food has grown over the past few decades. Just one year after I started the first community gardens in San Diego in 1970, there were sixty such gardens throughout the city. More consumers are aware of the life change that occurs when communities control the production of their food. The commercial food system has succeeded in alienating people from their food. People no longer understand where food comes from. Many people are afraid to eat food unless it comes from a grocery store or restaurant. The beauty and the abundance of what the Earth gives us are lost on people who do not understand their absolute dependence on the Earth for sustenance. With such a warped perspective, how can we expect to have peaceful and productive individuals, families and cities?

The new agriculture establishes a fully connected, accessible, equitable agricultural system in which neighborhoods, communities and cities maintain sovereignty over the food that sustains them. No people should be without control over their food. Food sovereignty is a basic human right and responsibility. It is fundamental to effective functioning on this planet. Stewardship of food is our birthright. We have to end the monopolization of the available supplies of food and land. Quality food must be a right, not a privilege.

War capitalism and industrial capitalism changed the relationships that people had with the land and their food. That dynamic has to change. It is changing. Building local food economies gets more local people involved with the creation of their food. The world in which people lived within walking distance of where their food was produced does not exist anymore. But the process of recreating elements of it is underway, so that people can regain control of their food.

Folks in poorer neighborhoods have to work extraordinarily hard to avoid eating garbage food. First of all, many people still don't know the difference between nutritious food and harmful food. Second, access to quality food is severely limited. I don't like the term, "food desert," because the phrase is racially charged. It's really about economics, it's about education, transportation and housing. These elements are determinants for why people don't eat well and don't live well. We want people to truly live well.

The USDA adopted use of the term, "food desert" in 2009, after the phrase had been in general use since around 1994. In 2008, Congress directed the Agency to research and report on access to quality food in the United States. The term has come to be associated with Black and Brown people, people of color, whose only access to fresh food is the apple and banana purchased at the corner gas station. Computerized foods from McDonald's or Burger King are always available. Fresh, quality food is not. Unfortunately, it has been documented by dozens of studies that supermarket and other fresh food access is vastly more limited in lower-income neighborhoods.

The definition of a food desert has evolved since 2009, and now includes four levels of income and distance from a supermarket. Frequently, the second level of the definition is used, which refers to an area that is more than one mile from a supermarket. The joke is that rich people travel just as far to get quality food as many poor people. The difference is that poor women must take a bus and train with shopping bags and children in tow, to get to better food choices. Rich folk just jump in their Mercedes and drive to the food. It is an issue of economics and education, not color that makes the distinction.

Just around the corner from where I live, there's a grocery store that sells garbage food. That's the only type of store that opens up in many Black neighborhoods. The big grocery stores chains will not provide service. But you can go up on the corner and purchase from Church's fried chicken, Checkers and every other hamburger joint known to man.

Community gardens, urban farms and farmers' markets have begun to fill the spaces left by the flight of large supermarkets from Black neighborhoods. There is a long way to go to completely fill the gaps in access. Often, the only people selling decent food in Black neighborhoods are the Africans who sell their own native food. They don't grow it; they have to import the ingredients. The problem is, even when you make good food available to community folk, they still don't buy it in sufficient quantities to support business people, because they don't know any better.

An educational process is essential. The best store in my neighborhood is a West African shop that sells a lot of vitamins, pills and supplements. The owner, who is from The Gambia, keeps his store stocked with fresh fruits and vegetables. He has his West African customers, and I guess other folks in the neighborhood come there and buy his wares as well. Otherwise, there is no quality food in the community at Campbellton and Delowe in Southwest Atlanta.

Parents and grandparents used to grow their own food in backyard gardens. The generation of freedmen, right out of captivity, saw many farmers go back into the economic slavery of sharecropping. Others fled the newly-minted slave conditions. They traveled north and went to work in the factories. Henry Ford and the railroads started bringing people up north and out west. That trend went on for a large portion of the twentieth century. Black people became wage slaves and got away from the land in huge numbers.

Generally, the elder generation that preceded me doesn't want to grow food anymore, because it reminds them of slavery or sharecropping. It's so fascinating to see their children and their grandchildren, even some my age, coming out to our gardens saying, "Wow, I remember that my grandmother grew food. I watched my grandfather raise all of us on the farm; then we left to go to college to get good jobs." Young people have been taken far away from the land.

Agriculture is no longer seen as a noble profession. It's seen as the last thing anyone would want to do. The average age of farmers is over 60 years old. The slave-on-the-plantation paradigm is one of the reasons Black people have been losing so much land. We've lost respect for the land and what it can do for us.

It is just nonsense to foster the idea that global population growth is outstripping the available land and that farmers are unable to produce enough food to feed the people. That is a Malthusian concept. Thomas Malthus was an economist of the 1700s who created the theory that populations would outgrow the supply of food. Commercial agriculture and the lobby supporting it have built upon that theory since then.

Overpopulation has been part of the rationale for eugenics, for imperialism and colonialism. These are efforts to control people and their resources, and it undergirds racism and classism. Westerners want to use the world's natural resources to take care of White folks. That's a racist notion and concept. The people of Africa were not starving until Europeans started colonizing them. Colonialism, neo-colonialism and massive economic inequality are some of what the politics of food is all about.

Malthus' doctrine of increasing numbers of people and diminishing supplies of food has no supporting evidence. In fact, what we're finding now is that with GMOs, the cost inputs continue to increase, and the benefits are not apparent. Scientific studies are now reporting that GMO production does not continue to increase yields. A 2015 article by the Environmental Working Group reported that GMOs have not actually increased yields. The article cited several studies on corn and soy yields, comparing U.S. production utilizing genetically engineered seed versus non-GE seeds in Western Europe. There were no significant differences in yields. The articles can be accessed at https://www.ewg.org/agmag/2015/03/claims-gmo-yield-increases-don-t-hold and https://www.ewg.org/release/claims-gmos-will-feed-world-don-t-hold#.Wor8UxPwbFw.

Testimony given to the U.S. House of Representatives has refuted claims by companies like Monsanto, that GE crops increase yields. View reports on House hearings at https://www.motherjones.com/food/2013/02/do-gmo-crops-have-lower-yields/ and https://www.cornucopia.org/2015/04/claims-of-gmo-yield-increases-dont-hold-up/.

The cost of producing GMOs has gone up and up. The modalities are producing super weeds, which require more chemicals to make GMO crops grow. Chemical agriculture is a zero-sum game, as has been demonstrated. We need to get out of that paradigm. It's broken. It does not work. History—our current reality—has proven that to be true. Malthus is dead.

The ramifications of chemical agriculture manifest in many other areas, such as eugenics. Eugenics started as a way to control the population of people of color here and around the world. The concept was repackaged as birth control, in order to make it more palatable, following the hideous applications of eugenics in Germany prior to and during WWII. In 1954, when Rockefeller interests invested money to help start Planned

Parenthood, it was White women who availed themselves of birth control modalities. Eugenics has backfired. Overall, White people now have negative birth rates, while the rest of the world has increasing birth rates. The total global population is increasing.

The lens of race is appropriate in this analysis because the intent of eugenics was to eliminate people of color around the world. The growth in population of people of color has contributed to an international resurgence of White nationalism, politics of White supremacy and fascism. Fear, based on a sense of scarcity of natural and social resources, is fueling the rejection of migrants and refugees globally.

Thomas Mboya, from Kenya, bought into the failing paradigm of scarcity. I was reading his book when I had my burning bush experience. He believed chemicals and technology could solve hunger problems. Mboya wrote <u>Freedom and After</u> in 1963. His approach to taking on the challenges of feeding his people was a Malthusian response. Mboya was sold a bill of goods.

One sentence catalyzed the burning bush experience that led me into agriculture and ultimately, urban agriculture. Mboya wrote, "With all the technology available in the world today, there is no reason we cannot chemically synthesize enough food to feed all the people." Now I have come full circle. I know with clarity and certainty that natural urban agriculture is a system that can get us out of the cycle of chemical denaturing, nutrient-depleting, Earth-alienating approaches that we have applied to our food and our lives.

All wealth, all health, all life begins and ends with the soil. All the resources needed to live as human beings come out of the Earth. All the trees, all the plants, everything is connected to the Earth. The gold, diamonds, silver, all the minerals, all the strategic metals that are primarily in Africa, where Black people live, come out of the Earth. I don't think we show enough respect to the Earth. There are many societies around the world that do respect the Earth—the Pygmies, the Aborigines and other indigenous peoples of the world, have great respect. Each of those societies has tens of thousands of years of history, which they are able to relate and recount orally. Their story goes back to the origins of the Earth and the connections that we have with the Earth.

By disrespecting the Earth, we are disrespecting human life. We are disrespecting all life, because all life is connected, and it's the Earth, the soil, that is the beginning and the end of life. Even the scriptures say that: ashes to ashes, dust to dust. We come from the Earth, and we're going to go back to the Earth at the end of our time, one way or another.

The new agriculture is being constructed around local food economies with more small to medium farms, owned by the farmers and their families, in cities and suburbs, as well as rural areas. Eugene Cooke trademarked the phrase, "Grow Where You Are," which is so true. Trademarking that phrase is difficult, because it comes up in the conversations of so many people in the New Food Movement. But it's true—people need to grow food wherever they are. You can grow food in your front yard, your back yard, on your patio, on your balcony, in your kitchen window. Wherever you are, you can grow something, and I think people should do that. It will help people be grounded and bring them many benefits.

However, one aspect of the new agriculture begs careful scrutiny and understanding. There are many folk pursuing indoor agriculture. Hydroponics has become quite popular, but the techniques continue the paradigm of commercial agriculture. Instead of focusing on building soil to produce healthy crops, commercial farmers use dirt only as the receptacle to hold roots and the chemicals they feel essential to growing plants. Likewise, hydroponics uses water as a receptacle for roots and chemicals. This is yet another implementation of Justus von Liebig's "Law of the Minimum." Indoor agriculture in its many variations is fine, as long as soil is the basis of food production, not chemicals.

This country has become more urban over the past century. 82% of Americans live in cities. Our food must be produced in urban environments as well. Those who remain in rural areas need to grow food there also. The best food for you is food grown in the same locality where you live, the same longitude and latitude, because that food is going to be in tune with your vibratory rates.

Creating local food economies is central to creating a healthier food system. We have to get the chemicals out of our food. If you were to ask the commercial agricultural industry, they'd say we're going a step backwards. But, even if you go to the top of the food chain, to folk that want to eat meat, you have to ask: Why would they want meat that's coming from confined animal feed operations? You are what you eat. Confined animal operations have cows and pigs being raised on concrete, lying around in their own filth, being given antibiotics and other drugs to keep them alive, in situations that are inhumane. It's just not right.

In <u>Genetic Roulette</u>, author Jeffrey M. Smith recounts numerous studies showing links between GMOs, the popular herbicide, glyphosate, and disease. The connections are further demonstrated in the scientific report titled, "Genetically Engineered Crops, Glyphosate and the Deterioration of Health in the United States of America," published in the September 2014 issue of the Journal of Organic Systems. Researchers showed strong correlations between the surge in rates of 22 chronic diseases and the increased use of glyphosate since 1994. There has been a consistent rise in chronic dis-ease in U.S. populations since the introduction of hybrid foods, particularly since the 1940s.

The system is broken. We need to go back to smallholder farms rather than large farms. We need more people involved in agriculture. People need to get out of these unhealthy work environments—factories and tall buildings—where there's artificial light, no air. The systems we live in now are unhealthy. It has to change. It is changing.

Each community has to figure out what is the best arrangement for their situation, considering the amount of arable land, open urban land, climate, infrastructure and investments. Whole

Foods in Atlanta considers their local food region to run from Florida up to Virginia, all the Southern states. Every climate has a specialty that it can grow. What we don't need to have is lettuce coming from California to Atlanta. That makes no sense, when we can grow lettuce all year round in Atlanta. Disparities like this one are amenable to swift correction.

The Metropolitan Atlanta area has almost a million acres of land not occupied with roads, buildings, or houses. It would take maybe 25,000 or 30,000 of those acres to provide all the fruits and vegetables to feed everybody in the metro area. Is that going to happen overnight? No. Meat and grains will always be grown in rural areas. There are limits to growth, limits on the range of what we can do. I think we need to make agriculture less *ex*tensive and more *in*tensive.

Georgia's climate and soils can grow wheat in the southwest and rice over on the coast. The Gullah people of the South Carolina Sea Islands grow rice, just down the road from Atlanta. In addition to wheat, South Georgia can grow oats, corn, and rye. A lot of people are now into what are called the ancient grains—those varieties that have not been tampered with over the years, like spelt, amaranth, quinoa and a few others. Amaranth grows wild down in Southwest Georgia. Georgia is suitable for cows, pigs, chickens and sheep. A good variety of fruit can grow. Apples tend to need a little cooler weather, and they can grow in the mountains of Georgia.

In some northern areas, like New York, they grow food on rooftops. A lot of acreage is available on rooftops. Greater New York, the metro area, used to be fed by farms in the Connecticut River Valley, in Massachusetts and Connecticut. They used to bring food down to the city. To have it come from all the way across the country makes no sense. Like other areas, they would have to source their grains and meats from rural areas regionally.

Growing seasons can be extended in several ways. Go back a couple hundred years and see how the people in the north ate in the winter. They grew their food and stored it over the wintertime. They had root cellars, which are just cool places where they could store their cool season crops—carrots, potatoes, rutabagas, beets, sweet potatoes, and squash. Bring them indoors, and they can last the wintertime. Root vegetables store well over long periods of time. Even cabbages can last for quite a while.

Food can be preserved in so many ways, dried, canned, pickled—which is what people have done traditionally for thousands of years. In Korea, where it gets very cold, they eat a lot of kimchi and other fermented vegetables. Fermentation is an excellent form of preservation of food that was grown in the summertime, so it lasts over the winter. People look forward to the springtime, when they can grow new crops again. I don't know of any culture that does not have a harvest festival, when you celebrate the new crops. In Africa, West Africa in particular, folks eat a lot of yams. You harvest the yams in the fall, and they have big parties around those yams. Yams last all the way into the next year, when they grow some more and then have another harvest festival. The feeling is, we've made it through the year, so let's have a party around food and be grateful.

Food sovereignty and food self-sufficiency are very important. Food self-sufficiency is people having enough food to eat. Food sovereignty is having control of the food being produced. Knowing who grows your food, the quality of your food, and where your food comes from is horticultural literacy. When you buy a bag of food from the store, you usually have no idea where it was produced, who produced it, the modalities, or the methodologies that were employed to produce that food.

It's important to dissociate farming from slavery. When I began to farm, I met many folk who didn't really want to farm because they connected farming with slavery. My son has a brother-in-law from South Carolina who never brought his family out to the farm because the experience felt too much like slavery to him. I witness this attitude a lot, typically with seniors who don't want to have anything to do with working the land. Part of my work is to help people regain an appreciation for the land.

I remember one time a lady came out to the farm on a Sunday after she had attended church service. She was dressed in her Sunday best, either on her way or coming back from the DeKalb Farmer's Market in Atlanta, which is a very large arena with food displayed from all over the world. She looked at the food, and said, "Rashid, you know, this food looks, looks...."

I said, "What, it looks dirty?"

She said, "Yeah, it looks dirty."

This food was fresh because I was harvesting it right there on the spot. The food had just been removed from the ground. From her perspective, it looked dirty. It could not be as good as that imported, hybrid, GMO food that she was going to buy at the market, which looked pristine clean. The food being harvested before her eyes was dirty; it had soil on the roots. It didn't look clean; it wasn't packaged pretty; it didn't have a ribbon tied around it to make her feel good. Naturally, food in the ground is going to have dirt on it! Food prepared for sale would be washed thoroughly. Even so, you wouldn't have to wash it to the same extent as the food from the grocery store because there are no chemicals used on it.

The new agriculture is not about everybody farming. Everybody is not going to grow food. You would have to completely disassemble the current economic system if you anticipated everyone growing his or her own food. We're way past that. In a local food economy, we have people who are growing food, taking it to a farmer's market and selling it. The farms are close to where people live, and you can get to know your farmer, visit his or her operation, and see what they do and how they do it. There is a cohort of entrepreneurs who create added value products and bring them to the market and sell it. It's local people trading with local people to feed local people.

Operating a small to medium farm may not be a million-dollar business, and you are unlikely to get rich, but you can make a good solid, middle-class income for your family. Like any other business, you have to plan and work strategically. Depending on what you're growing, how you're selling and your merchandising approach, you can do very well. Of course, some people are going to do better than others.

It's important to know that small-scale food production is more efficient. Natural agriculture is just as productive, if not more so, than commercial agriculture. This is a big surprise to most people, because it is contrary to the fiction that industrial agriculture represents salvation for the world. Cuba is an excellent example of what can be done. 90% of the food that the people in Havana eat is grown right in Havana. The global embargos against Cuba were a blessing in disguise. They were banned from trading with the rest of the world, particularly with America, which is only 90 miles away. Cubans were forced to creatively feed themselves. They had to grow their own food, right there in the city. They feed themselves. And I think that's a model that can be used in many places around the world.

Urban Agriculture is happening now. The question is, what are the requirements needed to sustain the local food economy and make it even more successful? The answer is increased and greater community support. In Atlanta, municipal support is growing. Only recently did we obtain zoning regulations that make it technically legal to grow food. The zoning ordinance that the City Council passed in 2014 was the most progressive in the U.S. at the time. Other cities, other mayors, have also given great help. In Chicago, for example, if you live on a block and there's an empty lot, you can buy that empty space for a dollar or lease it for an interminable amount of time. Cities are putting regulations in place, providing the inputs and financial support to increase food production that takes place in urban spaces.

Urban agriculture needs government support, academic support, financial support, foundations, corporations, as well as the will of the people. Understanding has to increase. An educational process is underway, but it's a long way from being accomplished. To a large extent, we find ourselves preaching to the converted, preaching to the choir around these issues. We have to expand our outreach.

Part IV

STRUCTURE & SKILLS
– SECTION A –

—✺✺✺—

Travel is perhaps the most all-encompassing way to develop life skills. Education through travel is unparalleled in its efficacy. Learning geography in school, studying world cultures and watching nature shows are all very useful. However, they do not compare to the benefits of travel. Witnessing the sun rise and set from different parts of the globe, observing the night sky, standing on different terrains and interacting with people from different cultures transmits ancient understandings that transcend anything a classroom could offer.

Social structures worldwide provide pathways and support for action. When change happens, it will soon make its way through a social structure, though it may begin in the mind of an artist or the heart of a lone pioneer. It is essential for revolutionaries to be aware of available social structures and the capacity of those structures to launch the envisioned transformations. As revolutionaries, we often seek massive restructuring and loathe participating in current social structures. Change, however, is built upon what is. If we are to build, we will build on the ground and shoulders upon which we stand. Greater success comes when we honor and appreciate what has come before, even as we take it to higher evolution.

Travel has been a motif permeating my life. I wanted to know the world as well as I knew the United States, and I wanted to learn the world through my work, not as a tourist. My work was the social structure that provided the pathway and support for my travel, learning and skills development. The next chapters outline travel and work opportunities that unfolded for me in a way that was divinely inspired. Each new adventure logically built upon the previous to continually expand my agricultural knowledge and human experience.

My agricultural skills and intellectual tools were developed at each node along the way, building upon previous experiences. Section A chronicles my early professional years. Eager and—I thought—unstoppable, I took up my mantle and dashed out into the world to save the day. My travels took me throughout the United States, on small farms and large ones. I sampled the red clay soils of Georgia, and the rich black loam of Mississippi. The people who produced in those soils shared their wisdom with me.

Included here are mistakes made and lessons learned. I introduce you to some of the wonderful characters I met along the way. Hopefully, the reader is able to see the pictures of the many disparate places that I visited, and the people who inhabit the many lands in which I have worked. I urge you to travel to many lands for yourself. There's nothing like it.

Practical aspects of agriculture and the geographic distribution of produce are described. The county committee system, cotton ginning, big farms, carrying charge markets, rubber manufacturing, grain origination and international grain trading will all be discussed. How all these elements of agriculture connect is elucidated.

Observing and participating in the journey from seed to the table created a paradigm within which I could achieve my goals. The arrangement of and relations between the elements crafted a structure. The complexity of the structural elements morphed into an operational design quite simple. The quality of being functionally organized to build institutions able to endure and stand the test of time is truly revolutionary. Rebellions tear down structures. Revolutions rebuild.

When after acquiring proficiency in these sciences,
I turned my attention to the methods of the Sufis.
I came to know that their method attains perfection
by means of theory and practice.

Imam Ghazzali

Chapter 9

Early Professional Years

The very first work I did out of university was to install organic community gardens and build farms around San Diego County. I was teaching children in school about edible crops that grow above the ground in contrast to those that grow below. It amazes me to look back and see that, from the moment agriculture became a divine imperative in my life, I have traveled a wide but straight path in that pursuit. I truly have been given a broad understanding of food production, distribution and nutrition "from the seed to the table." Ironically, the activities that began my professional career are exactly the same undertakings that completed my mission. Little did I know!

I left my growing family temporarily in Massachusetts with my in-laws and returned to California in late 1974 to look for work. The plan was for them to join me after I had obtained a position. California is the richest agricultural producing region in the history of the world. I figured there would not be a better place to observe the principles that I had learned at UMass than California, the place where I came of age. I traveled up and down the state, investigating all aspects of agriculture. That was one magnificent tour. It was likely the single most exhilarating educational experience of my life.

I toured the San Joaquin Valley to see animal feed lots and dairy farms and cotton production and vegetable production and almond groves. I saw the artichokes in Watsonville and citrus groves in Ventura County. I visited the wine country in Santa Clara, Napa and Sonoma Counties. I saw table grape production in many places. There was just so much to see. I visited the University of California at Davis, which is the premier agriculture school in the country. The men and women who run big business in California agriculture were very kind and patient in answering my many questions. I traveled around the state for two months. I did not land a job, however.

My travels included King's Canyon to see the giant Sequoias, truly some of the greatest wonders in the world. The canyons of the Kings River are actually the deepest canyons in North America, deeper even than the Grand Canyon, although they lack some of the spectacular topography of that area. From the bottom of the canyon to the top is fully 8000 feet in places.

The Grant Grove area of Kings Canyon contains some of the most massive trees on the planet. The largest sequoia in the Grant Grove is the General Grant tree. This giant is the third largest tree in the world. It stands 267 feet tall and 107.6 feet in circumference at its base. Actually, at breast height, its diameter is greater than any known tree in the world.

Giant sequoias can grow to over 300 feet tall, with diameters of 20 feet or more, and live for over 4000 years. It is difficult to appreciate the size of these giants because neighboring trees are so large. The largest of the sequoias are as tall as an average 26-story building. Their diameters at the base exceed the width of many city streets. The sequoias produce about 40 cubic feet of wood each year, approximately equal to the volume of a 50-foot-tall tree one foot in diameter. The ages of the General Sherman, General Grant and other large sequoias are sometimes estimated at 3500 years old. Botanists believe that the other giants in the grove are between 1800 and 2700 years old. These trees have seen civilizations come and go, have survived countless fires and long periods of drought, and continue to flourish—inspiring yet another generation of admirers, especially me.

When I arrived in San Diego, I went to the extension service and asked for a job. The County Extension Director, Victor Brown, said, "Well no, we don't have any money to hire you. But if you can find some money, I'll let you work here." That was good news to me. I still had many connections in San Diego from my high school days.

I reconnected with David Hermanson, my high school counselor. He created and managed the gifted student program for the San Diego Unified School District. Hermanson was eager for me to meet one of his protégés, a young woman from Texas of terrific intellect. Brenda Boles Richie was brilliant and engaging. She and I linked on many levels, and our relationship eventually resulted in the birth of my fourth child, Khadir Nuri Richie.

I went to see a County Supervisor named Moon. He knew me from my days as President of the Associated Student Councils and Representative to the Board of Education. The Supervisor had money set aside that he was able to invest in my project, so I could hire myself out. My first job out of college was with the Cooperative Extension Service.

My primary responsibility was to establish community gardens and work with school children in San Diego County. In the early 1970s, the concept of organic farming was not respected. Although ancient in origin, many people thought the techniques were new and exotic, with limited commercial value. I fought successfully to establish organic gardens throughout the county, despite the skepticism of my colleagues. I was most closely associated with the 4H staff. The staff relished the idea of involving so many people in community agriculture, but none of the 4H folks would support me during debate with the extension staff members. All they knew was "traditional" chemically based agricultural production and dared not venture into this controversial territory. Over time, the community garden concept and organic agriculture were embraced, and they have proliferated. Staffing for the 4H program increased. Twenty years later, the U.S. Department of Agriculture was developing national standards for organic agriculture.

I was teaching myself practical agricultural skills. I said to Extension Director Brown, "I need to learn. I don't really know how food grows, so I want to plant a few crops." The amazing thing is that my agricultural course work had provided no practical skills. Director Brown allowed part of my work during the day to include cultivating my own garden. I watched and learned how vegetables grew. I saw how seeds germinate and emerge from the soil. I saw how different cultivars manifested their leaves and what they looked like. There are differences between root crops like carrots and beets. There are similarities between cabbages, collards and broccoli in the early stages of their development, but major differences as they mature.

This was all new to me. The extension service published pamphlets and brochures on vegetable production. I collected and studied these, along with numerous books on vegetable and fruit production. I was able to translate, transfer and share that information to people in the community.

I completely landscaped my house with vegetables and created a living, edible landscape. Around the driveway, I had different colors of cabbage and carrots. In the backyard, I grew peas, beans, broccoli, spinach, squash and melons. We also had some citrus trees on the property. The only exception to the edible landscape was a rose bush I had planted in front of the house. Little did I know the significance that roses were going to take in my future. Again, the ground we stand on creates the pathway to the next level.

I helped Brother Randy, my original agricultural mentor, put together a large organically grown community garden in southeast San Diego. That was 1975. The school children that I worked with were primarily in the Black community. White folks, mostly rich, continued widespread development of community gardens in the County. The leadership for advancing the food movement primarily came from a small group of people who were receptive to what others and I had to say about the benefits of organic agriculture.

The gardens I worked with and started during my time with the Extension Service were the first community gardens in San Diego County. When I came back a year later, all the people at the Extension Service said, "Well, thank you so much, Rashid. You made this happen, and now we have 60 community gardens around the County." It turned out that community gardens were the mother lode for 4H programs. The gardens provided an entire arena where they could excel. I was proud to say that it was predicated on the work that I had begun.

Later, the wife of one of the San Diego city councilmen took the garden away from Brother Randy. As a person of influence, she supported the idea of urban agriculture, and found it necessary to take his garden as her own. Consequently, Randy and Ben Bella were displaced and left devoid of their large urban farm site. The woman who executed the eviction proved unable to properly manage the farm, and it disappeared.

It's crucial for communities to have sovereignty over their own land and food production. Whoever controls your food, controls you. Blockages to land and food production are compounded by the legacy of slavery and sharecropping, which has caused many Black people to turn away from the profession of agriculture. The importance of Black people controlling land became apparent later that year when I began working in Terrell County, Georgia on the farm owned by the Nation of Islam.

*No nation will ever respect us as long as we beg
for that which we can do for ourselves.*

Elijah Muhammad, *Message to the
Blackman in America*

Chapter 10

The Nation of Islam
Terrell County, Georgia

The fight for dignity and equality is futile without economic power. Power begets power. In 1975, I knew of only one organization in contemporary America that acted on the concept in a practical manner.

In my view, The Honorable Elijah Muhammad was the only man living in America teaching Black people to build institutions and businesses that were self-dependent. He demanded freedom, justice and equality for American Blacks. Mr. Muhammad did not rely on moral suasion, trying to get White people to be nice to Black people. Most of the major civil rights organizations have unsuccessfully attempted to secure gains for Black people through persuasion. Unfortunately, that tact has been the essential history and operating motif of many of these organizations. But hope is alive. The face of Malcolm X now adorns a U.S. postal stamp.

The country has yet to acknowledge the work and contributions of The Honorable Elijah Muhammad. However, the consciousness that his work evoked has made its way into all strata of American society. Attention to a healthy diet and expressions like "eat to live" and "do for self" have become commonplace.

Shortly after the turn of the century, in the early 2000s, Kweisi Mfume, former President and CEO of the NAACP, spoke at the annual Black State of the Union meeting hosted by Tavis Smiley to assess the Black State of the Union. Mfume espoused a program that sounded like a recitation of "What We Want" from the back page of the *Muhammad Speaks* newspaper. Freedom, justice, equality and reparations for the history of chattel slavery are the essence of what was wanted.

Savior's Day is the national holiday of the Nation of Islam. On Savior's Day in February 1975, the leader and teacher of the Nation of Islam, the Honorable Elijah Muhammad, dropped his body, and his son took over the leadership. That spring, Minister Louis Farrakhan came to California and gave a talk at San Diego State University. There must have been 3000 people in the audience that day. He called me up on stage and told all my home people that Mr. Muhammad's son, Warith Deen Muhammad, had invited me to Chicago to become involved with the farms owned by the Nation of Islam. At the time, I was one of the few members of the Nation who had formal training in agriculture. Leadership in Chicago learned this because Minister Amos of Temple No. 8 in San Diego knew my family and me and had forwarded information about my education and work to Headquarters.

Warith Deen Muhammad oversaw the largest conversion of any people to orthodox Islam in the history of the religion. He invited all the educated Muslims to the Chicago headquarters to help him in his work. An incredibly sharp group of Black men and woman gathered in Chicago, the most intelligent group of people with whom I have ever been associated.

The Honorable Elijah Muhammad reached out to Black

people of all classes, from former criminals to highly educated professionals. I spoke to a number of brothers who held the false perception that the Nation consisted of the "lumpen proletariat," poor and uneducated Black people who were attracted by the call of the brothers who sold Muhammad Speaks newspapers to "Come to the Temple and learn the truth." Therefore, it sounded like the Nation was anti-education. In fact, Elijah Muhammad encouraged people to gain knowledge to help build the community. There was a sizable number of educated people in the Nation, many with Ivy League training. It was sad that we had not even known each other. The months in Chicago provided an opportunity for us to meet and know each other. I established some lifelong friendships with members of that phenomenal group of people.

The Nation had four farms. The Michigan farm was approximately 160 acres. There were two farms in Alabama, 5000 acres in Marengo County and 4000 in Greene County. The Terrell County, Georgia farms comprised over 4200 acres. The National Business Manager asked me to do an analysis of the farms and create a work plan.

I toured the farms, together with Mario Abdus Salaam Ahmed, another of those called to Chicago. It was the first time I'd ever visited the Deep South. Before we took this trip, if you told me America still had slaves, I would have been incredulous. Sharecropping is a form of bondage. The system ties farmers and their families to a single piece of land, sometimes for generations, living in the same cinderblock house, with a single light bulb and no running water. That is slavery. Exploring the rural south, seeing people, both Black and White, sickly, living in abject poverty, left an indelible imprint of the raw cruelty and oppression that persisted in the Deep South.

After submitting a trip report in Chicago, I established Salaam Agricultural Systems and was appointed Director of Farm Operations. What an amazing opportunity! I was in charge of 13,000 acres of land on the three farms in Georgia and Alabama. When we first moved from California, my family lived in Montgomery, Alabama, which is right in the middle of all those farms. My fifth child, Kwesi Khalil Nuri, was born in Montgomery. We eventually moved over to Terrell County, Georgia, which is about 30 miles northwest of Albany.

I leased out the two farms in Alabama to provide working capital for the Georgia farm. I learned so much through the conversations and the explorations of doing this large-scale agriculture. The 4200-acre farm in Terrell County, Georgia was probably the most beautiful place I ever lived. Our house was canopied with oak trees and surrounded by two acres of pecan trees. The rustic beauty of the farm contrasted with the scenic oceanside wonderland of San Diego, my other "most beautiful" home. The Terrell County farm fulfilled my image of a place to raise children and build community.

I learned the farm by getting on a horse and riding around the boundaries. I wore dashikis and big Panama hats. Every day, I would get on a horse, ride and learn about another little piece of the land. We grew chickens and maintained a processing facility; our dairy cows lived near the milking barn, and beef cows lived under the trees. Our crops were cotton, corn, soybeans and peanuts. We leased out the peanut allotment. At that time, the USDA limited the number of acres of peanuts that a farmer could grow. The acreage was referred to as an allotment. I never really had to teach my children about the birds and bees; they watched the animals and figured it out. It was an idyllic location. Contrasted with this beauty were the shocking images of people still sharecropping under slave conditions. Seeing those economic relationships and living situations, years after desegregation, was scary.

We had several families living on the farm, each desiring to participate in the creation of an Islamic farm community. I wrote a document entitled, *Salaam Agricultural Systems Annual Report*. In it, I made recommendations to Chicago about how to build a substantive community around the land. The report did not get much attention because of the turmoil of reorganization that was going on within the Nation. The most frustrating part of the experience was that we never got any money from Chicago for development. It was nearly impossible to make a crop without working capital. We ended up selling livestock and other resources to sustain ourselves as time went on.

Joining the Nation of Islam came after working in many of the human and civil rights organizations of the 1960s and 70s. The Nation was the only group I saw that was actually walking the talk. Members created and owned businesses of all types. The philosophy of do-for-self is a serious construct when taken to heart. My dear friend, Arthur Kempton, told me I was the only person he knew who joined the Nation of Islam as a career move. When he first said that, I rather resented it. Looking back, I understand exactly why he thought that way. I joined the Nation in 1969. The prospect of living and working in an environment of full equality was unparalleled in America. Joining the Nation, for all of us, encompassed career, home and community. We joined to be a part of a collective movement to build community for Black folk.

Art's perspective was that I was taking advantage of a grand opportunity, in my mid to late twenties, to manage 13,000 acres of farmland. I agreed that it was an incredible opportunity to be able to take on that level of responsibility with little prior professional background. Opportunities like this one were often closed to Black men and women in America, regardless of experience. It was a tremendous learning experience. The farms made the promise and potential of the Nation come to life for me. The Nation of Islam represented much more than morality and a worship experience that takes place in a particular building on a particular day of the week. It represented being a whole person, able to carry my philosophical canon, not only into my spiritual life, but also into my daily work. It was a way of life.

Warith Deen Muhammad was still trying to solidify his place and determine what he wanted to do as leader of the organization. The biggest mistake he made, which he acknowledged before he dropped his body, was dismantling the economic structure that his father had created, through a new policy of decentralization. Decentralizing the organization was a good thing from a religious point of view. Individual communities need their own Imam or leader. However, the decision was economically devastating. As a result, the farm received no support from the national community.

On top of the fact that The Nation did not provide any financial support for our work on the farm, the White folks in Terrell County did not share what they knew about the help that I could have received from the U.S. government. There were very few Black farmers in the area and, being a newcomer, I did not know anyone who could have helped. I knew nothing about what the U.S. Department of Agriculture had to offer.

The existing social structures did not support the revolutionary work we were undertaking. We struggled financially. There was one man named Bobby Locke, who did give us some credit at his grain elevator. Credit was hard to come by, and the tricks that those folks would use to hold Black people back were downright treacherous. Occasionally, I was able to use the existing structures to mitigate some of the difficulties that we faced.

One spring, I sold several thousand bushels of soybeans in advance at a very good price to Calvin Lee, who owned the grain elevator nearest the farm. As it happened, we had a crop failure that year. We contracted the beans to him at $7 per bushel at the beginning of the season. Between spring and harvest time, the price of beans had dropped to $4 per bushel. When fall came, and it was time to deliver on the contract, I went to Calvin and asked him to pay me $1 a bushel to *not* deliver the beans. He was incredulous. How could I ask him to pay me for beans I did not deliver? I explained that I could go down the street, buy beans at $4 and deliver the beans to his elevator and collect $7. He had to think about it for a day or two and finally called and paid me not to deliver the soybeans.

Sometimes, folk in the north underestimate rural southerners, particularly the farmers. You see Uncle Bubba out there in his overalls and muddy boots. He owns a $50,000 tractor, and a $300,000 combine. However, we look at him as if he is the poorer relative. The folks up north, like my father, tend to think they have it made. My father dressed well, owned nice suits, a pretty car, high limit credit cards and he bought himself a piece of the sky—which is what I call a condominium, because you don't actually own land. He bought a piece of the sky. My father did very well by New York standards, but who had the wealth? Was it my father, who had mortgages and car notes, or Uncle Bubba, who owned land and accessed half a million dollars in capital every year to grow his crops?

Years later, I learned how White people would use the system to bankrupt Black people and steal their land. Farming is an expensive enterprise. Now, when Uncle Bubba went to borrow money to make his crop, he had to get that money in January or February in order to start planting in March. A producer borrows money at the beginning of a season to purchase the seeds, fertilizer, pesticides and other inputs he requires to make a crop. He pays back the loans after selling his crop at harvest in the fall. Many Black farmers would not get loan proceeds until late in the season. The farmer would still try to make a crop and fail. The land put up for collateral would be lost when loans went unpaid on time. This was just one of the conscious tricks that White folk instigated to keep Black folks down. You just did not get access to the resources

The USDA County Committees held life and death power over agricultural resources in local economies. The institutional decentralization of the county committee system meant that local people made all the decisions about who would benefit from federal money. The conduct of the county committees mirrored the attitudes and prejudices of the local power structure, which invariably is a White male world hostile to non-Whites. They were able to block or exclude Black folk from the benefits of federal payments. This is one of the problems: the U.S. Department of Agriculture is the last and the greatest plantation in government. The discrimination within federal programs comes straight from the top.

Years later, when I worked at the USDA, we were able to prove that the Department explicitly discriminated against Black and poor farmers. Some of the situations I experienced down in Southwest Georgia are examples of the systematic racism and classism that are ingrained in government and business. It is important that folks involved with agriculture avail themselves of all the resources provided by the USDA. This requires inquisitive visits to the local USDA office. They are now much more accommodating than in the past, primarily because of lawsuits, legislation and recognition that times have changed.

Farmers still have to do their due diligence and review all agreements with a fine-toothed comb. Old plantation-based policies can easily be slipped into beneficial-sounding arrangements. Oversight of USDA practices cannot let up. Racism and classism are alive and well.

Another obstacle I had to face was my own inexperience. On one occasion, my naïveté could have cost me my life over a bale of cotton. After cotton is grown and harvested, the cotton lint is taken to the cotton gin. Ginning cotton is separating the seeds from the cotton boll. The end result is a bale of cotton with just the seeds remaining. After my cotton was ginned, I told the gin owner, "I want my seeds back." He said, "That ain't how it works down here. I keep the seeds as payment. That is how the system works."

The ginner actually gets to keep those seeds as a matter of course. Linty fuzz covers the seeds. He puts the seeds in acid and removes the lint. He gets to keep the cottonseeds, which he can sell, crush for oil or meal, or process the seeds so they can be sold for the next year's crop of cotton. What the grower gets out of the deal is a bale of cotton.

A bale of cotton is about the same size as a 55-gallon drum of oil. However, where crude oil is selling for less than $100 per barrel, a bale of cotton sells at around $350 to $400. Cotton is the most valuable crop in the world, with the possible exception of marijuana and cocaine. The difference is the economic value added to a bale of cotton through manufacturing. The manufacturer's tag in a cotton garment can tie it back to the very farm on which that cotton was grown. That is how valuable it is. Cotton is still king.

I got into a big struggle with the cotton ginner over my seeds. I wanted my seeds back, and he would not give them to me. It was a very heated argument that almost came to blows, when his son stepped between us and broke up the fight. Later, I'd find out that this man was head of the local Ku Klux Klan. The only reason I didn't hang right then is that I was associated with the Nation of Islam. The Klan knew if something bad happened to me, the brothers from the Nation would come down there raising hell. The community I belonged to protected me from some of my own ignorance.

Walter Clyde, our farm manager, was the ramrod of the farm. He had worked for the same KKK ginner. One day, to punish Walter for marching with Dr. Martin Luther King in Albany, Georgia, the ginner switched on a cotton picker while Walter was inside repairing the machine. He cut off all of Walter's toes. The gin owner was a cold-blooded cracker. I walked away from my run-in safe and intact; that was just God's grace.

I did not know much about large-scale farming. Not yet. I tried to grow organically in the red clays of Southwest Georgia. If you step out in that stuff when it's wet, you will end up with six inches of clay stuck on the bottom of your boots. By the time the soil was dry enough to get in the fields, it would rain again. The weeds overtook the fields, and we lost many of the crops. We did not have particularly good years, because I wanted to grow organically. Forty years ago, I did not have the experience to do that very well.

There were a few other Black landowners in the area. New Communities, built by Charles and Shirley Sherrod and other local activists, was the first land trust in the country. They had 6000 acres on the east side of State Highway 19, in neighboring Lee County. Mrs. Shirley Sherrod was the USDA Rural Development Director for Georgia during the Obama

Administration. They fired the Director because of false allegations that she discriminated against White farmers in the South during the 1970s. Realizing their error, they wanted to hire Sherrod again in another position, but she refused the offer. The Sherrods' organization, the Southwest Georgia Project for Community Education, continues to work for small farmers to this day.

Black people owned and controlled more than 10,000 prime acres in Terrell and Lee Counties. This upset the landed White aristocracy. One thing that people don't know is how Dr. Martin Luther King and other protesters were able to get out of jail after being arrested during those marches in the South. Somebody had to post bond. Black farmers would often put up their land as bail to get all of those activists out of jail.

This upset the White folks tremendously. They set about a concerted effort to get the 10,000 acres back. Later, they tried to steal land from the Nation of Islam. They finally did steal New Communities. The 5700-acre land trust and farm collective were owned and operated by approximately a dozen Black farmers from 1969 to 1985. In what can only be construed as an outright swindle, the USDA took the land from New Communities by fraudulently withholding loan proceeds and demanding payments that were not due. USDA eventually paid the Sherrods very, very well for the injustices that they endured, but it took almost 40 years for their loss to be compensated. In truth, the loss of 40 years of production, development and progress can never really be justly compensated.

The biggest accomplishment I made at Salaam Agricultural Systems was to prevent the larger landowners, like Don Bridges, from stealing the land owned by the Nation of Islam. Despite the Nation's teachings to do for self, the heirs of Elijah Muhammad eventually succumbed to the same problem that other Black families have historically. Cash money to spend in northern cities was more important to the heirs and others than retaining the real value and wealth of rural land ownership.

They did not have an appreciation for the importance of

Black land ownership, so they were not alert to the impacts of Black land loss. African Americans had eighteen million acres of land back at the turn of the 20th century. In 2019, we have less than two million acres. The Chicago heirs of Mr. Muhammad were forced through probate court to sell the farms and divide the money amongst them. They had no real connection to the land. Furthermore, the land was owned privately by the Muhammad family, rather than being owned by the Nation. This unfortunate arrangement proved devastating, nearly destroying the results of years of development.

The people who wanted to take the land in Terrell County from the Nation of Islam eventually had to pay for it. Don Bridges, the very man who was trying to steal the land from us, wound up buying it. Many years after that, Minister Farrakhan and the renewed Nation of Islam bought back a third of the farm, including 1400 of the original 4200 acres. The purchase of an additional 300 acres brought the total to 1700 hundred acres that they now own. Thankfully, Minister Farrakhan has embraced the importance of agriculture, and now part of his theology is going back to the land.

The three years I spent in the Deep South were mind-blowing. Every single day brought an immense lesson. William Muhammad, a retired Detroit Chrysler employee who also worked on the farm, was one of my greatest teachers. William taught me how to navigate the local brand of racism. I found the racial hostility in Southwest Georgia the most blatant I had ever encountered.

William taught me how to hustle in the countryside. I knew nothing. William taught me little things that had great significance. He showed me how to be aware of things that were going on and how to respond properly. He taught me how to trade—how to barter for what you need out there in the country. Oh, it was a tremendous, tremendous learning experience. The lessons paid great dividends when I began to travel the world and visit places where everything is bartered.

I remember a time we were selling a plow to a local farmer. I said, "How much are you willing to pay me for this?" The farmer said to me, "I'm not buying, you selling. What you want?" That stuck, because I knew whatever price I gave him, he would offer me less. That made me stop and think. That was learning how to trade, how to negotiate.

William was funny. He was in his mid to late seventies and had a wife who was a year older than I was—somewhere around 28—and stair-step children. William used to say, "If the battery in your truck runs down, you don't go get an old battery to jump off the truck. You get a new, young battery to start the truck." Hence, his young wife.

One day, we pulled up to a field where Big John was supposed to be plowing. Here this big man was sitting, asleep, with his back to the tire of a large John Deere tractor. William said, "Watch this." He pulled the truck over, got out and tiptoed up to where John was sleeping. He leaned over and whispered in John's ear, "Brother, as long as you sleep, you got a job. The minute you wake up, you're fired." I thought that was hilarious; it was his way of letting people know there is no time to play. You have to do the work.

I learned how a grain elevator works; how they handle your grain when you bring it in; how to till the soil; pivot irrigation; the importance of knowing your tractors and equipment and how to take care of them. A big one: the value of working "from cain't see to cain't see." I mean, the lessons were just immense, and they built upon all the lessons that I had learned previously.

I met many characters down on the farm. I remember one time, I was driving with Hollis Watkins from Georgia over into Alabama, and I had to relieve myself. I stopped the car to go over on the side of the road to urinate. Hollis said, "No brother, you better not do that here." If a state trooper had come along and seen that, they would have arrested me. The only reason I'm still alive today is that I got away with a whole lot of stuff down in South Georgia, just because I was young and dumb.

I met C.B. King, the renowned civil rights attorney. He is the lawyer who represented me—rather, he wrote the order when

I had my name legally changed from Keith Freeman Woodard to Keith Rashid Nuri. When I went to court, the judge for my case was a very old man who had emphysema or something like that, and he did not talk very much. He had pre-printed posters that he used to manage his courtroom. I learned years later that, when he was running to be elected judge, he had signs that read, "No nigger votes wanted." That was his attitude. He would write on a card and give it to the clerk to read when necessary. I was sitting in court, and he said out loud, "Well, why do you want to change your name?"

I said, "I don't want no slave master's name." There I was down in Southwest Georgia, where they would still lynch Black folk. I am standing in court telling the judge I don't want a slave master's name. I thought I was being big and bold.

When I was done, he said, "Okay, where's the order?"

I said, "What?"

"Where's the order?"

C.B. King happened to be in court that day. He heard this whole exchange. I was bold, standing there telling this red neck cracker I did not want a slave name, going on and on and on, and C.B. just burst out laughing. I did not even know what an order was. Attorney King took over. He said, "Come here, I want to help you." He took a yellow legal pad and wrote out the order. The order is what the judge signs to say what is going to be done. I felt honored to have a real live connection to C.B. King. He did that for me, simply to help a young Black man, with no thought of compensation. This man represented Martin Luther King, Jr. during his campaign in Albany, Georgia. He also represented the Americus 4. He was a legendary legal activist.

On another occasion, Sonny Spraggins, who was a big-time farmer, wanted to rent some land from us. He flew in his own private airplane from Alabama, parked at the local airport, and came out to see me. I jumped up and down, eager to make the deal and collect the money I said, "Can we sign these papers?" Sonny said to me, "I don't know about you, Rashid, but I've been in this business over forty years, and one of the things that

I've learned is, these things take time."

I said, "Whoa!" That was another epiphany, a moment of stark revelation. Things evolve; they take time. Very few things happen overnight. You plant a crop, it does not grow overnight. You plant a tree, it takes sometimes years to get any fruit. You make a baby, it takes time to gestate. Things just do not happen instantly; things take time. Moreover, you have to be in tune with that time in order to prosper. That was a BIG lesson.

At every stage of my life, I've been able to say this is the best work that I've ever done. There is nobody that grades harder than I grade myself. To look back on my work and be satisfied with what I gave means a lot to me. The work in Southwest Georgia was more than satisfying. I learned and grew professionally and personally. I had five children at this point, and I was able to transfer some of those lessons to them.

Unfortunately, by 1978, the farm had run out of money. There was nothing left to do except shut down the farm operation and move on.

From cain't see to cain't see.

William Muhammad

Chapter 11
Louisiana – SCDF

$\mathbf{I}$n 1978, I moved from Terrell County to Lafayette, Louisiana. Louisiana is Cajun and bayou country, a whole world away from Southwest Georgia. This is where the Acadians from Canada who migrated south and mixed with the French culture in Southern Louisiana in the 17th and 18th centuries. It was an entirely different environment. I met different people, eating different food and living a different way of life. Lafayette is in the southwest corner of the state, just up the road from New Iberia and Avery Island, where they grow peppers for a plethora of famed Louisiana hot sauces. This is the home of alligators and Tabasco, just two hours from New Orleans.

Father A.J. McKnight hired me as an Agricultural Specialist to work at the Southern Cooperative Development Fund (SCDF). The organization financed Black agribusiness farming cooperatives throughout the South, using federal monies. A cooperative is a business owned and controlled by its members, who are generally the major users of the business. The members share in the benefits and risks of the business. Through cooperatives, individuals are provided the opportunity to strengthen their individual skills and resources in ways they could never or rarely accomplish as an individual.

Cooperative economics has long been studied as a promising antidote to persistent racial economic inequality. This structure is considered a solution that will bring meaningful economic development to urban and rural communities around the world. Varying forms of economic cooperation among American Blacks have been recorded since the end of the Civil War. Du Bois' 1907 monograph entitled *Economic Cooperation among Negro Americans* describes many forms of Black American cooperation.

In my capacity with the SCDF, I traveled to the Carolinas, Georgia, Alabama, and Mississippi, all up and down the Mississippi Delta, Arkansas and Louisiana. I visited co-ops, saw how they operated and worked with them on their business plans and internal organization. I saw how food is grown, from the deep, black soil that spilled out of the Mississippi River, all the way to the red clays of Georgia. I saw what the different soils looked like, and how they were organized. I sat down and talked with brothers who, for generations, had struggled economically to grow food. I was able to see up close the oppressive measures that were imposed upon the farmers over the years. My understanding of the totality of the agricultural system was growing by leaps and bounds. The need to evolve the structure of the agricultural system was without question.

The SCDF had brought a White man in to build a new farm for the organization. The farm was called SLADCO: St Landry Agricultural Development Corporation, located in the Ville Platte neighborhood of St Landry Parish. The man they brought in was trying to build a new vegetable farm—growing cucumbers and cabbages—on office hours, from 9 am to 5 pm. That just did not work. I fussed with the people, who were acting like a farm is a factory. Farm work in Georgia had taught me that you farm "from cain't see to cain't see." There is always work to be done. The SCDF finally fired the White manager, and I was appointed General Manager of the farm and finished its construction. Unfortunately, I had to fight my way through the process, mainly with the local homeboy, whom I called Golden Boy. I eventually lost the fight.

The underlying concept for the farm was to coordinate the collaborative efforts of sharecroppers and train them in new techniques. My opinion was that the farm should be a commercial venture. I did not want it to become a typical poverty program. My argument was simple. I had been involved in Johnson's so-called War on Poverty and Nixon's Model Cities. From experience, I knew these programs did not help the community at large. Poverty programs failed because the only true beneficiaries were the people hired to administer the programs.

The farm was funded by money from the Department of Labor as a job creation program. Unfortunately, with such programs, after the money was gone, there were no institutions, organizations or businesses left in the community. Nonetheless, I was determined to make the farm self-supporting. That is, my vision was to have the farm earn money. Once the subsidies were taken away, the sharecroppers would still be in a business they could call their own.

I brought Walter Clyde and his nephew Tom over from Georgia to help me build the farm. We put up sheds, erected buildings, bought equipment, did all the installations, worked the land and planted the crops. We attended to all the details involved with constructing the farm, which was geared to both training and production. I bought pegboard to hang the hand tools in the storage unit and painted silhouettes around each tool so you could just look and see if there was a tool missing. Father McKnight brought in an Israeli engineer named Dagi Schmuelly to put in the irrigation. Dagi had farming experience with drip irrigation that he applied to growing roses and other crops in Israel.

We succeeded in planting cabbage and cucumber crops. Dagi and Wilbert Gillory, who managed the farm after I left, were initially critical of my work. The fields did not look pretty because the seedlings were yet to catch. They eventually understood that I was going to do whatever it took to get the work done. Louisiana soils were quite sandy and drained well. It would rain in the morning and, after 3-4 hours, we could get back into the fields. We were out in pouring rain at times, getting plants in the ground. That's the determination with which I approach all my work.

As I look back at the intensity of the work, it amazes me. Some of it was just stupid stuff, but we did it. Dagi said, "Oh, this is not going to grow, it's not going to work." I fought the status quo like a blind man with a pistol. I wanted the project to be real. At the end of the day, the farm was properly constructed, but it cost me my job. The impatience that rode on the back of my revolutionary spirit failed to properly honor the existing structure and its quirks. A blind man hoping to use a gun effectively has to pause and allow his other senses to direct his aim. Instead, I operated with my traditional "Ready, fire, aim" sense of urgency.

At the same time, I carefully thought through the processes of building and putting systems in place. That's why the details seemed so abundantly clear to me. One day, we were putting in a walk-in cooler. I told the workers, "Put it over here in this corner." I left those instructions and drove away from the farm to run some errands. When I returned, an intern had repositioned the construction of the cooler in the market shed. He didn't understand; I had to explain my reasoning. He said, "Well, I thought it would be better to have it here."

His comment took me back to something Sadikifu used to say to excoriate people, "You have neither the ability nor the right to think in that situation." The intern's decision meant that we ended up with a bunch of dead space in the storage area. My lesson from that was: you have to attend to the details. You can't leave any instructions unclear if you're in charge, because other people are not going to take care of it the way that you do. I was so irritated. I had been gone for about two hours. By the time I got back, the contractors had gone too far to change the positioning; it would have cost too much for the workers to correct the problem. Most of us working on the farm were Black people. I think the young intern exercised his White privilege to override my decision without checking back with me. He had no concerns; he did not think he needed to get my permission. He assumed his decision was more correct than mine.

The Golden Boy that I mentioned was Mike Darnell, my manager. He wrote the proposal that obtained grant money from the Department of Labor for the SCDF Cooperative. Darnell did not know the first thing about agriculture and continually wanted to argue with me about my area of expertise! We fought tooth and nail. I was adamant that the government tail should not wag the dog.

Two major blowouts over having the Department of Labor dictate how we managed the farm demonstrated that the relationship was coming to an end. I said on several occasions, "No, I'm not doing that." After the third blowout, I knew it was time for me to go. Father McKnight, the founder of SCDF, was not going to tolerate the fighting anymore. I admit to a certain level of arrogance on my part. During the initial pre-employment interview, I sensed we were going to clash, right from the very beginning. When Mike asked me a question, I would say, "That's a good question."

He said, "Stop telling me my questions are good. I know they're good."

I said to myself, "Whoa, here we go."

Mike grew up in that area; he had the last say on all arguments. At the end of the day, I had to go. The farm that I built is still there. I don't know what my colleagues thought, but our fights created a lot of discordance in SCDF. This is one of the problems that I've had in just about every place I've been. After the deal goes down, after I've had these fights with folks over various issues and principles, at the end of the day, they would come back and say, "Wow, Rashid. Thank you for what you did. We appreciate the leadership role that you played here."

My attitude was, "Well, where were y'all when the deal

was really going down? Why did I have to fight this battle by myself?" Then it comes back to the moving-on thing: let that go, move onto whatever is next, disconnect. I was either fired or quit (same thing) from many of the jobs I've had during my life. It was always for reasons of principle. I was very focused, very opinionated. I was very clear about certain values and would come into conflict with people around those principles and values. But I can look back and see that, what was structurally accomplished and what I learned from the experience made it all worthwhile. Now I'm closer to the understanding of who I am and what my role is. I am Ogun, the builder, and the one who establishes. I can now peacefully leave the ongoing management to others.

Part V

SUSTENANCE

—∾⊘∾—

Spiritual teachings manifest through prayer, chants, meditation, asanas and other physical activities. Often, the focus is metaphysical. When I met Baba, my spiritual guide, I made the erroneous assumption that these types of practices would be part of the gifts he would bestow on those who came to him for spiritual sustenance.

I was pleasantly surprised to hear him chastise young people who walked around trying to be holy—or worse—to act holy. Instead, Baba admonished everyone to be normal and live a normal life as the path of spiritual sustenance. He wanted us to get jobs, go to work and provide service through excellence to the community. He demanded we take good care of our families, demonstrate kindness and courtesy to our spouses, pay our bills and be good citizens. Most of all, Baba wanted us to BE love.

One of the many things I learned from Baba was to be in the world, but not of the world. He taught me to maintain a detachment from the fears and franticness of the world, while still being engaged with the world. Indeed, the task of the spiritual life is not to make an "either-or" choice between the active and contemplative vocations, but to create a "both-and" synthesis. It is all about balance.

Service through excellence is one of the most revolutionary things that we can do. It is one of the principles that Baba lived and demonstrated. He helped me acquire the tools necessary to successfully do my work. As revolutionaries, we need to ensure that we pack our bags with physical and spiritual food that will not only keep us alive, but will keep us truly living well. This next chapter introduces you to the man who was a father figure and spiritual guide for me. May we all find sustenance in our spiritual lives.

*This moment is filled with joy. I now choose to
experience the sweetness of today.*

Louise L. Hay

Chapter 12

BABA and the Rose Garden

Baba was sitting in an overstuffed chair on the second
floor of his modest home in South Minneapolis. Around the
small room, eight to ten people sat on the floor in rapt attention. Baba grunted softly, as a young woman in close proximity
translated his hand signs, using her voice to communicate his
words. Baba did not verbally speak. He was in silence.

After a brief introduction, Baba asked about my personal
history, the origins of my name and my practice of al-Islam. In
an apparent test of veracity, I was instructed to demonstrate the
postures of Salah, the Islamic mode of prayer. That night, he
sent me to stay in Eden Prairie, at Everblooms Under Glass, a
series of Greenhouses containing 32,000 rose bushes.

Meeting Baba was the beginning of my next life-defining
moment and the beginning of a life-long spiritual relationship
with him.

Minneapolis, Minnesota became the next stop in my
agricultural journey, shortly after I left Louisiana. I met Baba

in 1979 through my wife, Lauren. She spent some time in Minnesota with an old friend named Renee, who had spoken to us about Baba many years before. When she returned to Massachusetts after visiting Renee, Lauren told me, "You need to go see this man." So I did. I planned to visit for three days and wound up staying for several months. All told, I spent thirteen years with Baba. He and I traveled in Asia, Africa, Europe and America together. He became a loved and trusted part of my family. All of the 80s and early 90s, I was with Baba.

Baba maintained three permanent residences. He had a home in Minneapolis (which he said would someday be the capital of the United States because of its central location), a home in the United Kingdom and his farm in India. The farm in India was located in a small village near Cheravthur in Cannanore District, in the northernmost part of Kerala State. Kerala is a highly politicized region, but has a long tradition of religious amity. It is an educationally advanced state with its own language, Malayalam. It has the highest rate of literacy (96%) among all the states of India. Women in Kerala enjoy a high social status, thanks perhaps to its historic matrilineal system.

A Dravidian Malayali (speaker of Malayalam), Baba stopped talking in February 1962 and did not speak for 48 years, until he dropped his body in 2010. He communicated with a sign language of his own invention. There was a specific hand position for each letter of the alphabet. Rapid movements of his hands would spell out the words he wanted to communicate. Certain individuals were chosen and trained to vocally translate his hand movements and thoughts into words. He usually kept paper and pen nearby for times when there was no one around to read his hands.

After that first "interview," Baba asked me to put together a vegetable plot in a grassy area outside the greenhouse. It was late June, and I knew that Minnesota had a very short growing season. I doubted the garden would yield very much. It took several days to remove the grass, prepare the soils and get seeds planted. One day, I removed my shirt and worked bare-chested under the sun, which rose quite high in the sky of this northern latitude. A couple of days later, I felt a tingling on my back, and my skin began to peel. Only then did I learn that Black people could also be sunburned.

One night, about two weeks later, Baba came to inspect my work. He walked into the garden and urinated on the ground. I thought nothing of it until five days later, when we began to harvest vegetables. I realized that some sort of horticultural miracle had taken place. In my 50 years of agricultural experience, I have never again seen this much produce materialize from a plot of land so small, in such a short period of time. I became a believer in miracles.

Baba was once a plaintiff in a lawsuit and retained Bruce Douglas to represent him. When it was his turn to testify, the clerk asked Baba to swear he would tell the truth, so help him God. Baba retorted in his sign language: "What does God have to do with it? I will tell the truth because that man is wrong," pointing to the defendant. As part of his testimony, Baba explained how he loved everyone. During a recess, the defendant approached him and asked, "Baba, you say you love everyone. How can you love me when you are suing me?"

Baba replied, "I do love you, very much. I love you like a tiger loves a deer!"

I was looking for some short-term work to earn a little money. Baba said, "Put on your business suit and go see Bruce. Tell him I sent you and see what he can do to help." As instructed, I donned my best outfit and drove downtown to Bruce Douglas' law office. We sat and talked about my background and the projects that involved him in addition to his law practice.

I asked if there was anything I could do to help and at the same time generate some income. Bruce was very straightforward. "Did Baba send you to see me?" he asked. I replied affirmatively, and he said, "You did not tell me that. You came here as if on your own. Had you acknowledged that Baba sent you, I would have something for you to do. Since you didn't, I don't!" I was wrong and humbled. Lesson learned.

Eventually Baba allowed me to read his hands. Only those he chose could actually do it. I never saw anyone able to decipher his words without permission. I accompanied his travels over four continents. I drove, carried his bags and ran his errands, delivered messages, made tea, wrote letters, washed dishes and performed all other tasks he requested.

Rarely did Baba directly praise me for any of the assignments I undertook. It was always clearly understood that excellence was the standard, as well as its own reward. I was astounded, however, at the complimentary things Baba would sometimes relate to others about me. When I was introduced to his circle, he would often say I was like a son to him. Being with Baba was an education. Through this training, I came to understand how the practice of excellence could be the highest form of rebellion and creates its own revolutionary dynamic.

Baba and I had a number of interests that connected us. One was roses, and the other was gemstones. My relationship with him was like that of a gemstone to a gem cutter. A raw gemstone has beauty in and of itself, but the expanded value and worth are only revealed after it's been cut and polished. That's what Baba did for me. In order to do excellent work, when people get a call to service, there has to be a spiritual well from which to draw. Baba showed me how to find the well.

I had been very deeply engaged, particularly throughout the 70s, very deeply engaged in inner space exploration. To meet the man who would become my spiritual guide was very, very, very, very significant. In all aspects of my life, I now begin by asking myself, how would Baba handle this situation? What would he say or do in this setting? That notion has informed me ever since I met him. His influence has permeated my life. Baba insisted upon honesty and self-examination. He did not tolerate hypocrisy and would call you on it if he felt you were being deceptive in response to inquiry. His probing of the individual psyche was laser-focused, making it difficult to hide in his presence. His influence manifested in a personal credo or technique that I continue to employ in my quests, both spiritual and temporal. The four-part process helps me to unfold most issues I encounter.

1. Truth-seeking – inner space exploration
2. Recognition – seeing conflicts and/or contradictions
3. Acknowledgment – of the realities and problems
4. Resolution – dealing with what has been discovered

Some years ago, I noted that John Coltrane had created a similar motif in his album, *A Love Supreme*. That monumental piece, published in 1965, was a spiritual declaration that Coltrane's musical devotion was now intertwined with his faith in God. Trane performed his credo:

1. Acknowledgment
2. Resolution
3. Pursuance
4. Psalm

Coltrane's music was part of the canon I absorbed in my youth. It was not until I reached middle age that I made this personal connection of his music with my spirituality. I was happy to find the correlation with the credo that I had absorbed from Baba. What I realized is, once one has come to a resolution about an issue, that resolution must be pursued, which then leads to psalm or peace. Lessons from Baba, reinforced through music.

"Everblooms Under Glass," in Eden Prairie, a suburb of Minneapolis, had seven greenhouses containing 32,000 tea rose bushes under glass. It was mind-blowing to watch those roses grow and to see the spiritual lessons that were contained in their development.

Tea roses are actually man-made. They are grafted and hybrid. There is nothing natural about them at all. An old rose, an original rose, is just a little flower with none of the magnificence found in the roses we give each other these days. A rose plant is usually grafted to the roots of an old rose to minimize fungus infection. The metaphor of the rose is this: as a rose blooms, it unfolds, like knowledge in human beings. It is constantly expanding until it eventually withers and dies.

The rose business is intense but beautiful. Commercial roses must be harvested twice a day, every day. The process is similar to the care required at a dairy farm. Cows must be milked twice a day, which leaves little time for a vacation. In order to get a continual supply of roses, you have to cut them. If you leave the rose on a bush, it's going to create hips, rose hips. Rose hips are very rich in Vitamin C and useful for health purposes, but if you want to have roses, you have to cut them so more can grow.

I had many interesting experiences trying to give away roses, particularly at the airport in Minneapolis. People got very suspicious as I tried to share the roses that were our "seconds." In order to sell them wholesale, roses have to be perfectly straight. When we had some that grew crooked, I would give them away or keep them in the house. And it's just incredible how people thought I was trying to hustle them, when, in fact, I was literally trying to give away the roses.

I managed the business of the garden and increased the production significantly during the short period I was there. Baba told me years later that I had increased production by twenty-five percent through my work. While working in the rose business, I realized what my next career step would be. I wanted to know how food is moved around the world. Cargill, one of the biggest commodity traders in the world, had their headquarters right down the road in Minnetonka. I was able to get a job with Cargill that began the next phase in my career.

Part VI

STRUCTURE AND SKILLS
– SECTION B –

⸻⟨ఌఌఌ⟩⸻

The spiritual sustenance that I received from Baba continued to nourish me through my journey. It was a pure blessing to be able to spend those initial months with him. It was a kind of intermission that blended professional and spiritual growth in a wonderfully balanced way. The time with Baba, in fact, placed my next professional steps right before my eyes and spiritually powered me for the journey.

My travels became even wider when I left "Everblooms Under Glass" and joined Cargill. The Cargill structure afforded both expanded and detailed examination of the movement of food around the world. The U.S., Europe, Asia and finally, Africa, opened up before me. I was able to see the huge footprints of Cargill and other trade giants that aggregate agricultural commodities from growers. Cargill trades and processes the commodities into ingredients that it then sells to food manufacturing giants like Frito Lay, Kellogg and General Mills.

The minute details of these large exchanges were no less essential. Commodities exchange, feed formulation systems, foreign agricultural business development and country-specific growing systems were all areas in which I had to gain skills in order to fulfill my responsibilities. It is not hard to imagine how structures this large and intricate would collapse under their own weight and complexity. Is it really necessary to have this type of structure in order to effectively feed people? My answer is emphatically no.

The aggregation and concentration of the wealth that is fundamental to existence—the wealth of the land that feeds us—is a fatal imbalance that is replicated throughout our economic system. Inequality is unnatural, yet it is the norm. As food revolutionaries reclaim food sovereignty for our communities, cities, states and regions, we have to consider how to right-size the industry. We have clear techniques for sustainable production of fruits, vegetables and herbs. It is important to also optimize the production of grains, meats and nuts, opening production to a larger number of players.

The opportunity to see how other countries manage their food systems, and the culture that is built upon those systems, was equally valuable. I observed cultural practices at the macro and micro levels, and learned simple phrases in several languages—enough to get me through most practical situations. I learned the power of China in the world and the beauty of the sunlight in a variety of terrains. Travel is, indeed, second to none as an educational tool.

The international grain merchants are a secretive lot....

William Diebold, Jr.

Chapter 13
Cargill Econ Analysis and Gainesville

Minnesota-based Cargill, Inc. is one of the largest private family-owned companies in the world. Founded in 1865 by W.W. Cargill, the company has been owned and run by the MacMillan and the Cargill families for its entire existence.

Cargill has many lines of business:

- Trading, purchasing and distributing grain and other agricultural commodities, such as vegetable oils;
- Trading in energy, steel and transport;
- Raising livestock and producing feed;
- Producing food ingredients such as starch and glucose syrup, vegetable oils and fats for application in processed foods and industrial use.

Cargill also has a large financial services arm, which manages financial risks in the commodity markets for the company. The name, Cargill, is not well known by most consumers because the corporation deals at the bulk level. They sell corn to Kellogg, cocoa to Hershey and Mars, and orange juice to Minute Maid.

It was tough selling my interviewers on why I should be hired. At that time, Cargill rarely hired people with any experience. I was already 32 years old and had acquired 8-10 years of practical agribusiness understanding, which my younger colleagues did not have. I was ten years older than the other trainees. The company wanted to have fresh minds to train in the Cargill way. They wanted all potential executive leadership to be solidly acculturated in the Cargill way of doing things.

I made it clear during my interviews that my career objective was to live and work in Africa. They hired me, after going through twice the usual number of interviews, with a 55% reduction in salary from my previous work. I took a $20,000 pay cut from what I earned at the SCDF. They said, "If you're crazy enough to come and work for what we'll pay you, we'll bring you on."

I began work with Cargill on the first day of business in January 1980.

The company had a very intense orientation process for new employees at the Minnetonka headquarters. The trainees were generally college graduates and mostly White males. Executives from various departments would make presentations to the group about their jobs and what trainees could anticipate. I had studied a book entitled <u>Merchants of Grain</u> by Dan Morgan, which described the seven secretive families and five far-flung companies that controlled the world's food supplies at that time. Informed by this knowledge, the depth of the questions I asked made an impression on the senior executives. I emerged as a leader of our group.

Economic Analysis

The company orientation lasted about a month. The newly indoctrinated employees were assigned to different divisions within the organization and moved to sites around the country.

Not sure of what to do with me, they temporarily assigned me to Economic Analysis. This department, led by an economist, gave forecasts and analyses to Cargill executives. (It is hard to find a one-armed economist. Typically, an economist will posit, on the one hand, such and such, and on the other hand, such and such more. Rarely a straightforward answer.)

The Soviet Union's 1979 invasion of Afghanistan was met by the United States with numerous economic sanctions. By January 1980, President Jimmy Carter had imposed a grain embargo on Russia. In addition, the United States led a boycott of the 1980 Olympics, which were hosted in Moscow. It was an election year, and Republican nominee Ronald Reagan promised to end the embargo. Incumbent Democrat Jimmy Carter was not willing to reverse his policy. The embargo remained in effect until Ronald Reagan assumed the Office of President and ended it in 1981. American farmers felt the brunt of the sanctions, while its impact on the Soviet Union was inconclusive.

Early in January 1980, Cargill executives, along with executives from the other major grain trading companies, were in Washington making their case to the government about their concerns regarding the embargo. I had done enough homework and learned enough about the grain business to fully understand the arguments presented to the U.S. government about the grain in question. In the Economic Analysis Department, telexes were coming through about the impacts of the embargo on the markets. Reading the wires and seeing this information, I was able to get the full picture.

The United States had become a net grain exporter, and American grain companies dominated the international grain trade. Crop failures in the Soviet Union had produced shortages. They were experiencing famine in some places and needed grain imports to meet national requirements. It really did not matter to grain merchants where the corn, wheat and soybeans originated. The grain companies could sell to the Russians from storage facilities in other parts of the world. American farmers, however, suffered when the U.S. Government prohibited Americans from selling grain to the Russians. Prices for commodities dropped.

The grain companies prospered. These multinational corporations knew how to navigate the conundrum. Cargill and the other companies told government representatives, "Look, you're telling us we can't sell grain to the Russians, but we've accumulated all this grain to deliver against the contracts we have with the Soviet Union. What are we going to do with it?"

The government said, "We'll buy it from you." And the grain merchants were paid once.

Then, after the government bought it, the grain traders said, "Well, what are you going to do with the grain? Where should we deliver it?"

"The Government doesn't have any facilities. Will you hold it for us and store the grain?"

The frequent telexes revealed Cargill's answer: "Okay." So, they were paid a second time, this time to store the grain.

The company's next step, since they couldn't deliver grain to Russia from the U.S., was to use the grain originated in their South American facilities. They delivered their South American grain stores against the contracts they had with the Russians. So, they were paid the third time.

Finally, Cargill returned to the government to discuss the grain that the company was storing for them. They said, "Well look, what are you going to do with this grain? The price has gone down, and we can't ship out of the US; the grain won't last forever. We can buy it from you, but at a lower price." So, Cargill bought the grain back from the Government at a lower, distress price and sold it again on the open market. They were paid the fourth time.

Interestingly, a similar scenario is unfolding around President Trump's imposition of tariffs on soybeans sold to China. The script is recited that the U.S. farmers are the ones who will suffer and, therefore, the government will provide $12 billion to offset potential losses. Interestingly, the Market Facilitation Program will provide less than $10 million to commodity producers and

$200 million for Agricultural Trade Program China Embargo Relief for Farming Organizations, not farmers. The fact of the matter is that farmers do not ship directly to China. It is the grain companies who buy beans from the farmers. These same grain companies have facilities overseas, particularly in South America. It is those overseas companies who will profit from the tariff increases. Globalization enables the movement of goods and services that inure to the benefit of multinationals, such as Cargill.

I watched this scenario unfold and told them what I saw. I suppose that was somewhat problematic, because they recognized that "this boy knows a little something." They decided to get me out of Minnesota and find somewhere else to place me. My next assignment was in Georgia.

Gainesville, GA

I made my second trip to Georgia when I was assigned to work at Cargill's Gainesville soybean processing facility in north Georgia. Initially, there was concern about sending a Black man to work in the Deep South. It soon became clear that it would not be a problem, because I already had relationships with many of the elevators in South Georgia from my time running the farms for the Nation of Islam.

Downtown Gainesville had a 30-foot marble obelisk with a bronze chicken sitting on top. Gainesville is the chicken capital of Georgia, if not the world. Across the square was also a bronze statue of a Confederate soldier next to a cannon, both facing north in remembrance of the "War of Northern Aggression."

Processing facilities are always built in areas of supply or areas of demand. North Georgia is the center of the chicken business. There were numerous chicken farms and processing facilities in the area with a steady demand for soybean meal. We originated soybeans from the farmers in South Georgia. At the plant, we crushed the beans to create added value products: soybean meal for animal feed and soybean oil to be further processed into different forms of vegetable oil. We sold the soybean meal to feed mills for animal feed. The Minnetonka headquarters sold the oil to companies like Frito Lay for chips or grocery chains to make margarine.

The plant was quite large. It crushed about 50 to 60,000 bushels of soybeans per day, approximately 330 days a year. Beans were delivered to the plant in rail cars that hold about 3000 bushels, or trucks that carried 850 bushels. My job was to buy the beans from grain elevators and sometimes directly from farmers. I was responsible for protecting our margins by hedging the beans and oil at the commodities market of the Chicago Board of Trade. I dealt with all the big feed mills that served feed to chickens in the state. The chicken broiler business remains the number one industry in the State of Georgia, centered in Hall County.

Soybeans delivered to the plant were stored in large tanks holding hundreds of thousands of bushels each. A bushel weighs 60 pounds and comprises 79.2% soybean meal, 17.8% soybean oil and 3.0% hulls and waste. The raw beans are heated and put through large steel rollers and flaked. These flakes are dumped into a large vat of hexane to remove the oil. Hexane is the same fluid used to remove oil from clothes sent to the dry cleaners. The soybean meal is cooled for sale and the oil sent to a deodorizing facility to wash it of the residual hexane. The products are then loaded in rail cars for delivery.

Gainesville was quite an experience. Here I was, writing checks for half a million dollars to folks that really didn't want to do business with Black people. I can remember one time when I showed up at a grain elevator to talk to the man who was one of our bean suppliers. I walked in the store and stood there waiting to get someone's attention; I watched as White folk came in and out of the shop. I just kept waiting over to the side. Finally, after he finished doing business with everyone else, the proprietor said, "What you want?" I said, "Well, good afternoon," and he recognized my voice. I'm sure he was thinking, oh shit...because he knew he had been rude to the man who wrote checks to him. He took an entirely different attitude when he realized that I was "somebody." There was a lesson in that. Racial and ethnic disparities remain an essential element of American society.

Edgar T. "Terry" Savidge was my supervisor and account manager. It didn't take long for me to work my way up to senior merchandising manager of the facility. Of course, there were challenges. At one of my earliest evaluations, Terry said that I did not pay sufficient attention to details. I was surprised and disagreed. I went over to my desk, reached in my briefcase and pulled out a notebook in which I had recorded and accounted for every single penny I personally spent. Now he was surprised. Our reconciliation was that he would help me recognize the details he felt were important for the business. From that point, he and I did well, as I continued to learn the business.

After a couple of years, I was asked to help design and develop a computer model that would automatically conduct a margin calculation. PCs were new in the early 1980s and generally not part of business models in the grain business. In the soybean processing business, we bought beans and sold the meal and oil. The margin was the profit that resulted from the crushing process. We designed a program that would do this calculation and include the hedges placed at the Chicago Board of Trade. It was a complicated analysis requiring many months of work, several iterations and testing before it was completed.

I learned much about the movement of commodities, learning how to trade commodities on the Chicago Board of Trade and all the dynamics of running a soybean business. We even experienced a labor strike. I traveled all over the back roads of Georgia, seeing how the grain and soybeans were grown. I had the authority to buy the beans, sell the meal and trade the futures contracts. I learned the industrial and trading side of agriculture. I gained a broad array of skills: marketing, merchandising, trading, managing and training the young merchants who came into the company.

My sixth child and second daughter, Afua Zarinah Nuri, was born when we lived in Gainesville, Georgia. Gainesville, at that time, was still a very segregated town. Railroad tracks, for the most part, separated Black people from White. While I was there, we organized the largest interracial gathering the town had ever had. We were working to keep the Boys' Club open. We brought the Black folks and White folks together to file a petition and raise money to invest in the club. Nothing like this had ever happened in Gainesville.

Later, I organized a demonstration against the KKK. I found out that the Klan was planning a recruitment march in Gainesville. I went to the officials and said, "Sheriff, give me a permit so we can have a counter march."

He said, "Are you out of your ever-loving mind?" I probably was, but he gave us the permit. I promised no violence would occur. The Klan was marching in their robes, and we were carrying signs that read, "Tell the Klan to go home." I was involved in the community, both from the business point of view and socially.

At the same time, I kept my eye on the prize of going to Africa. When I first came to Cargill, I told them I wanted to go to Africa, and I continued to beat that drum. Finally, after about three years of my repeatedly telling them that, the company decided to grant my request. I was invited to an interview with the President of Cargill, Jim Spicola. Recognizing my seriousness and rewarding my good work, they decided to send me to other points in the U.S. for training, and then Asia, before Africa.

I spent six to nine months traveling all around the United States. I was in Arkansas learning about poultry production; in Florida learning about broiler production; in Kansas City seeing how feed mills are run. I spent time in the feed business, the seed business and the poultry business. I was in Fayetteville, Arkansas; Jacksonville, Florida; Kansas City, Missouri; Memphis, Tennessee as well as headquarters in Minnesota.

I always wanted to know the world as well as I knew the United States. Cargill sent me all over the place. They designed a special fast-track program for me that finally took me out of the States. My youngest son and seventh child, Yawo Abd'allah Kareem Nuri, was born just before we left the country.

He who returns from a journey is not the same as he who left.

Chinese Proverb

Chapter 14

Cargill Southeast Asia

My first overseas travel was an around-the-world trip. I visited England, Netherlands, Switzerland, Germany and Singapore, which eventually became my Southeast Asian base. I went to Indonesia, the Philippines, literally around the world, visiting different facilities owned by Cargill. I was exposed. I learned.

Europe

On that first trip abroad, I landed at Schiphol Airport in Amsterdam. I had a several-hour layover before I caught my next flight to Germany and took a mini-tour of the city. I was standing in the downtown square, when this brother runs up to me and says, "Hey man, you want some cocaine?" I freaked out. I'm looking over my shoulder, everywhere around, wondering who's coming to get me, until I realized that the Dutch are free like that. You can go to a café or bar and purchase all the reefer you want, all the marijuana and hashish; you can walk along the canal and see women sitting in windows along the canals offering their wares. Europeans have a different sense of freedom; they're not uptight like many folks are in this country.

Amsterdam would become more directly related to my work when, years later, I worked for Cargill in Africa. When I traded cocoa in Nigeria, the cocoa went to Amsterdam, where it was processed into cocoa powder, cocoa butter and cocoa liquor. From these ingredients, all the fine chocolates of Europe are manufactured.

Of the many things I learned from Kwame Nkrumah, an important lesson came through the mistakes he made in managing the economy of Ghana. All over Africa, the countries did very little added-value processing. At independence, African nations had infrastructure problems. Instead of processing commodities into added-value products, they began to export raw materials, mostly to Europe, and then import finished goods from Europe.

It made no sense to ship all your cocoa to Europe and then import Hershey bars or Nestlé's Kwik. Africans needed to break those raw materials down right there in their home country, do the added-value processing on the continent, then ship those products to Europe and thus control the trade and expand their profit margins.

Nkrumah borrowed money against his cocoa crop—which is still the finest cacao in the world—to build the dam that provided electric power for the country. The Europeans did not approve of the positions Nkrumah represented in international politics. He was a threat to the status quo. Nkrumah was the leading pan-Africanist of his time and wanted African nations to unite across the continent to thwart continued exploitation of the continent by Westerners. The Europeans and Americans worked to get rid of Nkrumah with a series of economic sanctions. They lowered the prices on the cocoa, stopped buying it and then called in the loans, because the fledgling economy no longer had sufficient export income to pay its bills. Cacao amounted to as much as two-thirds of Ghana's exports.

Western interests set up the economic and tactical conditions that led to the coup that deposed Nkrumah, who became one of the leading Pan-Africanists in history. BBC News' 2016 article entitled, *Four More Ways the CIA has Meddled in Africa*, cites several sources that confirm U.S. involvement in the coup. Unlike BBC News, Ghanaian-born author and Professor, Charles Quist-Adade, also includes the British role in the coup in his 2016 article, *The Coup that Set Ghana and Africa 50 Years Back*.

Nkrumah's leadership was important to African liberation movements on the continent and throughout the diaspora. He was stymied by the colonial relationships that served to keep emerging nations dependent on their overseers. I learned at the beginning of my career, the importance of added-value processing to establish one's self-dependence and independence. Not having that structure in place made Nkrumah more vulnerable to the whims of the European governments, markets and multinational corporations.

Neocolonial efforts continue with organizations like the New Alliance for Food Security and Nutrition (NAFSN), a UK organization with strong corporate ties, that has been accused of massive land grabs in Africa. Similarly, the Cotonou Agreement between the EU and countries in Africa, the Caribbean and the Pacific, also has neocolonial provisions.

England was the European and African headquarters for Cargill. I did not enjoy the UK at all. It's too far north; the reason the Brits have stiff upper lips is that the weather is so bad. Their food is awful. When you go to London, you can get some of the best cuisines from all over the world, but British food itself did not appeal to me. There is very little agriculture in England. The British import considerable amounts of their food. That's another reason the British needed to control the world, so they could bring the resources of the world back to the British Isles.

Over the years, I saw a lot of England, including Liverpool and Manchester. I traveled it by road and by train. That's the first place, and probably the only place, that I took a tour. On one trip, I had a two-week layover; I couldn't do anything else while I waited to get my visa to go to Nigeria. I took a tour bus and visited some of the historic sites. Westminster Abbey is where Newton is buried, along with Dickens, Disraeli and seventeen European Monarchs. It was remarkable. The British have a history that is 1,000 years old. That's impressive, I have to admit. It's an old country, a citadel of Western culture. But I did not like the place.

Southeast Asia

Cargill transferred me to Singapore in 1985, where I was given the position of Regional Investment Manager. I eventually traveled to and worked in all the non-communist nations in Asia, identifying investment opportunities for Cargill.

I worked with seed, feed, poultry, oilseed processing and grains, all the areas in which I had been given special training. I spent three years traveling around Asia. The travel gave me a chance to get a better understanding of how food is moved around the world, what's involved in that process and to see it at a lot of different levels. There are a lot of people who have a greater depth of experience than me in any particular area of agriculture, but that work gave me a chance to see it from a very broad point of view that few have experienced.

Feed formulation is somewhat like cookie making. You put all the ingredients in a big mixer, and you come out with an animal feed product. Until that time, feed formulation had been done overseas by hand with paper and pencil. The perfect feed formula has specific percentages of different nutrients that enhance animal growth. Feed ingredients change price on a regular basis, based on market supply and demand. Given a wide variety of potential ingredients, the feed manufacturer purchases the cheapest ingredients possible and mixes them together to meet the formulation requirement. The technique is called least-cost feed formulation. Doing feed formulation on a personal computer saved much time. I introduced the usage at all of the feed plants in Japan, Taiwan, the Philippines, South Korea, Taipei, Indonesia, Malaysia and Pakistan.

This is back in the mid-80s, when we used 5½-inch floppies. When 3-inch discs were introduced, we thought it was such remarkable technology. Running MS-DOS on desktops was still commonplace back in those days, so teaching farmers and managers how to use personal computers to do the feed formulation added a great deal of efficiency. Instead of using paper and pencil to do the calculations, the merchants could input cost data in the computer and run the feed formulations proficiently. We designed these programs in the States before I took them over to Asia. That was fun.

One of the most important things I did was to put together a quality control manual for all the feed plants. The manual analyzed every single aspect of the feed business. Doing that work gave me greater insight into the processes. We ended up with a quality control audit that was used in all the Cargill locations in Asia. That gave me a chance to get deeply involved in the processes in those plants and to learn everything about how they worked. Performing quality audits of all those facilities exponentially expanded my knowledge of manufacturing processes.

I trained folks. I looked for possible investment opportunities in the countries I visited. In a lot of ways, I was a troubleshooter for the company, particularly in the area of animal feed. In Malaysia, I looked for investments in palm seed oil. I did the same thing in Bangladesh. I traveled to see if we could build an oilseed processing plant in the country. That required doing the research and the investigation and making a decision. Quite often the answer was no, based upon the best information available. Many times, saying no to an investment was just as important as the possible yeses.

I did this all over Asia, in all the feed operations that Cargill owned. Poultry and animal feed were the principal businesses of interest in most countries. We also looked at other enterprises. Rubber and other products were traded, but I wasn't much involved with those commodities. I was primarily focused on the feed.

I worked in Sri Lanka, Malaysia, Taipei, Hong Kong, Japan, and the Philippines. I probably spent six months in Indonesia. I got to see local food economies, how people feed themselves and, in most of those places, except for the big cities, the majority of the population still lived within walking distance of where their food was produced. They had lively and thriving farmers' markets in all the cities, where I had the opportunity to buy fresh food. I thought that was very important for me to see, and certainly informed the work that I instituted with Truly Living Well.

Pakistan and India

In India, I stayed at a five-star hotel. The city now named Mumbai was still called Bombay at that time. When I came out of the hotel, I had to step over the people living on the street. Right outside of the hotel was a tent city. I was walking in the tent city one day, and a young man invited me into his tent, saying, "Come have a cup of tea with me," in impeccable English. It turns out that he had been injured on the docks and couldn't work. He served me tea and rolled the cigarettes he smoked with paper from a brown bag.

I smoked Dunhills back in those days, which are still one of the most expensive cigarettes you can buy. They tell me now that they are $10 a pack. It's a pure, clean tobacco. That was my way of rationalizing my smoking cigarettes, because they were clean. Of course, I shared my Dunhills with him; I ended up giving him the pack. This was a young man, who lived in a tent, crippled for life and probably would never really work again. What was impressive was he invited me into his home and served tea with dignity and grace and self-respect that I had not seen in a lot of places. Oh, that really touched me.

I remember on that first trip to India, I was taking a long walk on the beach in Kerala State, on the western coast. An older man came up to me, put his hands behind his back and walked along beside me. He was an accounting clerk. He started to ask me about Michael Jackson and Muhammad Ali, and the conversation went on and on.

After we finished, I realized that this was one of the few opportunities he had to speak "American." His cultural references for America were the two American names most well-known at that time. This was post-Thriller, and Michael Jackson and Muhammad Ali were the two prominent American names that were known around the globe. He didn't ask me about the President; he wanted to know about those two men. I thought that was good. It was a simple conversation. We connected on a human level, and that was beautiful.

Baba arranged for me to meet significant personages on my first trip to India. I got to meet the mayor of Delhi and some poets and influential politicians in India. The introductions earned me a certain level of respect because Baba was a man of respect. I went to his village in Kerala State and spent time with his mother on their farm, named Prasanth. I slept in the marble cave shrine. Carved in the floor of the marble cave is a beautiful footprint. The cave is lined with gemstones, with lights shining through them that illuminate the shrine. I found out when I returned to the States that not many people were accorded the privilege and honor of sleeping in the shrine.

Baba sent me to meet a poet who venerates rats. I was sitting in this woman's house having tea, and all these rats were running through the house, just as bold as you please, while we sat there, drinking tea and eating biscuits. The things you learn! The Mayor drank his urine every morning as a health ritual. I met a Fakir in Lahore, Pakistan, a big man with a grey beard. He was sitting outside, completely naked. He looked at me with such piercing eyes. I could imagine how he would terrorize people. I looked right back at him, caught his gaze, and he caught mine. He was just sitting there in the street naked, and that's part of his spiritual practice. He was Fakir—God infused.

I asked Baba if I could take a gift to Savathri, his lifelong companion who lived at Prasanth. He said, "You can buy her some cloth." So I did. I saw this beautiful piece that had silver threads running through it; it was really wonderful, and I bought it and gave it to Savithri. She said, "Oh, Rashid, thank you so much, this is so beautiful." It wasn't until many months later that I learned about the laugh they had on me. What I had done was propose marriage to her. This was a marriage sari. Savithri accepted it very graciously, but it was a cultural faux pas.

One of the things you have to do when you're in a new country is learn their customs, how people do things. One way for a Chinese person to insult you is to hand you something with their left hand or give you money back with their left hand. In most of the world, you DO NOT use your left hand in polite company, because that's the hand you use to clean yourself after you use the bathroom. In Arab countries, when a thief gets his hand cut off, they cut off his right hand, so that all he has is his left hand. You cannot sit down at a community table and eat with your left hand; the thief can't eat with community people anymore. As I often say, sharing a meal with someone is one of the most intimate things you can do. The thief can't do that, and that's part of the punishment.

I traveled all over India, north and south. The rural areas of South India contain tropical jungles, where palm trees and fruit trees grow. All the aromatic spices can be found there. When you start moving into North India, all the way up to the top of the subcontinent, including Pakistan, you find dry lands just before the Himalayas. The Punjab is very dry, and stretches across Pakistan and northern India. I took about a dozen trips to Pakistan.

The Indian subcontinent encompasses everything south of the Himalayas. You'll find the Aryans in the north and Dravidians in the south. They say India is the place where racism first raised its head. This developed among the Aryans, Iranians, Greeks and all of the fair-skinned people who traveled to India versus the Dravidian people of the south. The Dravidians are jet Black people with jet Black hair and thin noses and thin lips. Then there are all colors in between that you will meet when you travel. There are seven races of Black people on Planet Earth as described by cultural anthropologists. It's really remarkable to see them all.

My first stop in Asia was Pakistan. After getting my bag at the Karachi Airport, I hailed a taxi to take me to the hotel, which luckily was only a mile away. Just before leaving the airport, a large man jumped into the front seat and said hello. He told me that he remembered me from my last trip. Now, I had never been to Pakistan before, so I had no idea what he was talking about. He said, "Don't you remember that I helped you hide a package of brown to get through customs?" Brown is heroin.

I got scared. I didn't know where he was going with this conversation. I denied any and all connection. The driver had no reaction. We pulled up to the hotel, and I disembarked quickly. Finally, I figured out the man must have been a policeman trying to lure me into a crime. That was my welcome to Pakistan.

Cargill already had a sunflower seed business in Pakistan. I went to investigate buying into the poultry and animal feed business. In Bangladesh, east of India, I looked at oilseed production and processing.

It was just astounding to experience a traffic jam in Lahore and Karachi, Pakistan. There were cars, trucks, motorcycles, wagons with donkeys, and herds of goats, all converging on one big intersection in a mad cacophony of sounds and smells. Adding to the exotic picture were the different types of dress that people wore. Many Muslims in America take on cultural customs in the name of religion. When I hear people say that someone is "dressed like a Muslim," I just realize how off base that is. With some major exceptions, Muslims dress according to cultural dictums, not necessarily religious.

A World View

Travel is very exciting and very educational, giving you a fuller appreciation of the nuances in culture and tradition. I have had a chance to see, feel and taste the world. More importantly, I was able to look back at America from overseas. Some of the cynicism that I have about America, its empire and its systems, comes from having lived in other places, from which I viewed America through the eyes of non-Americans, non-westerners. It gave me entirely new perspectives, which have stayed with me.

Most people overseas have no problems with Americans, but they hate America because of what the American empire represents in their experience: pervasive invasion, imperialism, exploiting the resources and the riches of people around the world. The British controlled India for a very long time, since the Boxer Rebellion of 1856. They crushed the Indians and took over their country for nearly a century. Europeans maintained their tightest grip on the world from the end of the First World War until 1947, when India won its independence. That's very significant for my lifetime. 1947 is the year I was conceived. My life spans the post-colonial world, which is what I set out to study during my break from Harvard.

Following India, Egypt was next to win its independence, and then Vietnam almost gained its freedom. The Vietnamese beat the French, but then the Americans intervened and also lost. In 1957, Ghana won its independence. After Ghana, other African nations began to break from European colonialism. The Europeans fought hard to prevent this, but the time had come for self-rule and national independence.

As I stated previously, the contemporary attempt to re-colonize Africa has the Arabs and Chinese very much involved in the race to control the strategic metals and other riches that are found in Africa. President Obama invited many Africans leaders to visit America for discussions. In 2013, there were three U.S. presidents visiting Africa at the same time: Obama, Bush and Clinton were all there, right after they established the AFRICOM Command post. That was America telling the world that Africa is a vital interest of the United States. Presently, there is more reporting on African politics and social affairs in the American press than ever before.

Gaddafi was killed to assert American influence on the continent. In the same effort, U.S. intelligence created a coup in Egypt. Hosni Mubarak had been running the country for 40 years as a friend of the U.S., and Israel and Egypt received more foreign aid from the United States than any other countries. After 40 years of rule, this 80-year-old man was arrested and hauled to court chained to a gurney. It's disgusting. America has permanent interests, but no permanent friends. As long as you can do something for America, they will like you. But as soon as you stop representing American interests in the way America wants, America will turn on you.

The only country in the world to drop an atomic bomb and ruthlessly kill hundreds of thousands of people was America, when it bombed Japan. The Japanese are not going to forget this. The Russians entered World War II against Japan and ran the Japanese out of Manchuria. Crushed them. The Japanese were just days away from quitting the war. Truman decided he had to drop a bomb on them anyway—not one bomb—he dropped two. Oh, it's disgusting. So, from other parts of the world, they view America as a big bully.

America has about 1000 military installations around the world. We have planes with no pilots—drones—dropping bombs, killing women and children. We live in the richest country in the entire history of the world. Yet we have people who are hungry, people who have no place to live, people who are not getting health care, and people who are illiterate, not going to school. How are American values going to be held up as a virtue for the world? No, I don't buy it. When the complete history of this country is written, it's going to be very ugly. We've killed people, dropped atomic bombs on people; we send our army and military all over the world killing folks. We take our citizens and test mustard gas on them and give them syphilis so we can see the scientific test results. That's not the world that I want to live in. That's not the way I think it should be.

America claims to fight terrorism. Yet, there has never been a nation in the history of the world that is more terroristic than the United States. Chattel slavery was a brutal reign of terror. What could be more terroristic than to have some white-hooded people standing in your front yard burning a cross? Terror is the

Seventh Calvary of the U.S. Army riding down on a camp where people are living on the plains, killing women and children, as they did to Native Americans. That's terror. That's how this country was built, around terror.

The balance of power is changing. Countries are not as afraid of the United States as in the past. Take the TPP, for example, the Trans-Pacific Partnership trade agreement that Obama put in place and that Trump has opposed. The U.S. has led economic policy in the world since 1945. Backing out of this trade agreement around the Pacific Rim means that the Chinese are going to step up and take over. Their influence will be felt even stronger. The Chinese are building islands in the China Sea, telling people you can't come to Chinese territory anymore. They are exercising hegemony by investing money. Contrast that with British colonization by conquest and America through military superiority. The world is changing.

It was when Cargill based me in Singapore that I learned that the economies of all the Asian nations, except for Japan and Korea, are run by the Chinese. In Indonesia, I learned the quiet influence of Chinese heritage. Indonesian citizens of Chinese descent would use their Indonesian names to do business and live in the country, but they would use their Chinese names at home. The Chinese control all those economies, and they have for centuries. You have to go to Asia, breathe the air and see the daily lives of the people, to fully understand how pervasive Chinese culture is and the Chinese people are. Every place I've been in the entire world, no matter how far in the backcountry, I could always get a Chinese meal. Think about the intelligence network that the People's Republic of China possesses. They have people all over the world, with their eyes and ears open, bringing or sending information back to Mainland China.

Britain leaving the European Union is huge. Germany is on the rise, and they already dominate the economy of the EU. Britain was their only rival. So, with Britain going out, that leaves Germany as the dominant force. The Germans have started militarizing again, the Japanese are militarizing again.

It's not a pretty picture.

The only people that ever invaded the U.S. were the British, and the last time was in the War of 1812. Other than the 9/11 bombings that took place, no other country ever invaded America. But at some point, these shores are going to be invaded. The vast majority of the American people live on the two coasts, East and West. The Interstate Highway system that Eisenhower started will have to fulfill its original purpose, to move the military back and forth across the country.

America has a thousand military installations around the world, in about 130 or so countries. What if the Italians had a military base down in Columbus, Georgia? Would Americans go for that? I don't think so. But that's the kind of practice that America exports. We have bases everywhere. Imagine if the Dutch had an airbase in South Carolina or Texas. We would not like or stand for that, yet the U.S. does that all over the world. It can't last forever.

Thailand

I expected Thailand to be similar to Pakistan, but it wasn't. Bangkok is quite modern, with many tall contemporary buildings. However, you can see elephants walking down the streets of the capital, Bangkok. I love Thai food. It was in Thailand that I learned to eat with a fork and spoon instead of a fork and knife. The spoon is what mostly goes into the mouth while the fork is used to hold the food in place for separation by the spoon into smaller bite-size pieces. My Thai hosts tested my taste buds on my first trip, wanting to see if I could eat spicy hot dishes as they did. I passed!

I traveled with one suit on my first trip to Thailand, made of raw silk. I sent it out one afternoon to have it cleaned. When I put it on the next day, it did not fit. Instead of dry-cleaning my suit, the cleaners washed it. The suit shrank! Thailand, the land of silk, mishandled my suit. The hotel paid for a new suit to be tailor-made, overnight. Impressive!

The Thai are very gentle people; they're so polite to each

other. There are instances where the military would rise up and have a coup, and the general who led the coup would lose. He would go to the king and apologize, saying, "I'm sorry, Sir, we made a mistake." Then he would get another job, instead of being executed. That is the level of politeness exercised by the Thai people. I learned little subtle things. Never put your hand on a person's head in Thailand. That's the spiritual crown. You know how, with children, you sometimes pat their heads? That would be the highest insult. Learning what is a cultural faux pas and what is not is extremely important.

Indonesia

Indonesia is just beautiful! I never knew there were so many different shades of green until I went to Indonesia. On my first trip, all I could say was, "Wow," because it was so strikingly beautiful. Verdant, I guess is the word to describe the landscape there. Everything you would think a tropical paradise would have, Indonesia possesses.

Indonesia has a diverse topography and diverse people. It's a nation of 3000 volcanic islands stretched across an archipelago the size of the United States—big islands, small islands. People grow rice in paddies on the sides of these volcanoes, many of which are still alive, with volcanic smoke steaming out of the top. We would climb up the mountains and look down into the valleys to see all the places where people were growing rice and corn. What I did not see is big fields like farmland in this country.

The varieties of foods found overseas are just incredible. Chiquita and Dole, the princes of banana imports, bring us one main variety of bananas. They change it every ten or fifteen years. There are over 250 different varieties of bananas and plantains. If you look at the bananas that you eat, you'll see that there are no seeds in them. They're solid flesh, which is not natural. Most likely, it is a GMO.

Indonesia is the singular most populous Muslim country in the world. It also practices Buddhism amongst the Javanese, woven within Islam. If you take the entire subcontinent south of the Himalayas, including Bangladesh, Pakistan and India, most of the Muslims in the world live there. Indonesia is next. Today, over 250 million very busy people live in Indonesia. The people are small in stature and very warm and friendly. I love the way they eat. Well-seasoned rice, fish, vegetables and other seafood are the stapes of their diet. It is very much how I eat today.

Before I left the States the first time, I obtained a book on the Indonesian language. I wanted to learn to speak Bahasa, the language of Malaysia and Indonesia. If you learn 500 words of any language, you'll be able to communicate. I didn't quite get up to 500, but I learned how to count, say please and thank you and where is this, where is that, good morning, good evening, etc. When you greet someone in his or her native language, it goes a long way. They'll give you a double take. I still remember a little bit of Bahasa.

In Jakarta, where the main Cargill Indonesia office is located, you find these big mansions erected right next to raggedy little shacks. They didn't really have any zoning codes. Scattered throughout the city and the countryside, there were mosques. So, when it was time to pray, everywhere you turned, the call to prayer was being made.

We went to a park outside the Bogor, near one of our feed mills. Walking through the park, I saw all these large objects hanging from trees. I thought it was the fruit of a type of tree I had never seen before. The man who accompanied me started making a lot of noise. The trees came alive. The objects turned out to be fruit bats hanging from the branches. Fruit bats are somewhere around 16 inches long, with wingspans of five feet or more. They were huge things and completely harmless; they only eat fruit. To see them hanging there was just absolutely incredible.

One of the first places that I insisted upon visiting in Indonesia was the zoo. I wanted to see a Komodo dragon. They are the world's biggest lizards. Again, I'm talking about huge animals—they look more like alligators and crocodiles, they are so big. They walk very slowly until they smell blood. Then they'll outrun a person. The dragons originated on an island called Komodo. People put goats down on the shore and watch the lizards come out of the hills and run to eat the goats. They have dangerous, nasty mouths. They have teeth, but the real danger from the Komodo dragon is their saliva, which is full of poisonous bacteria. Their average length is 3 meters, about 10 feet, and they weigh about 150 pounds. You can get one as a pet and grow old with it.

My interactions with the people of Indonesia were mostly based around work. I didn't really create a social life within the community. Every time I went, I stayed in the same hotel mini-suite. Occasionally, I would go to a club at night, but mostly I played tennis when I wasn't working. The Indonesian Country Manager was Dutch, and his wife was a native Brazilian of Japanese descent. After work, I would go to their estate and play tennis with the manager and his wife at their home court, and that's where I began to improve my tennis game. My six months in Indonesia were some of the most beautiful of my Asian adventures.

Singapore

Singapore is a pristine island at the tip of the Malay Peninsula. When the British colonized the island, Singapore was a trading post for the British East India Company. It is so clean, you can eat off the streets. Prime Minister Lee Quan Yew ruled with an iron fist for more than 30 years and built a country that was extraordinarily disciplined. You don't spit in the streets, you don't chew gum on the streets—you'll get a fine if they catch you chewing gum. Even back in the 80s, if you violated a driving regulation, they did not pull you over to give you a ticket. They had traffic cameras all over the country, and the government would send your ticket in the mail. If you came to the Singapore airport, and your hair was too long, Customs would make you cut your hair before allowing you to enter the country. One time they whipped a young Australian boy—literally, with a cane—

for marking up some cars.

Singapore has four national languages: Mandarin Chinese, English, Tamil and Bahasa, and many people speak them all. They are regimented and disciplined people. That is why a lot of companies like it as a place to have headquarters for their Asian businesses, along with the fact that it's centrally located.

It was easy at that time for expatriates/expats, people from other countries living and working in Singapore, to settle on the island and live very well. The apartments are huge. You could get a four or five-bedroom apartment in the city. We did not have a driver, but most expats had servants to keep house. My family was the only one in the Cargill cohort to live in a house, because I had my mother and six of my children in the country with me. All the other Cargill employees lived in apartments. My son graduated from the Singapore American school; all my boys played basketball and baseball there.

The entire three years that I was stationed in Singapore, the longest I ever stayed was two and a half weeks during one holiday season. I had two passports. I could leave one in an embassy to obtain a travel visa and use the other to travel, then come back and switch them up. I was on the move. Having my mother, wife and nanny in the country enabled me to travel without worry for my children's welfare. Up until that time, I had no appreciation for what it meant to fly first class or business class. Spending all that time on airplanes, the extra comfort made a big difference. It was nice to have plenty of seat space on the plane and somebody to pick me up at the airport. My family thoroughly enjoyed the luxurious lifestyle that expatriate living provided

Malaysia

Malaysia is a very wealthy Muslim country. They have the world's tallest buildings, and a lot of electronics are manufactured there. It's on a peninsula, surrounded by water on three sides. When you travel north of Malaysia, you come to Thailand, Cambodia, Vietnam, Laos, and other countries further up the peninsula. You go west, then you see what used to be Burma, now called Myanmar, and China on top of all of them, geographically and figuratively.

Malaysia has huge palm plantations. We considered buying a palm oil facility. The headquarters of one of our largest poultry businesses was in Kuala Lumpur. One of my functions was evaluating different projects. The boss would say, "Rashid, go up to Kuala Lumpur and tell me what you see. Go down and take a look at this, go there and take a look at that." I would go up and take a bunch of pictures, describe it, write my report and make a recommendation. That is why I got to travel so much.

Hong Kong

Hong Kong is a crowded, bustling place. There is an astounding number of skyscrapers on that small island. You see a lot of Rolls Royce and Mercedes Benz vehicles. And this was before they rejoined China. There is a strong impression of riches and wealth in Hong Kong. Cargill maintained a cotton trading business, and the office was the base for the company's involvements on Mainland China. This was many years before the islands were annexed to the mainland.

The Philippines

The Philippines is another county with lots of islands. Radical Muslims live on the southern island of Mindanao. They are still rebelling against the central government in Manila. They are small people, who eat a lot of fish and rice. You can find Negritos, very small African people, up in the mountains. Every place you go in Asia, you can find Black people. Every place in the world you go, there are Black people. I remember when I first saw Black Chinese people. I was thinking, they are working hard out in the sun, and that's how they got so dark. No, they are Black people. J.A. Rogers, a Jamaican-American author, journalist and historian, clearly points that out.

Korea

Korea is cold. I only went there once. They have so many American military men stationed there. They eat pickled, fermented food, like kimchi, and lots of ginseng. They've got ginseng tea, ginseng chicken, ginseng in every meal. That is one of the reasons why the Koreans are so physically powerful. You ever see them doing their native Tae Kwon Do, how fit and strong they are? Many have ginseng loaded up in their bodies—they can walk through walls. Ginseng is good stuff, though, beautiful and tasteful. I have been eating it for 45 years.

Japan

I didn't like Japan. The feeling was mutual—they didn't really like Black people where I was. A couple of places I wanted to go, they told me "no," I couldn't come in. I guess that's because of the Yakuza, the mafia. They didn't want Black men messing up around there.

My hotel room in Japan was so small that the bellman had to walk out of the room so I could walk into the room. They utilize very small, compact spaces. They build each room in their houses to be very versatile. The room that you sleep in is where you may also have meals. You just roll up your mat and put it in the corner.

Black People in the World

Black people are not welcome in many places in the world; we may be tolerated, but not welcome. You can go all the way to the middle of the Pacific Ocean and find people who are jet Black, with big noses and big lips, far away from the African continent. Those folks from New Guinea, the Negritos in the Philippines, the Black Chinese, all of these people and others let you know the extensive reach of Black people around the Planet Earth. It was incredibly eye-opening for me. I still have a picture that hung in my office in Singapore. It is of a Black man from Papua, New Guinea. The story of most Black people in America coming from Africa to the Americas may be true, but it doesn't provide the full scope of where Black people live and have been living on this planet. The Black Aborigines of Australia have a 60,000-year history of which they are quite proud.

Black folk have been everywhere on the planet since time began, but the history books don't tell it that way. We have not learned these facts because we have not written our own books—others have written the books for us. The longer I stayed away, the more I realized that I am an American, and my tribe is here in America. Black folk, who have undergirded the development of America for 400 years, are the people with whom I have the most cultural affinity, who recognize and appreciate the cultural symbols that make up the stories of our culture in the United States. Travel brought this understanding.

I am an African, not because I was born in Africa
but because Africa is born in me.

Kwame Nkrumah

Chapter 15

Cargill Nigeria

I wanted to go to Africa through my work and not as a tourist. I made that decision as an undergraduate. It took 18 years to get there. On my first trip, Cargill sent me to Nigeria. I spent a month exploring the country.

Nigeria remains king of all African nations. It is a big, rich, country. At that time, two out of every nine Black people on Planet Earth were living in Nigeria. It has all the resources necessary to build a great nation: land, labor and capital.

Nigerians are very vibrant, very much alive, very dynamic people. In many countries, the people are small. Nigerians are big, like African Americans. It's a very diverse country, with many different ethnic groups and 250 distinct languages or dialects. The terrain is equally diverse. There is the desert in the north, the jungles in the southeast and the forests in the southwest.

Natural wonders leave me motionless, completely awestruck at the magnificence of creation and the mastery of the Creator. Sleeping on a return flight to Lagos after several days of meetings in London, I was awakened by a bright, luminous, golden glow that enveloped everything. Looking out the window of the plane, I saw nothing, except a bright blue sky and a yellow Earth. From horizon to horizon, there were no clouds...only the vastness of the Sahara below, and my view from the sky 35,000 feet above.

The only true desert to be found along the 0° latitude line, the Sahara is also the world's largest desert. The Sahara covers most of North Africa, more than a third of the continent, and an area around the same size as the United States. It extends more than 3000 mi (4830 km) from the Atlantic Ocean to the Red Sea. All the standard desert landscape types are present in the Sahara, from great fields of shifting sand dunes or ergs, to vast plains filled with rocks, known as reg.

The African peoples living in this harsh environment created great civilizations that encircled the Sahara. For the most, they are Muslims practicing Islam and have community names like Berber, Taureg, Fulani, Soninke and Hausa. As part of their Islamic obligations, it was necessary for them to cross this vast nothingness to make a pilgrimage, or Hajj, to Mecca in Arabia.

Askia Muhammad Toure, 1443-1538, the ruler of Timbuktu and the Songhai kingdom, made his journey across the Sahara on camels with a retinue of 1500 princes and chiefs of the empire. He is reported to have given 300,000 pieces of gold to Mecca, Medina and other holy cities, and spent 100,000 pieces of gold among the Mecca merchants. Absolutely incredible!

I really enjoyed Nigeria, just the liveliness of the place. It was such a learning experience. Nigeria is where I learned African macro culture, the dominant and common cultural mores that define national institutions and human interactions. The other place that I lived in Africa was Ghana, many years later. It was there that I learned about African microculture, etiquette and protocols.

My work in Nigeria afforded the opportunity to do business in many other African nations. In West Africa, I visited Senegal, Togo, Benin, Cameroon, Cote d'Ivoire, Niger and Chad. In East Africa, I was in Ethiopia, Kenya, Tanzania, Malawi and

Mozambique. The contrasts between East and West Africa are vast. East Africans were colonized and directly ruled, primarily by the British. The history of direct rule rendered East Africans less aggressive than their Western brothers. West Africans, like the Nigerians, were never conquered. Those colonies were indirectly ruled through local Chiefs and Kings, which allowed tribes to better hold onto traditional customs and values. East African countries were colonies of the British and French, with the exceptions of Tanzania (Tanganyika), which was colonized by the Germans, and Mozambique, colonized by the Portuguese.

Cargill was not doing substantive business in West Africa. I wrote a book for the company on how to enter the market in Nigeria. I suggested we start green fielding Nigeria, i.e., creating an organization and business where none currently exists. The premise was to begin with basic commodity trading and eventually expand into added-value processing. I stayed in the Sheraton hotel in Ikeja, Lagos State for six months. I established Cargill Nigeria Ltd., opened an office, hired young people and trained them in the culture of Cargill, Inc.

Our office became the largest grain trader in Nigeria overnight. We established a carrying charge market. A carrying charge is the cost associated with storing a physical commodity over a defined period of time. Carrying charges include insurance, storage costs, interest charges on borrowed funds and other similar expenses.

In Nigeria, Star Beer was the market leader. There was a ban on the import of barley malt to Nigeria, a fundamental ingredient in many beers. The Federal Government of Nigeria instituted this ban in the early 1980s. This act saved the country huge foreign exchange and gave support to cultivation, malting and industrial use of sorghum in brewing and other food industries in the country. Nigerian breweries started substituting sorghum for malt.

Sorghum and maize grew plentifully in Nigeria. The flour mills used these grains also. Farmers from the northern parts of Nigeria, where the grain grows, would traditionally harvest their crops, load them on a truck, and transport these grains to the flour mills and the breweries in the South. Farmers took their crops to the food manufacturers to sell. They would sit and wait under the shade of their trucks until the purchasers were ready to buy.

My team of young Nigerians would go upcountry and buy the grains from the farmers. We stored it in rented warehouses in several different grain production locations. We would then sell the grains to the flour mills and the breweries for future delivery and earn the carrying charge. The premium charged for this service is how we earned our income.

We became the middleman in that operation, which relieved the farmers of the inconvenience of leaving their farms to travel long distances from northern Nigeria to Lagos. Having our service meant that they no longer had to pay the costs of transportation and lost productivity in order to sell. That was the first time this service had been provided in Nigeria.

In addition to maize and sorghum, we traded cacao, sugar, rubber and cotton. Cargill had an equity stake in the cotton gins that were owned by the British Cotton Growers Association, a subsidiary of Cargill Europe. The relationship was very much a vestige of British colonialism. In Sven Beckert's <u>The Empire of Cotton</u>, he explains how cotton was the catalyst for modernizing industrial processes around the world. Slavery and the cotton trade were the engines that powered war capitalism and industrial capitalism. Industrial manufacturing of cotton cloth ended up being focused in England, but it really began in India and China. Asians developed the production of cotton textiles, and the British brought cotton and its usages to Europe. The rest is history.

Aliko Dangote, a Nigerian billionaire, had a monopoly on the sugar trade in Nigeria before I arrived. I opened up the country for importing sugar by Cargill and others. No one else had traded sugar in Nigeria beside Dangote. He thwarted my best efforts by drastically dropping the price, assuring we would lose money on our trade. However, that trade made it possible for others to come in and do sugar business in the future, because the fear of Dangote was gone.

I learned a great deal about how rubber products were grown and processed. The jungles of Eastern Nigeria, Ibo Land, are where rubber trees are grown. Currently, rubber is harvested mainly in the form of latex from the rubber tree. Latex is a thick, sticky, milky substance drawn off by making incisions in the bark and collecting the fluid in vessels, in a process called tapping. The latex is then refined into rubber, ready for commercial processing. In major areas, latex is allowed to coagulate in the collection cup. The coagulated lumps are collected and processed into dry forms for marketing. In the processing facility, liquid latex is immersed in formic acid to make it congeal. The blocks are shipped off to Europe to be processed into tires and other products.

Palm oil was another Nigerian commodity. The palm tree is cultivated for its oils, rich in highly saturated vegetable fats. Palm oil is extracted from the fruit flesh, and palm kernel oil is extracted from the fruit kernel. Nigerians eat copious amounts of palm oil in their food. For domestic use, Nigerians harvest big bunches of palm fruit, drop them in hot water and boil them. The oil floats to the top and is skimmed for use. Malaysia and Indonesia, where they use commercial solvent extraction processes, are the world's leading producers of palm oil. Palm kernel meal is an important feed ingredient and the by-product of the process.

I saw many different kinds of fruits and vegetables that are never seen in the United States. Americans enjoy a very limited palette of fruits. A host of different kinds of absolutely delicious, nutritious fruits grow around the world. These fruits were, at that time, open-pollinated, non-GMO varieties. The high quality of the food Nigerians ate showed in the vibrancy of the people and the strength of their teeth. I would sit in a club in Nigeria and see a young woman take a beer bottle or a soda bottle and open it with her teeth. If Americans tried this, a tooth would pop out with the bottle cap.

It's been a long time since I've been to Nigeria, and I'm sure things have changed, but it was a cash society in 1987. There was no credit, no mortgages, no welfare and no social security. They barely had pensions. The social underpinnings that we have in the west did not exist in Nigeria. That means everybody did business. No matter what kind of work you did, you had something on the side, some additional income that you were earning.

One of the very first people I met in Nigeria was a man named Bernard Calil, of Lebanese descent. The Lebanese and Syrians controlled many of the flour mills and vegetable oil capacity in West Africa. Bernard was born in Nigeria, where his family had resided since the 1880s. Bernard carried two passports, Lebanese as well as Nigerian. Lebanese Nigerian citizens would go back to Lebanon to get married and go to college, but they maintained their businesses in Nigeria since the colonial period. Bernard told me, "Look, don't come over here talking to me about corruption. I don't want to hear it. If I want something from a politician, I take a bag of money and set it on his desk and tell him what I want. You all set up all these political action committees and campaign funds, and you're doing exactly the same thing that we're doing, only ours is more upfront. Here's the money. This is what I want."

I said, "Wow." That was revealing to me. It was the first time I had looked at it that way, and what he said was absolutely true. We bribe politicians in the United States every day, but we do it through our campaign contributions. I learned the story of the fox and the wolf, which teaches a moral about honesty and deception. Would you rather deal with a wolf, which will look you in the eye and tell you, "I'm going to eat you," or a fox that will smile at you and bite you as soon as you turn your back? I like wolves. I know what I'm dealing with, right up front.

The political process in America is hypocritical. If you made a $100,000 campaign contribution, you could get an invitation to sleep over in the White House. You can buy influence with any representative in America for $5,000, a senator for $10,000.

The leadership will cost you a little bit more. Politics is the same all around the world.

I had a very good relationship with Nonyelum Chris Okeke, who was our company lawyer and my best friend. Chris is an Aro Igbo and the firstborn son of the firstborn son eleven times removed. His father was the first Education Minister in Nigeria. Throughout the centuries, his people were master traders, trading everything, including slaves. Chris had been wearing tailor-made shoes and tailor-made clothes since he was ten years old. As a gift for me, he bought a pair of handmade English shoes that cost $1500 back in 1988. I still have those shoes in my closet. Through Chris, I learned a great deal about culture and etiquette. I learned the relationships between tribes and sub-tribes and how a Yoruba from Oyo was different from a Yoruba from Ondo, or from Ife. Chris took me by the hand and introduced me to people and places that would assure success with my business.

I met my "big brother" and lifelong friend, Ernest Dunkley, in Lagos. He is originally from Brooklyn. Ernest lived in Lagos for 18 years. Lloyd Weaver is another New Yorker who lived in Nigeria for over 30 years. They have remained friends since I first met them. Ernest and Lloyd would come to my house on weekends to drink fine liquor, listen to jazz and eat egusi soup, my favorite Nigerian meal.

I lived extraordinarily large. We lived in a big house overlooking Bar Beach. We had two cooks; one in the office and one at my house. There were probably 15 people that acted as servants one way or another. The position I held as Managing Director of an international corporation came with expectations of how I was to manage my affairs. If you're hiring people, putting people to work, there's a certain way that you're supposed to conduct yourself, and I had to learn that.

In Singapore, we had a Pilipino woman named Lita, who cleaned our house and acted as a nanny for the children. Lita really taught me how to deal with servants. Servants are not slaves. They have their own levels of respect that need to be honored. For example, the man that washed my clothes had somebody to wash his. There's a hierarchy that's in place that needs to be understood and respected.

Many of the homes and office buildings in Nigeria are gated. The person who opens and closes the gate is called a "magadi." Most of them came from the North. Every morning when I pulled in to my office compound, the young man who was our magadi would open my car door, take my bag into my office and set it down next to my desk. If I did not allow him to do that, I would be taking away some of his dignity and the respect that came from his occupation. As the magadi, considered one of the lowest positions on the staff, he could only come into the inner sanctum of our office building to bring in my bags. Otherwise, he couldn't come in there. It was a privilege that he appreciated. These are some of the cultural nuances that I learned.

I learned how to eat with my hands. You do that in India as well. Asians use chopsticks. Knives and forks are a very European thing. In most of the world, people eat with their hands, including people of high society, who don't spill a drop on their clothes. In the West, we tell our children, "Don't eat with your hands," but food actually tastes better when you eat it with your hands, because there are enzymes on your fingers that get into the food and enhance the flavor.

The social hierarchy is another important nuance. I was the MD, the Managing Director of Cargill Nigeria. Calling people by their first name is part of the Cargill culture. The Chairman of Cargill was Whitney MacMillan, a family member. Everyone he encountered called him Whit. So, I asked our Nigerian staff to simply call me Rashid. That was a mistake. It created an atmosphere of familiarity that was not appropriate in Nigeria. I should have insisted they call me MD.

I used to ask the young people I was training what they thought about different aspects of the business. In Nigeria, if you're a senior person, you don't ask a junior person's opinion. You tell them what to do. That was another cultural faux pas. They thought that because I was asking their opinion, I did not know, when in fact, it was my way of testing their knowledge. They stepped over the line and assumed they knew more than I did, or that I did not know. They took advantage in many ways that were not appropriate. But it was my mistake, because I allowed them to approach me that way.

As I said, Nigeria had a cash economy. There were virtually no credit cards, and people did not readily accept checks. I had to learn how to manage major transactions. Once, I wrote a check to buy three automobiles. I handed the dealer the check and wanted to drive out with the cars. The salesman said, "Oh no, Oga [master]. You have to wait for the checks to clear, and that will take five days." At the end of the five days, I went back to collect the cars, and he told me the price had gone up. I said, "Well no, I am not paying more. Please give me my money back."

He said, "No, I can't give you your money back. That money is spent already. So, if you want your cars, you will have to pay more." I was stuck. Had I come to the dealership with a bag of cash, there would not have been an issue. After that, we rode around with carloads, suitcases full of cash to purchase grain. Many times, we would sit on the grass on a rug underneath a tree and open up a bag with the cash money for a grain transaction. The Nigerians would take it out, smell it, look at it, and when they were satisfied, they would say, "Ok, give him the grain," which they had stored somewhere.

I traveled all over Nigeria, working in 20 of the 21 states then extant. I saw doctors and lawyers, robbers, rapists, businessmen, judges and bankers, but no niggas. None! Africans will fight over money; they will fight over religion; they will fight over women; but it is never, ever, about the color of your skin. And that was just wonderful; to be amongst all those people who looked like me and accepted me as a whole human being. It really was quite rewarding.

In 1991, I attended the First Pan African Congress convened by Revered Leon Sullivan, in Abidjan, Cote d'Ivoire. It was a gathering of Black people from all over the African Diaspora.

Cargill helped sponsor the conference by donating $10,000 to Rev. Sullivan. It was at this meeting that I met Joia Jefferson, who was covering the conference for Black Entertainment Television. We began a conversation that eventually led to Joia marrying me some years later. Although we are not married now, we have worked together in one capacity or another ever since.

I met an Afrobeat musician in Nigeria named Fela Anikulapo Kuti and spent considerable time with him. Fela had come to the United States and lived in Harlem and Los Angeles. He learned American music, then returned to Nigeria and created a whole new type of music. He was a cultural icon, and very well-respected. Fela would come to my house and bring a large entourage. We had a wonderful time. He had a venue space in Ikeja called the Shrine. It was like going to church. Fela had dancers and a huge 26-piece band. The show began at midnight, and people would be there celebrating until the early hours of the morning.

Fela was a rabble-rouser, a man of and for the people. Many in Nigeria were threatened by his anti-government stances. At one point, the military invaded Fela's compound, and his mother was thrown out of the window and subsequently died. He wrote a song afterward, called *Coffin for the Head of State*. He took his mother's coffin to the Office of the Head of State, dropped the coffin and told him, "You killed her. You bury her."

Fela got away with that kind of thing. One time, we were leaving my house and encountered a police roadblock. They had armed police everywhere; some were more ruthless than others. We were rolling by in several cars filled with Fela's entourage, and the police demanded we stop. Officers came across the road with their guns drawn. When they saw Fela, all they said was, "Fela e day! [Fela's back here]!" The officers stood at attention and saluted him. The Inspector said, "You all can go on through." Fela was stronger than armed soldiers.

People often look at the role of women in African society as women being oppressed. What I saw in Nigeria is that women really run the place. If you go out to the market, you see these sisters wearing market clothes that may not appear to be neat and pretty. But what you think is a fat stomach is actually a large roll of money wrapped up in those clothes. When departing the market, many jump into their Mercedes Benzes and go home. The women run the economy. The men are out front flashing, but the real deal is that the women actually control the local food economy. Women are now working to ensure that they get proper pay in other economic spheres, as well as appropriate education and public credit for the contributions that they make.

Family is the ultimate relationship of importance, and Nigerians understand that much better than we do. The thought of having a family with everybody in a different room, eating a meal just doesn't make sense. We're family. We sit down and have dinner together. We eat out of the same bowl. You don't have your meal in this room, and another whole menu for someone else in another room. No, no, no. That kind of activity did not happen in Nigeria.

London was the headquarters for all of Cargill's business in Africa. I was Cargill's first Country Manager in Nigeria—first Black Country Manager anywhere—and the first to do business for Cargill and set up a foreign office. London headquarters refused to accept any of the fifteen or more investment opportunities that I presented for Nigeria. My operation did not receive the equity capital promised. This meant borrowing working capital at interest rates as high as 37% to keep the doors open. I lost money. In corporate bottom line parlance, I failed. It did not matter that the Nigerian operation received less support than other Country Managers learned to expect. After deciding that I had "gone native," they brought in someone else to manage what I had built. The rejection was painful, and the racism rampant.

Thirty-five years of hindsight helped me to understand the breadth of economic racism that may have come into play in corporate decisions. In the 80s, Nigeria, as did many African and Latin American countries, labored under a Structural

Adjustment Program imposed by the International Monetary Fund.

Until the 1980s, Africa had been 90% self-sufficient and exporting its raw materials to finance its development. Beginning in the early 1980s, the world dollar price of raw materials began a tremendous free-fall. In 1980, one Naira, the Nigerian currency, bought US$2. In 1987, US$1 bought 17 Naira. This was a tremendous devaluation of the currency. Inflation was rampant. Coupled with an increase in its international debt load and the lowest commodity prices in almost 50 years, Nigeria was having problems servicing its international debt.

Western banks were making US$ billions on the so-called African Debt Crisis, and wealthy bondholders reveled in the double-digit interest rates being paid. Debt rescheduling and various IMF interventions into African economies more than doubled the amounts owed to international bankers. This was the neo-colonialism Nkrumah warned us about.

I have no false pretenses about racism in corporate America. Cargill was only the second organization I worked for that did not have Black people as its customer base. Very few of the senior managers were non-White or women. Here I was, a bald-headed Black man, who wore fedoras, dressed in decent clothes, kept my shoes shined and my nails cut. I did my job and did it better than most. Nevertheless, the distrust of me because I was Black, was quite evident.

On one occasion, my boss came to visit, and we got embroiled in disagreement about the direction for the Nigerian company. He said, "Rashid, you don't look like a Cargill man." He instantly transported me back to Harvard, where they told me, "You don't look like a Harvard man." He was quite surprised when I agreed with him. There had recently been an international Country Manager's meeting at a resort just south of Barcelona on the Spanish Mediterranean coast. At the end of the meeting, the 150 participants posed for a group picture.

The framed photo was on the floor next to my credenza. I pulled it out for my boss and said, "Let me show you something.

Can you find the Chairman in this picture?" My boss pointed his finger and pushed up and down the rows until he found our CEO. It took maybe thirty seconds. I said, "Now find me!" It took all of five seconds for him to point me out. "Of course, I don't look like a Cargill man. I can't and never will, as long as only White men are in charge." He was red-faced, embarrassed and stammered a defensive explanation that race was not what he meant. He actually called ME a racist for pointing out his blindness. It wasn't long after that I was told it was time for me to leave the company.

The President of Cargill Europe came to see me to let me know that my boss was my boss, even though we disagreed on how things were being done. I was able to keep that business going, despite the fact that I didn't get the kind of help from headquarters that I thought was appropriate. Meanwhile, some of my Country Manager colleagues told me, "We get lots of help." The truth of the matter was that, in Nigeria, we did not get the support required.

I was asked to leave Cargill, not only because of the run-ins I had with management of the company. Cargill thought I had become too much of an advocate for Nigeria. There are certain requirements, or prerequisites, for doing business anywhere, and Cargill was not prepared to give up any company equity in Nigeria. We argued about that.

I advocated for and was promised a million dollars in equity money from Cargill. It was never invested in Cargill Nigeria. The Federal Republic of Nigeria required that all foreign corporations have Nigerian partners. Cargill was not prepared to partner with Nigerian businessmen. I never got the money. The plan that I had laid out worked perfectly, but borrowing foreign money at 35% interest to do business made it impossible for me to make the business successful. Despite the fact that I opened up Nigeria for Cargill, I was set up for failure in that regard.

I negotiated a financially comfortable separation package. I spent considerable time contemplating whether I would stay in Nigeria or return to the States. After all the years it took to get to Africa, I was not in a hurry to return to America. At that time, Chief Arthur Mbanefo was my mentor and advisor. He eventually became Nigeria's Ambassador to the United Nations. He said, "You can do more to help Nigeria from America than you can from here." That was very striking to me and pretty much the decisive argument.

The longer I stayed out of the U.S., the more I realized how much of an American I actually am. African Americans are my tribe. A Black person from Boston will probably have difficulty communicating with a Black person from South Alabama because each of their accents and experiences will be so different. However, they will still have more in common with each other than with somebody from the Yoruba tribe in Nigeria. The Yoruba man is not going to know who the Lone Ranger is. He may not know who Richard Pryor is. He may not know the taste of cherries. These are the types of things that bind us to our cultural traditions versus theirs.

I realize that the anger that I have about who and what America is has certainly not subsided. It has probably increased over time. But my work is in America. My work is with my people, right here in this country. I did go back overseas to Ghana later on to do some work, and I felt the differences between Africans and Americans of African descent even more distinctly. I am a Pan-Africanist, but America is home. If I'm going to provide leadership and direction, America is where I should do it.

Part VII

SYNERGY

Synergy is the benefit that results when two or more agents work together to achieve something, which neither one could have achieved on its own. It's the concept of the whole being greater than the sum of its parts.

Successful synergy lies in finding the right people with whom to work, to develop and manifest the potential that exists within the institutions of society. I have not always been successful in finding the right folk. I had to look at why and attempt to resolve the answers that came to me.

These chapters reflect the transition from skill development to implementation of the skills and tools acquired. They reflect attempts to create structure around the principles and values underlying my work. The principle of synergy reflected a core issue for me as a food revolutionary. As revolutionaries, we see what "needs to be done" and set about the business of bringing our visions into reality. Implementing my vision ultimately required making space for the visions of my comrades. The flowering of synergy helped me to heal wounds, pave roads and build sustainable institutions.

*This moment is filled with joy. I now choose to
experience the sweetness of today.*

Louise L. Hay

Chapter 16
Baba

After I left Cargill in 1992, Baba invited my children and me to live with him in Minnesota for a year. I said, "Baba, let me think about it." I called him back ten minutes later and apologized. It occurred to me that Baba is a mystic, a highly spiritual man. It was crazy for me to hesitate about doing what he suggested, and I immediately began preparations to leave Lagos for the Twin Cities.

I had become a single parent. Four of the children were still enrolled in college. Kamal was finishing Harvard, Koro was at Tufts, Aliyah at Smith and Khadir at the University of Texas. Khalil, Zarinah, Kareem and I went to Minnesota and lived there for a year at Baba's feet, helping him with his work.

Over the Cargill years, whenever I had any free time or when I came back to the States on vacation, I would spend time with Baba. Baba devoted 8 years in tutelage with his spiritual master, and I spent 13 with Baba before he sent me out into the world to do my own work.

Cargill paid me a decent amount of money to leave them, so I had money in the bank that we lived on for that stage. This period is the only time my children ever lived in an apartment. We had two luxury high-rise apartments overlooking the Mississippi River in downtown St. Paul.

During that year, I observed how Baba handled relationships. People came to him with their problems, and he would help them. He often said, "If you listen to me, I will help." Start a new life beginning today. Baba said, "In the lives of all human beings on this planet, there come good times and there come bad times. The pendulum of happiness and sadness, laughter and sorrow, and light and darkness swings constantly from side to side. Sometimes, when the pendulum is in the extreme of darkness in whatever form, Baba appeared, to help that person. There are many people who have been lucky to be seen, touched and in many ways helped by Baba. When the night was very, very dark with not even a glimpse of light visible, that is when Baba would find his way to enter that person's life. From the darkness, Baba appeared like the Morning Star in the sky and shone on that person to show them the right way. He sought fairness, honesty, justice and equity amongst all people. He did much of the cooking at our home, where we often had guests. I washed a lot of dishes and drove him wherever he wanted to go.

The vow of silence that Baba took in Delhi in 1962 had lasted 48 years, until he dropped his body in 2010. It was an honor to have been chosen on occasion to serve as an interpreter of his sign language. The messages that he transmitted continue to resonate and ripple around the globe.

There are very few actions I undertake without thinking, how would Baba handle this? He remains my spiritual guide.

USDA: The last and greatest plantation in America.

K. Rashid Nuri

Chapter 17

United States Department of Agriculture

When it was time for me to leave Minnesota, I thought, "I've never lived in Washington, D.C., let me go there." I interviewed as many agencies as I could discover, looking for work around the issues of agriculture and Africa. As it turned out, the easiest place for me to get a job in DC was to obtain an appointment in the new Clinton Administration.

Most times, when people get political appointments in a President's administration, they have worked in the campaign or contributed a lot of money. I did neither. But I did have a friend named Mike Williams, whom I knew from grad school in Amherst. He was the Chief of Staff for a congressman and Godfather of my daughter, Ama Aliyah Nuri. When Aliyah was born, Mike babysat my two boys while we were away at the hospital in Boston. Mike and Joia, my future wife, introduced me to the right people in Washington, D.C.

You have to campaign for those jobs. The list of supporters

and references that I had in my package was pretty impressive. My list included Congressman Mike Espy, who soon became Secretary of Agriculture; the current Speaker of the House, Tom Foley; Senator John Kerry; and even Whitney MacMillan, the Chairman of Cargill at the time. They all wrote letters in support of my obtaining a position in the Clinton Administration. My package was quite powerful.

The interview process included meetings with the White House Liaison, Undersecretary of Agriculture and several other Administration officials. Initially, I was under consideration for two jobs, both the Administrator and Deputy Administrator of the Agriculture Stabilization and Conservation Service (ASCS), which was later named the Farm Service Agency. Eventually, I was appointed Deputy Administrator for Management, and Grant Buntrock became the Administrator of ASCS. Grant previously served in the Carter Administration. This often happened. After 12 years of Republican control of the Executive Branch, many former Democrat employees were brought back to serve as political appointees in the new Democratic administration.

In September 1993, I was appointed Deputy Administrator for Management. I had a tremendous amount of responsibility. Through my Division Directors, 2200 employees directly reported to me, and I oversaw an $18 Billion budget. I handled human resources, information technology, finance and budget, contracts and facility management. Most everything that happened in that agency came across my desk one way or the other. Eventually, I also worked for the Foreign Agricultural Service, with the same number of responsibilities.

After about a month on the job, Gene Moos, the Under Secretary, called me to his office and asked, "Rashid, you know, the Commodity Operations Division is open, and that's really more in line with what you've done before. Do you want to change positions?"

I shared that conversation with Charles Duncan, the White House liaison. "Charles," I said, "I have a typical Negro job handling administrative stuff. Should I accept the offer?"

Charles said, "Man, what's wrong with you? You've got jobs, money and contracts. That is where the power lies. Go back over there and do your job."

I said, "You're right." I told the Under Secretary, "No sir. I've already made some commitments to my people. I'm going to stay right here." The problem was that they knew I had too much power. I got things done. I was determined to help as many people as possible. Mary Lawrence once said that I needed a food taster, because I was doing too many things that were not in line with the status quo.

In my family, a very high value is placed on education. Prior to my coming, Department employees were allowed reimbursement for continuing education. However, the rules stated that you had to take courses that were directly relevant to your position. For example, a secretary could take shorthand classes, and an accountant could take bookkeeping classes. My education philosophy is, if you just read a book, you're going to be a better human being. I told my people, "If you take a class, we'll pay for it." I had a couple of people finish college while I was there. Expansion of educational opportunities for employees was one of the first things that ended after I left the Department.

Our computer systems and data center were managed in Kansas City, Missouri. A woman in our division worked in Kansas City. Her husband worked for another USDA agency in St. Louis. They lived in the middle, and each had to commute, in opposite directions, every day. They were both career employees. One day, she came to visit my office and asked, "Can you help us? We have done all this travel getting to work and would like to spend more time together." I immediately said, "I can get you transferred if you like." All I had to do was pick up the phone and say, "Fix it," and it was done. I could not understand why this situation had not been corrected many years before.

The bureaucracy is so intense. Folks would come into my office with speeches written for what they wanted to talk about.

I would say, "Don't read to me. Just tell me what you want." They would tell me, and I would sign the papers and get on with business. Then I'd holler, "Next!" and just run them in and run them out. My boss and peers did not like my style. I was not following the normal slow-moving protocols of government. Things were getting done at a much faster rate than the norm.

Dallas Smith was the highest-ranking Black career employee at the USDA. He told me, "You're a good manager but a terrible politician." He was right; I was doing what I knew needed to be done. I handled my business and responsibilities. When I came in the morning, my desk was clean and when I left at night, the desk was clean, because I got things done. I did not let work or decisions pile up. I made sure that the management part of my job was completed, but that's not how you're supposed to do it. The rhythm of government was one that I was not interested in pursuing. As usual, I swam against the stream.

We tend to blame civil servants for many of the problems of government. Before coming into government service, I bought the fiction that bureaucrats and civil servants were the problem with getting things done in Washington. It is not the civil servants but the political appointees, like me, who create problems. There are highly competent and intelligent people who do good work, particularly at the higher levels of the senior executive service. Their problem is that they work for the politicians, and the politicians won't listen.

Too many political appointees are most concerned with the non-issues, such as the length of their title, size of their office and the amount of their check, instead of dealing with trying to help somebody. For the most part, the senior career government employees are hard-working, intelligent, dedicated people, who work hard to get things right. They get in trouble because politicos attempt to lord over them, feign superior knowledge and demand ill-informed actions. When things go wrong, the bureaucrat receives the blame.

Another problem with government is the perpetual backbiting. At Cargill, if I wanted a promotion, I had to train somebody to take my place. You fed your colleague as much information as possible, as soon as they were able to absorb it. But in government, you don't want anybody to know what you know, because they might try to get your job. So that's what keeps information on a need-to-know basis. In the business world, it's more like, "Here is everything I know, so now can I move on up." In hindsight, I can see that continued education created unwanted competition for career employees.

The Miller Report

In 1993, President Clinton appointed Mike Espy, a Black Congressman from Mississippi, as Secretary of Agriculture. Mike had been the first Black official elected to a Federal office from Mississippi since Reconstruction. His selection by Clinton was a hugely important and highly symbolic event. Espy made it clear to everyone that he intended to rid the Department of its institutional racism and general hostility toward non-White employees and farmers.

Coming from Mississippi, Mike Espy had considerable knowledge of the struggles Black farmers faced in his home state and across the South. Since Ronald Reagan abolished the Office of Civil Rights at USDA, virtually nothing had been done to assist Black farmers. Black farmer complaints gathered dust at the USDA and were ignored altogether, as there was no staff to address the issues. Widely known were the efforts of Black farmer organizations to address the discrimination their members experienced. Yet the government was nonresponsive to these protests. I recognized that something needed to be done to make a difference and help Black farmers find relief.

The 1993 Farm Bill and Reorganization legislation helped by directing the Secretary to conduct an audit to determine the nature and extent of discrimination in the administration of farm programs. The Secretary delegated responsibility to conduct this study to the Farm Service Agency. Espy hoped the report would provide facts and data upon which he could act to mitigate the discrimination. Managing contracts within USDA agencies was under my supervision.

D.J. Miller and Associates, a Black-owned Atlanta firm, was engaged to conduct the disparity study and prepare the report. I delegated signing authority for contracts to my deputy, which allowed flexibility for me by providing plausible deniability. He said, "Rashid, I'm going to sign this contract, but this is going to be the end of you." At the end of the day, he was right.

Dave J. Miller survived numerous attempts to scuttle the project. He came within 15 minutes of being disqualified for non-performance by the contract office that reported to me. Based on information from the contract office, I was going to dismiss him at 6:00 p.m. Dave came to my office at 5:45 and explained that he had been blocked from accessing data from the record and data processing center in Kansas City, Missouri, which also reported to me. Without that information, Miller could not measure the impact of the discriminatory USDA conduct. He was set up to default on the contract because he had proved to be a major threat to many key USDA officials involved with maintaining the status quo in the Department. In thwarting the attempts to impede the report, I made enemies who succeeded in eventually engineering my departure from the USDA.

Miller conducted extensive field investigations at the local, district and state levels of the county committee system. He looked at many aspects of the USDA's farm support programs, including discriminatory treatment in the loan and disaster programs. The D.J. Miller Report demonstrated comprehensive fieldwork. The actual data provided by the USDA itself had a profound impact at the agency. The report proved, beyond a doubt, the impact of discrimination on non-White farmers. We proved that the U.S. Department of Agriculture was discriminating against not only Black farmers, but also poor White farmers, Hispanics and Native Americans. The study found that USDA officials, in the administration of federal farm loan and payment programs, treated non-Whites and women unfairly. The study collected evidence of discrimination from non-White employees at the department. It also recommended changes in the County Committee election process that would increase non-White and female participation in the farm loan and complaint review process. The institutional response was to discredit both Miller and the report.

D.J. Miller & Associates had to sue the USDA to receive the contractually agreed upon payment. The suit against the Department of Agriculture alleged that federal officials "unreasonably and without justification delayed, disrupted and interfered" with a study that was performed under contract. The suit sought $400,000 in damages for costs associated with producing a report commissioned by the Department's Farm Service Agency in 1994. He won.

Miller's report was buried deep within the bowels of the USDA. It was difficult to find copies of the multi-volume document. However, the Miller Report became the benchmark for many subsequent studies and reports about USDA discriminatory practices. Despite proof that there had been massive discrimination at the USDA in the past, not a single USDA employee has been either fired or reprimanded.

I didn't realize at the time, the work we did at the USDA would have sizeable reverberations beyond assisting Black farmers. With the report as a predicate, Black farmers filed suit against the U.S. Department of Agriculture in 1997 because of the long-standing racial discrimination in services and credit opportunities. The Pigford lawsuit was the largest class action suit ever filed against the U.S. government, settling for a total of $2.3 billion, paid to claimants in 2014. Official documents related to the case are available at www.blackfarmercase.com.

Settlement of the suit did not solve all the problems for Black farmers, but it did bring attention to the issues and some financial relief to thousands of individuals. The Pigford Settlement led to successful lawsuits by Native Americans, Latino and women farmers. Women and Black staff at the USDA also began to organize against the discrimination they experienced at the Agency. Anti-discrimination efforts are ongoing.

Commodity Credit Corporation

There is a little-known agency within the U.S. Department of Agriculture called the Commodity Credit Corporation (CCC). Secretary Espy did not know as much as he wanted to know about the Commodity Credit Corporation, and he asked me to prepare a report for his edification. Commissioning the Miller Report and writing the CCC paper for the Secretary were likely the two most significant acts of my tenure at the USDA.

The USDA Farm Service Agency website states that the Commodity Credit Corporation (CCC) was created "to stabilize, support and protect farm income and prices. CCC maintains balanced and adequate supplies of agricultural commodities and aids in their orderly distribution." This is the same agency that made deals with big grain companies during the Russian grain embargo.

The Secretary of Agriculture is Chairman of the Board of Directors of CCC. The Board consists of seven members in addition to the Secretary, who are appointed by the President of the United States. All members of the Board and Corporation officers are USDA officials. There is no organization chart readily available, nor would you see names of the officers posted on the wall.

CCC has no operating personnel. Its price support, storage and reserve programs, and its domestic acquisition and disposal activities are carried out primarily through the personnel and facilities of the Farm Service Agency (FSA). I was a Deputy Vice President of CCC and responsible for executing financial aspects of the Corporation. I had the money part of it.

In the early 1990s, the CCC had an $18 billion revolving line of credit from Congress. The CCC Charter Act authorized the sale of agricultural commodities to other government agencies and foreign governments, and the donation of food to domestic, foreign or international relief agencies. CCC also assists in the development of new domestic and foreign markets and marketing facilities for agricultural commodities.

The CCC facilities supported the use of American commodity production as economic and political weapons. Ronald Reagan used the CCC to finance Saddam Hussein in the Iraq/Iran war. He shipped grain to Iraq that was sold for cash to finance Saddam's military. My predecessor as Deputy Administrator for the ASCS had 55 shredders in her office and papers stashed up in the drop ceiling. She was busy cleaning up evidence of the scandal around Iran Contra. The President of the United States, through the offices of the Secretary of Agriculture, had the authority and latitude to utilize the CCC in most any way the Administration deemed useful.

Food and agriculture are of vital importance to the U.S, even in the country's position as the world's leading manufacturing and service provider. Food and agriculture are even more critical to developing countries. Adequate and affordable supplies of food and fiber in these countries determine, more than any other single economic factor:

1. Their political stability;
2. Their capacity for economic growth and infrastructure development;
3. Their ability to participate in international markets; and
4. The health and quality of life of their people.

The richest nations and the poorest nations of the world, therefore, share at least one common and enduring characteristic—an absolute dependence on the viability of the food and agriculture sectors of their economies. This shared dependency demands a global strategy to pursue complementary international, domestic trade and development opportunities from the most powerful and influential food and agricultural organization in the world—the U.S. Department of Agriculture.

Federal budgetary and fiscal realities substantially limited additional funding for trade and development programs. New and innovative uses could be made of the funds and authorities that already existed. The Commodity Credit Corporation could and should have been the catalyst within the Department of

Agriculture for the initiatives that I thought were needed in the areas of domestic and international trade and development.

At the request of the Secretary, I wrote two papers suggesting programs he could initiate through the CCC. The first paper addressed providing aid for trade and development, particularly involving African nations and disadvantaged communities in the U.S. It was entitled: *GLOBAL TRADE AND DEVELOPMENT: Expanding Domestic and International Trade and Development Opportunities through the Authorities of the Commodity Credit Corporation*. The paper provided background material for the Secretary on the role and function of the CCC, as well as a rationale for a change in direction. Below are the recommendations from that report.

RECOMMENDATIONS TO ACHIEVE INTERNATIONAL STRATEGIC OBJECTIVES

1. TRADE AND AGRICULTURE DEVELOPMENT. Sell agricultural commodities to developing countries for local currencies, which can, in turn, be used for development purposes.
2. INFRASTRUCTURE AND FACILITIES DEVELOPMENT. Establish and improve facilities in emerging democracies to improve handling, marketing, processing, storage or distribution of imported agricultural commodities and products.
3. MARKET PROMOTION. Pursue important foreign market development opportunities through the co-financing of projects with U.S. trade organizations.
4. FACILITY CONSTRUCTION AND INFRASTRUCTURE IMPROVEMENT. Provide assistance in the administration, sale and monitoring of food assistance programs to strengthen private sector agriculture in recipient countries.

RECOMMENDATIONS TO ACHIEVE THE DOMESTIC
STRATEGIC OBJECTIVES

1. SMALL AND DISADVANTAGED BUSINESS PARTIC-
   IPATION. Increase the participation of small, small disadvantaged and women-owned small business in CCC
   commodity acquisition and distribution programs.
2. ASSISTANCE TO SMALL AND DISADVANTAGED
   EDUCATIONAL INSTITUTIONS. Use the CCC to
   fund appropriate research activities, particularly at 1890
   Land-Grant Colleges and Universities, and at other historically Black or Hispanic institutions.
3. RURAL DEVELOPMENT. Use CCC funding and programs to leverage and complement other programs and
   funds for rural development, extension and research
   available through USDA, other Federal and State agencies and the private sector.

The second paper prepared for the Secretary focused on
inclusion. How could the USDA expand opportunities for those
who had not been significant players in the commodities trade,
and who were not beneficiaries of the largess provided by the
USDA to the agricultural industry? It was entitled: *COMMODITY
CREDIT CORPORATION GRAIN AND PROCESSED
COMMODITY ACQUISITIONS: Increasing the Participation of
Small, Small Disadvantaged, and Women-Owned Businesses.*

One of the most significant opportunities for increasing the
participation of small, small disadvantaged, and women-owned
businesses in USDA programs is through the commodity
acquisitions of the Agricultural Stabilization and Conservation
Service (ASCS) (now the Farm Service Agency) and the
Commodity Credit Corporation (CCC). During fiscal years
1992, 1993 and 1994, the ASCS and the CCC acquired more
than $5 billion in grains and processed commodities for use
in the USDA's domestic and international sales and donation
programs. Participation of such firms in these programs during

those three years had been virtually negligible, particularly for small disadvantaged and women-owned small businesses.

Funds for the USDA's commodity acquisitions were provided through the CCC, with the actual purchases being made by ASCS's Kansas City Commodity Office (KCCO) on a competitive bidding basis. The number of individual solicitations and contracts issued by KCCO during FYs 1992 through 1994 exceeded 15,000.

The analysis that followed was an examination of actual and perceived barriers that served to inhibit and restrict the participation of small, small disadvantaged and women-owned firms in USDA's commodity acquisition programs.

PART I was an analysis of *Perceived Barriers* to increasing the participation of small, small disadvantaged and women-owned businesses in USDA's commodity acquisition programs.

PART II was an analysis of the *Regulatory/Procedural Barriers* to increasing Commodity acquisitions from small, small disadvantaged and women-owned businesses.

PART III was a *Proposed Strategy* for increasing the participation of small, small disadvantaged and women-owned businesses in the USDA's commodity acquisition programs. The strategy proposed went well beyond the elimination of existing barriers.

PART IV was a *Statistical Compilation* of CCC grain commodity acquisition for FYs 1992 through 1994. It provided a very clear indication of the limited number of U.S. firms that dominated grain sales to the CCC.

PART V contained *Summary Recommendations* for eliminating barriers and obstacles, institutionalizing meaningful procurement preference for commodity acquisitions, and establishing a long-term, fully integrated program that substantially increased the participation of small, small disadvantaged and women-owned businesses in the USDA's commodity purchase activities.

These papers got me into trouble for sharing some of the Department's secrets. I shared the papers with the lawyers and my peers; perhaps that was not smart. Secretary Espy wanted to know what all the information meant. I told him, "Mike, you're the Secretary. It means whatever you want it to mean. You can do anything you want with the money."

Barry Ohler was one of a cohort of senior staff who would arrive at the Department very early each morning to meet and share information about what was going on in various agencies. One day, as I was managing by walking around, I visited a very large office located at some distance from my own. Barry, the IT Director, asked, "What are you doing up here? You are supposed to call me down to your office." He took me on a tour of his department. We went up one set of stairs and down another to a room lined with state-of-the-art computers. I sat down, and he turned on one of the machines and, step-by-step, zoomed in on a field of corn in Iowa. Barry demonstrated how he could count the ears of corn on a single stalk in that field. This was space age technology that I was responsible for managing but had no idea existed. I learned this because some of my staff would share with me some of the secrets. This same IT Director told me, "You know about eighty-five percent of what goes on around here."

I said, "Eight-five percent? I'm used to being an A student and that is a B at best.

"No, no, no," he said. "You're doing real good, because we like you. Your predecessor knew about fifteen percent."

My Deputy, who signed the Miller contract and said his doing so would be my end, was absolutely correct. The Administrator of FSA dismissed me for being too controversial. They chased me right out of there. Once something—as in a bureaucracy—is created, it will do anything to survive. In addition to White supremacy at the USDA, the comfort with the status quo from a huge, entrenched, racist, bureaucratic infrastructure resulted in an attack on those who would challenge it. I was one of those.

One day, a colleague, another political appointee, gave me lessons about hunting dogs and how you use them to hunt. He said dogs have to honor the pointer. If a dog doesn't honor correctly, you kill it. It wasn't until several years later that I realized he was talking about me. He told me straight up, if the dog doesn't honor, you kill it. They chased me out of USDA for being too controversial, for not honoring the status quo.

I went over to the Department of Commerce after that, as Senior Advisor in the International Commerce Division. I was fortunate and grateful to attain this position at Commerce. I was involved with several exciting projects before Secretary Ron Brown died. As soon as he was gone, they parked me in a corner office and literally gave me nothing to do. I knew I had knowledge and skills to contribute, but not even my Black colleagues would give me anything to do. I spent a lot of time doing absolutely nothing. I was approaching fifty, and all of a sudden, I was prematurely retired.

I was angry, and felt a profound sense of betrayal. I had expectations that people would welcome my enthusiasm and work ethic. I imagined that we would jointly approach problems of process and efficiency with a desire to maximize the effectiveness of the organization and do as much as we possibly could for the public. It was here that I began to understand the futility of projecting my values as expectations of others. I did not realize the extent to which collective values are developed collectively and agreed upon expressly. Truths that I held to be self-evident were not necessarily so.

The deeper discomfort was the extent to which I had departed from a life-long attitude about government. Prior to joining the Clinton Administration, I had little interest in the two-party politics of this country. I saw little fundamental difference between the parties in their relationship to Black people. A fox will smile in your face and then bite you when your back is turned. A wolf tells you he is going to bite and then does it. Either way, you get bit.

At that time, I saw no need to vote and had done so only three times in my life, and two of those votes went to Jesse Jackson. My attitude came from the Nation of Islam point of view. Let us get our own. The pettiness and hypocrisy of government were confirmed by my experience in the USDA and Commerce Department. Newt Gingrich led the attempt to impeach President Clinton for the exact same behavior he demonstrated. The pot calling the kettle black is beyond duplicity. I found people in positions of power and authority afraid to exercise their own will to help anyone but themselves, and afraid to take any risk that might expose them to any form of heat. Mr. Muhammad was demonstrably correct.

Trust demands predictability. The ability to predict the actions of persons yields conformity in an organization and creates a corporate culture. Shared corporate identity is important in building an institution that will last, that has stability. Breaking new ground and pioneering new vistas requires a different mentality, a distinctly different mindset. C.L.R James once asked: "What else do we have to do, to go beyond?" Beyond what? One might ask. My answer has always been to be useful, not according to our desires, but according to our powers. What can I do now, this day, to contribute to improving the world? How do I strip fear, deconstruct unreality and create new paradigms?

People without fear are fundamentally unpredictable, and thus become untrustworthy in the eyes of many. Fear is also a control mechanism. Those without fear suffer contempt. They become isolated because they are uncontrollable. They are themselves feared.

I have the distinction of having worked for two African American cabinet secretaries, neither of whom finished their full term of office, and both of whom left me in a jam. Mike Espy was indicted for corruption and forced to resign. He was subsequently exonerated of all charges. Ron Brown, Secretary of Commerce when I worked at the agency, was killed. Ron Brown was incredible. He is the one who brought the Democratic Party back to life. As head of the Democratic National Committee, he brought together the coalition that engineered Clinton's election.

At Brown's memorial service, Clinton said that he would not have been President had it not been for Ron Brown. The Secretary was an incredible man, who demonstrated little fear in his actions. His upbringing in a conscious atmosphere kept him grounded in a number of majority-White environments. Brown joined a fraternity at the White college he attended. He was a captain in the U.S. Army. Growing up, his father was the manager of the Theresa Hotel in Harlem. Brown was present when Fidel Castro stayed at the Theresa on his visit to the States, after his successful revolution in Cuba. He was exposed to a host of Black celebrities and got to meet all of the important folks in Black society. The exposure gave the young Ron Brown a very clear understanding of who he was and where he came from, which enabled him to move through all the worlds with wisdom. Ron Brown was just a really remarkable man. I'm honored to have had a role in his burial.

After I left the Clinton Administration, I did a lot of work with small businesses in DC. I helped Iyanla Vanzant put her business together. Her business was in boxes on the floor in her home. I organized her files, structured her business and put it all onto a disc. We were still using three and a half inch discs at that time. I helped her sort through and get organized, so she knew where her money was coming from and where it went. She acknowledged me in a couple of her books. I worked with a number of different businesses in that way. The National Black Chamber of Commerce wanted to publish a magazine. I did the desk research and showed them how to create a hard copy magazine. The problem for the Chamber was that the world was becoming digital. Joia and I also created business plans for a company named Medimmune and the Rev. Jim Webb.

I left the Clinton Administration at the end of his first term. I spent the next several years exploring inner space. What I had not acknowledged up until that time was the emotional impact that my various experiences had on me. I arrived at a point when I finally acknowledged my emotional pain. On most projects, I was always the pioneer; I was always pushing the envelope. I was the one who went to war repeatedly, in various situations. After it was over, I would say, okay, that's over. What's next? I was always moving on. My ouster from the Clinton Administration was deeply frustrating. I reflected on the repetitive error that led to turmoil around my departures.

The lesson that I had yet to learn was how to create synergy with my superiors and coworkers. Creating the community of my dreams would require a collective resonance with fellow change makers, bringing the sense that we were growing together toward shared goals. I had followed the Divine directive to learn all that I could about food, experientially. My path had zigzagged the United States and crisscrossed Asia, Africa and Europe. I had returned to the U.S. and found a position at one of the greatest centers of agricultural power in the world—the United States Department of Agriculture. How was I to apply the knowledge, skills and experience I had gained? I needed answers.

What forbids us to tell the truth, laughingly?

Horace, Satires, I. 24

Chapter 18

In the Meantime

I was around the age of 50 when I left the Clinton Admin-istration. I was hurting a lot, physically and emotionally. I had to explore the whys, the causes and the difficulties. I spent a cou-ple of years in that inner space exploration. Clearly, I needed to achieve a greater level of self-awareness. I was still doing some work with small businesses in Washington, D.C., but mainly just exploring inner space. Often, we look outside of ourselves for the causes and the reasons in our lives. People who pursue a spiritual path tell us that the real life is inside. Exploring inner space is a powerful counterpoint to the surveillance of outer space, of exploring the external world.

During that inner journey, I discovered and learned about my own vulnerability. As a child, I chose venturing outside of the house to explore life, rather than engaging in conflict at home. I avoided the pain of not feeling understood and embraced by my stepfather, and I avoided the power differentials inherent in parent-child relationships. I do not recall even considering talking with my mother about my feelings and issues. In my mind, she became a silent partner in the parental package and somewhat inconsequential.

My choice to change venues, instead of facing family conflict, undoubtedly limited my capacity to resolve issues with those in authority, or to at least stay in touch with my feelings about them. I channeled my energies into observation, analysis and decision-making. I became very good at those executive functions, without understanding the feelings that motivate people's actions. I was action-oriented, without the skills for integrating my and others' feelings into the processes of getting things done. My inner space exploration brought me face to face with vulnerabilities that I had not acknowledged.

I have a book in my library entitled The Universe in 40 Steps, which I remember finding in a Hollywood bookstore sometime in the 70s. The book has a series of photographs that begins with a woman sitting in a chair. The next shot is magnified 10 times, and you can see a giant mosquito on her arm. Then they move in closer and closer, in orders of magnitude of 10, until you get down to the cellular and molecular levels of her body.

The next series starts with the shot of the same woman in the chair and goes to outer space in magnifications of 10. Hence, it's The Universe in 40 Steps. You realize that what's inside looks just like the universe. The way the molecules of your body are organized looks just like the galaxies that you see in outer space. That knocked me out. I said, "Wow, inner space, outer space; it's all one, it's all connected." It's about challenging ourselves to find the God within. We frequently look for God outside ourselves, up in space. God is within.

Exploring inner space meant being able to sit with myself to come to know who I am and what my origins are—not lineage, but connection to creation, and how to relate. Hopefully, in meditation, one is able to quiet the mind in order to listen, to hear. We spend a lot of time telling God what we want, instead of listening to what God wants for us. Inner space exploration is a pathway to that peace.

Almost thirty years ago, my sister Kikanza sent me a

quotation. She typed it on a 3x5 index card, and I placed it in my date book. At the end of each year, before even transferring important notes from the journal, I would first shift the card she sent me to the new book. Over the years, the original became somewhat tattered from handling. I would retype the message and put it back in its rightful place. To this day, I have no idea where she found the quotation. I never asked. My sister, who is now an ordained minister, had skillfully discerned an aspect of my character, which at that time, I had not consciously realized. Since then, I have literally carried the thought and the words with me everywhere I have traveled. The quote read:

All men dream, but not equally.
They who dream by night,
in the dusty recesses of their minds,
wake in the day to find that it is vanity.
But the dreamers of the day are dangerous men,
for they act their dreams with open eyes,
to make it possible.
T. E. Lawrence

In my early twenties, I compiled a list of things I wanted to accomplish in life. At the time, I saw myself as a Black Nationalist. I desperately wanted to be an active participant in Black on Black nation-building. I fathered three children before I completed graduate school. I promised God to be a responsible parent, never allowing anyone else to raise them. I grew up with music. I wanted to DJ a jazz radio program, get paid to play drums in a jazz ensemble and learn respectable 3-5-1 chord progressions on the piano. Professionally, I was interested in health and nutrition.

I wanted to experience everything about the agricultural process from seed planting until food arrives on the table. I wanted to explore the world through my work, never as a tourist. I wanted to live and work in Africa. I wanted to fly an airplane. I figured it would take most of my life to get through this slate. I never imagined completing the list well before I was fifty years old. Flying is the only thing I did not accomplish.

At 50, I had traveled the world in answer to a divine call that came in a Harvard library. I had merged my understandings of the science and politics of food through study and experience. Yet, the nation had not yet been built. I desperately needed to determine what would be my next steps in helping to accomplish that goal. The achievement of my personal list left me with a huge problem. What will I do with the rest of my life?

Time is a measure of distance traveled. Time may confer experience, but it does not endow anyone with wisdom. I clearly remember the very first time I experienced the passage of a significant block of time. I could not have been more than twenty-one or twenty-two at the time. I recalled an event that had taken place maybe five years previously. It blew me away to think that my life could be viewed in such an expanse. At fifty years, half a century old, it was hard to believe—and even more difficult to comprehend—that I could consider the passage of time in terms of decades.

My birthday always initiated a foray of inner space exploration. I would examine where I was and where I still wanted to go. The trip usually lasted a week or two. Generally, I was not concerned about what I had accomplished. My focus was more on what I had yet to do. The trip actually began more than a year before my fiftieth birthday. Prior to that year, I was always perfectly clear on which road to travel. At fifty, it had become a struggle. I was looking for Plan B.

My path has always taken me to the edges, places where few dare to travel; a life lived with fearless abandon. I trod the edge with enthusiasm, no safety net of any kind. I carried a faith that God would always take care of me, because She always had. I walked with confidence and feared no one and no thing, except the wrath of God. I have never been afraid to die. There are some limits, however. Despite my lack of fear, I have never done roller coasters, horror movies or tattoos. With so many things possible to fear in this life, I never summoned the resolve to pay someone to see if they could indeed make me afraid. As I approached age fifty, I fell off the edge.

Joia and I married. Thereafter, my fiftieth year yielded monstrous new experiences. We struggled through what it means for middle-aged people to marry and merge families. I gained another daughter, India. India is Joia's niece and was just one year old when Joia began raising her. For the first time in my adult life, I was without a tangible source of income. My wife hospitalized me three times in the course of one month. On two of those occasions, I was painfully close to death. It felt like I had walked into the mouth of a tiger and pulled up a chair. Talk about a reality check.

Although I did not die, the physical and psychological pain was tremendous. Sometimes it takes traumatic events to demonstrate how tiny one is as a human being in the overall scheme of things. Life is truly precious.

There always seemed to be physical pain in my life, usually from pushing my body too hard. Earlier, I described how every seven years I suffered a major body trauma. On a Thursday night playing in a Cargill company basketball game in Gainesville, Georgia, I tore my Achilles tendon. I arrived late from the plant and neglected my usual stretching routine. My teammates kept saying hurry up, hurry up. Although my game could never be described as more than mediocre, it was good to be deemed a necessary part of the squad. I speedily ran onto the court. While reaching for an errant pass, I heard what sounded like a gunshot exploding. I felt the tendon roll up my calf like a venetian blind. My leg burned with pain. I hobbled off the court and sat on the bleachers trying to convince myself I only had a severe muscle pull. I managed to hop to my car and drive home. The next morning, I stopped at the drug store, purchased a walking stick and went to work.

I must have looked quite pitiful limping into the office, because all of the ladies insisted that I immediately go to the hospital, which I did. The intake nurse wanted to know how I arrived at the hospital. I told her I walked in. She was incredulous. I still had not fathomed the severity of my injury.

The first thing the doctor asked was what I had eaten for breakfast. Knowing he wanted to operate immediately, I responded, "No sir! I saw the movie!" Anesthesia on a full stomach is dangerous. It is possible to drown in your own vomit. Furthermore, I was the single parent of young children. I had to arrange for their care before admission.

The doctor put me in a short leg cast for the three days that I stayed at home before I finally allowed him to operate. They put a wire in my leg, creating a bionic tendon. It will never tear again. I left the hospital after a week in a full leg cast. Rather than staying home with my feet up, I immediately went back to work. I let nothing slow my pace.

Employees of the Cargill Soybean Processing Plant in Gainesville, Georgia were on strike. In addition to resuming my usual responsibilities as Merchandising Manager, I did all of the food shopping for the management staff that had been imported to act as strikebreakers. I stayed busy despite my ailment. I resolved myself to a strenuous rehabilitation program. Within six months, I was able to run three miles. I did that only once, and never played basketball again. Instead, I began playing tennis, and then my knees died, right on schedule—seven years later.

I remember a typical muggy day in Southeast Asia where the heat was on without relief. The president of our company had flown over to Singapore from Minneapolis to participate in a regional meeting. He sat in the back of the conference rooming nodding from a combination of jet lag and the heat. Later, we found out he was also dying from prostate cancer. Around him, other colleagues were also finding it hard to keep their eyes open. I could not possibly sleep because my knees were burning from pain.

I blew out my knees through twenty years of active running, mostly on pavement, playing basketball, tennis and other sports. I got a kick out of attacking hills, running up the down escalators of underground Metro systems and other similarly excessive exercises. My boss finally said, "Please go get that fixed. It hurts me just to watch you walk." Both knees required cutting. With my usual enthusiasm, I began a rehabilitation process. Rather than sitting around with my feet up for six to eight weeks, as recommended by the surgeon, I was playing tennis within three weeks, lifting weights to strengthen the muscles. I had resumed my heavy schedule of international travel.

For over a year before my fiftieth birthday, I had felt increasingly poorly. I would eat some food and literally fall asleep, face first, in my food. Talk about embarrassing. My feet and hands would swell. I was thirsty all the time and wetting my pants on a regular basis. My children were afraid to ride in the car with me because I would nod out at the wheel. I had an accident in Joia's car just four days before our wedding. I just blacked out. It was astounding to run into the back of another vehicle at 20 mph and see the car I was driving destroyed. I got to the point where I had difficulty walking and required a stick to support my weight. Health says no, so the body won't go.

The biggest pains were humiliation and bewilderment. We wear diapers in the early years of our lives. I had no idea the extent to which diapers reappear in the later years of life. Walk through any drug or grocery store, and you will always find at least one aisle committed to "diapery," the art of hiding the fact that more than 13 million American adults, mostly women, wet themselves each and every day. There are all kinds of euphemisms to describe the phenomenon. There is stress incontinence, overflow incontinence, functional incontinence, urge incontinence, over active bladder, etc. The products look like panties, underpants, over pants, briefs, wipes, bladder control pads and inserts. They come with garter belts, snaps and re-sealable tape. I recently saw ads on TV for pills to prevent adults from wetting their pants. Magazines sell the products. None of this meant much until it happened to me. All of a sudden, I could not get to the bathroom quick enough. For a while, I dared not leave the house without my own diaper strapped on.

Diabetes is one of the real cool killers, quiet and deadly. My daughter Aliyah told me she suspected I was diabetic. I chose not to listen at the time. Normal blood sugar levels range from 80-120 mg/dl. When I finally entered the hospital, my level was almost 800. I was unwittingly suffering diabetic comas. It took ten days to bring my level down to a point where the doctors felt comfortable enough to release me from the hospital.

I finally had to acknowledge that my extended birthday inner space exploration was actually a clinical depression. While depression affects about 5 percent of the general population at any given time, the rate is between 15 and 20 percent in patients with diabetes. Diabetics with depression have a very difficult time managing their blood sugar levels. Often, individuals with depression do not realize that they are depressed. It is easy to attribute the symptoms of depression to the diabetes.

Many newly-diagnosed diabetics go through the typical stages of mourning. These are denial, anger, depression and finally, acceptance. I felt betrayed by my body. I had spent years focusing on diet and exercise. I didn't even know it was possible for me to get diabetes. I had not resolved the inner issues that gave me a psychic connection to the disease. Louise L. Hay wrote a book about the mental and emotional causes for physical illness. She says the probable cause of diabetes is longing for what might have been, a great need to control, deep sorrow and no sweetness for life left. Depression, she says, comes from anger you feel you do not have a right to have, and hopelessness. After speaking to his mother about my condition, my son Kareem reported that whenever I was not working, I became depressed.

I was a terrible patient. The hospital staff got annoyed, because I challenged and questioned everything. I thought the food was terrible. The choices contradicted common nutritional sense. I made a list of questions for the doctor, who said he had to look up the answers. I seemed to know more about nutrition than the hospital staff. I left the hospital not knowing if my health was restorable. I faced the prospect of taking insulin for the rest of my life. I did not know if my eyesight would return to normal, how damaged were my liver and kidneys, or if I would ever actually feel good again.

Two weeks after leaving the hospital with a diagnosis of diabetes, I went out for a late evening of music. I left the small club in Northwest DC and walked toward my car. I had parked only half a block away. It had been a good evening. Riding alone in "Blue," my comfortable sedan, always afforded me headspace to explore inner and outer space. I had enjoyed the last set of music and was silently humming some of the riffs played by the tenor saxophonist, who reminded me of Dexter Gordon on *Our Man in Paris*.

I greeted a couple of young brothers who were relaxing on a stoop. They responded in what seemed a reasonably warm and appropriate manner. As I passed, one of them called out and said, "Hey, let me ask you something." I stopped, turned around and walked back the few steps to where he was sitting. As I leaned forward to receive the question, the youth cold cocked me with the full force of his young athletic body. I reeled back in total shock.

I clearly remember thinking to myself. 'What is this about? I am not going to fight that boy. Run man. Run! He is younger than my fourth son is. Let me just walk quickly to my car and avoid this altercation altogether.' That was my mistake! Seeing my back, in what they must have assumed was flight from fear, they swarmed me. After a couple more blows to the head, I fell to the ground in a fetal position, covering my head with my hands, as the youngsters continued kicking me everywhere. That was the last thing I remember of the incident. Later, I found out they left me lying in the middle of the street, stripped, bare assed naked and bloody. The beating was severe. The hospital attendants initially diagnosed paralysis. I exhibited no feeling in my lower body.

I was immobile for several months. Not from physical disability, but from the damage to my heart and soul. I am the one who loves the sights, sounds and smell of the street. Wherever I traveled, I made a point of visiting the richest neighborhoods and the poorest. I had never been afraid to enter any community, except South Boston. I would tell people who avoided certain locales that they have nothing to fear. People, like dogs, can smell fear, and will only attack those who appear weak.

I prided myself on an ability to speak many dialects of the American language. I can visit the White House and talk with the president, as well as stand on the corner and converse with the young bloods. People find so many things to separate and distinguish themselves from others. One can always find fault if one chooses. In the Holy Quran, God says He has made us of different tribes, so we can know one another. I always look for some area of commonality as a way to initiate communication with people. It has worked for me all over the world. Now, here I was in Washington, D.C., a genuinely Black metropolis, and boys who could be my sons, whipped me good. I just could not believe it. All around, I felt rejection. My health was bad. My own people beat me up. No one was calling, seeking my skills for work. What was I to do?

In my search for perspective, I reflected on the presence and writing of C.L.R. James. I greatly admire C.L.R. James for the sheer force of his intellect and the intensity of his analytic ability. James became one of my intellectual heroes during the spring of my last semester in graduate school. The Black academic community had organized a lecture series honoring Paul Robeson. James came as one of the invited lecturers and taught me a great deal on his evening. James' thought on Paul Robeson was significant, but that was not the major lesson. It was the paradigm of his thinking, not so much what he said, but how he structured it.

Already an old man, he walked into the room and sat down front on a straight back chair. He began his talk by listing five reasons he thought Robeson was a great man. Then he discussed and analyzed each of the five points. At the end of his two-hour talk, he reminded us that he promised five items and repeated them. It was a brilliant lecture, proving Mr. James one of the great thinkers of the twentieth century.

The role of the thinker is to make the ordinary citizen conscious of the process of which he or she is a part. In his book, <u>The Black Jacobins</u>, James said, "Great men make history, but only such history as it is possible for them to make. Their freedom of achievement is limited by the necessities of their environment. To portray the limits of those necessities and the realization, complete or partial, of all possibilities, that is the true business of the historian." I felt that these words held some insights into my personal circumstance and history. They helped me as I again undertook an inner journey to discover the origins of my repetitive interpersonal difficulties.

My professional life has been as painful as my physical life. I have tried to be a thinker, and a man of integrity. Integrity means having values and behavior in congruence. An issue I confronted during my transition to middle age was the seeming rejection of my work or perhaps a lack of vision by others. I have fought for causes and taken stances that somehow created disharmony, particularly with my "superiors." Most often, my work has been the startup or restructuring of organizations.

There is nothing more difficult to conduct, or more uncertain in its success, than to take the lead in introducing a new order of things. The reaction to and rejection of new concepts that I introduced was painful. I would leave a job in acrimony and turmoil. Ironically, years later, people who were part of the project would come and say thank you for the work I had done at the time. Gratitude is nice and appreciated, but I wondered why few chose to stand with me in the moment. Again, I asked myself the questions that had become all too routine: Why did I have to fight those battles alone and without support? Is it because I usually proved unwilling to compromise principle?

Years ago, I saw a movie starring Sir Anthony Hopkins and Brad Pitt called *Legends of the Fall*. It was a story about transitions, relationships, stretching of boundaries, conventions, expectations and assumptions. The film helped me to understand why I had so many problems with my "superiors." I was not trusted. The movie affected me greatly. It had a narrated prologue that began:

Some people hear their own inner voices,
with great clearness,
and they live by what they hear.
Such people become crazy,
or they become legend.

A central theme in the film was trust, which is so often based upon predictability and stability. There is also a trust that develops between a guru and his disciple, which contains no element of predictability. Trust even exists in the world of the trickster, where nothing is as it appears to be. The instability and unpredictability of breaking new ground and pioneering new vistas, more often brings the limited trust afforded the trickster than the devotion of the disciple to his master.

Sometimes Baba would instruct me to do something that defied all logic. It took a while, but I learned to hear and obey without question. I trusted his wisdom and knew that his guidance would open new spiritual perspectives for me. Trust, in the highest spiritual sense, made it possible to listen openly to his advice, secure in the knowledge that I would come to know how to create the new paradigms of service that I sought.

Patience is the art of hiding one's impatience. The impatience of my first 50 years mellowed through time. I am still learning patience. I no longer think everything must happen today. Some things can wait until tomorrow. Some matters, particularly those imposed by others, can wait until cotton comes to Harlem. It is just not that important. Ill health also contributes to learning patience. Diabetes requires a careful examination of your feet each time you bathe. Picking your toes takes time. However, several things still test my tolerance level: mendacity, incompetence, obfuscation and bovine scatological.

The impatience of my first round in life led to burnout. I never took a vacation until I was 48 years old. I was the consummate workaholic. Twelve or sixteen-hour days were no big deal. I lived to work, rather than working to live. I always thought it absurd for people to spend money, go to exotic places and do nothing. I could stay home and be very busy doing nothing, as well as saving the expense.

Q: What are you doing?
A: Nothing!
Q: Will you do thus and so?
A: No!
Q: Why not?
A: Because I am busy.
Q: Doing what?
A: Nothing!

If I wanted to rest, I could stay home, read a book, watch a game, make love and just chill out. Doing nothing could be a lot of fun. This was especially true since my work had taken me around the world more times than I could count. I have lived in more than thirty places in this country, spent time in forty-nine of the fifty states, lived overseas nine and a half years and worked in Africa, Asia, Europe and America. When it was time for me to rest, I just wanted to sit down, not have to pay to do so.

At fifty, God blessed me with a timeout. Being forced to sit down and do nothing—not out of choice, but from necessity—created the opportunity to examine my life. Again. This time, it was in even more strenuous detail than what I underwent in San Diego, those many years before. Both times, I bounced back after a deep dive into uncertainty that teetered on the edge of despair. It would be totally out of character for me to quit on life and just lay down to die. The examined life, the life of the mind, is a life well worth living. I was sure God still had tasks for me to accomplish. My service was far from complete.

Spiritual healing occurs as we begin to consciously reconnect with our essential being – the wise, loving, powerful, creative entity that we are at our core.

Shakti Gawain

Chapter 19

Los Angeles

I left DC in the winter of 2002/2003 and returned to California. I had found an internal place that was very dark and dealt with it through introspection and self-medication. A great deal of that was physical sickness. I hoped for California to be a place of restoration. I can attest to Louise Hay's analysis that diabetes comes when the sweetness goes out of life, because I was really hurting. I can remember sitting on my sister's back porch and saying to myself, "God can't be finished with me yet. I've got too much knowledge, too much experience. I just need to get through this, because something else is going to come." I didn't know what it was going to be or what it was going to look like, but something positive had to come.

Kikanza has a lovely home in West Los Angeles, near Interstate 10, which runs from the beaches in Santa Monica, all the way to the beaches in Jacksonville, Florida. She invited me to stay with her for rest and recuperation, and I did so for six months. My time was spent walking in the neighborhood or up the hills in Ken Hahn Park, which is part of Baldwin Hills. I learned my way around Chinatown, seeking herbs to address my diabetes. I spent hours talking with Diane Maxwell Brown, one of my oldest and dearest friends. My sister and I cooked and ate together. I wanted to heal and was driven to do so.

Etha Robinson taught biology at Dorsey High School. I met Etha in a Black book store on La Brea Avenue. Etha had founded and incorporated the African American Food Association and asked me to work with her to manage the organization. We rented a tiny office space located inside a print shop at the corner of Slauson Avenue and Overhill Drive in Windsor Hills. We did urban agriculture work in Los Angeles. Adonijah Miyamura El and Eugene Alala Cooke worked with us on the first Earth Day project organized by Black folk in L.A. I helped maintain a food forest at Crenshaw High School. Eugene worked with me to install a couple of home gardens in the area.

The most ambitious initiative of the African American Food Association was a three-day Agribusiness Symposium with the theme, 'From the Seed to the Table.' The intent was to organize a symposium that would bring 1500-2000 agricultural and agribusiness people to Los Angeles and attempt to address all issues affecting the African American agribusiness industry... from the seed to the table. We were unaware of any organization attempting such a comprehensive undertaking on such a fundamentally pertinent issue as Black food production. We proposed bringing together African American people at the right time in history, focused around the right issues.

The symposium would gather together members of the African American agricultural and food services industries, placing them in one location at the same time. Invitations would be extended nationwide to farmers, ranchers, horticulturalists, farm market managers, distributors, canners, food processors, bakers, caterers, candy makers, restaurateurs, wholesalers, distributors, grocers, academicians, researchers, extension services, farmer organizations, farm support groups, funding sources and students. The attendees would participate in lectures, seminars and hearings constructed with a fundamentally educational intent, similar to that of the Congressional Black Caucus' annual event. There would be general assemblies, large dinners and caterers/food vendors on-site.

A major expense we had to consider was both the written and video documentation for fundraising and for history. Unfortunately, our ambition was far too grand. Not only did we not have the requisite finances on hand, but we also did not realize it would take quite some time and immense community organization to make all this happen. We got no further than discussion and writing position papers. As the years went by, smaller regional events along the lines we were thinking did occur across the nation. The African American Food Association's biggest success was to produce a George Washington Carver event on the campus of the University of Southern California.

I first learned about George Washington Carver when I was very young, during the time that I was challenging myself to read a plethora of books, especially during the summers. Through the biographies that I read, Carver's life became like a North Star for me. His dedication to being of service touched me as a child and remains a guiding principle. I had no idea that I would grow up to emulate, not only his commitment to serve, but also his connection to the intricate, often indiscernible, life of the garden.

My awareness of Carver increased over the years. George Washington Carver is more than an icon. He was a multi-dimensional man. The levels of contribution he made, not only to America, but also to the world, are just absolutely miraculous. We continue to build upon the legacy he established so many years ago.

George Washington Carver was a shaman, a very spiritual man. He was also a plant scientist, earning a Master's Degree at Iowa State toward the end of the 19th century. Booker T. Washington brought Carver to Tuskegee Institute in Tuskegee, Alabama in 1896, where he remained for almost 50 years.

Carver, the botanist, soil scientist, inventor, community builder and educator died in January of 1943.

Carver's impact on American agriculture, American industry and American social relations was astounding. He single-handedly saved the South. A lot of folks think of him as having only worked with Black people because he was at Tuskegee. But the impact of his contribution literally saved southern agriculture.

Southern agriculture was built around cotton. At the time that he started doing his work at Tuskegee, cotton had just about played out. The boll weevil was eating the cotton crop all up, and farmers didn't know what to do. Carver came up with the solution, which was crop rotation. This is very simple stuff that we now know and certainly implement in our natural urban agricultural work. The standard catechism of agriculture is to rotate your crops. George Washington Carver is the man who introduced crop rotation to southern agriculture.

Carver introduced soybeans, he introduced sweet potatoes and he introduced peanuts into rotation with cotton. Crop rotation brought the soil back and saved the south. Until that time, farmers were mining their soils by planting the same cotton over and over and over again, perhaps including corn in the rotation. All the nutrients were removed from the soil. The plants were weak because the soil had been mined and depleted of nutrients and life. That is why the boll weevil infected the cotton fields so viciously. They attacked weak plants, grown in weak soil. With no living soil in sight to stop them, the insects spread from field to field. Planters were afraid of the boll weevil. Carver showed them how to resolve the problem.

We live in a world that's so reductionist—without an understanding of the whole. Organic, at its best, means whole, complete. Human beings on many parts of the earth today are disconnected from the soil. We are disconnected from the natural world. We feel that we are superior to the natural world, and thus attempt to conquer nature, instead of being in harmony and in tune with nature.

The plants and the animals formed a community that existed long before we got here. It will be here long after we're gone. So many folks say they are concerned about climate change and how people are going to destroy the earth. I am not worried about that at all. The planet has been here. It has been strong for gazillions of years; mankind has only been here for fifteen minutes. The real problem is, if we don't take care of the environment around us, we may kill humankind. It's the human beings who are going to have a problem, not Mother Earth. Mother Earth has been here and will survive anything humans do to it.

Carver talked to plants. No, actually the plants talked to Carver. Understanding the relationships between the plants and the earth and the sun and the water generates greater respect for the natural world around us and our connections and interactions with it. Carver would get up in the morning, take his walk in the fields and listen to the plants. The plants would tell Carver what experiments to do. Because he was a spiritualist, he opened himself, he allowed himself to commune with nature. When you're communing with nature, you're communing with God. Being with those plants is a meditative form. It can take you into a whole other realm, if you let yourself go and try to establish that connection.

We do that in the garden. If you go into the garden and listen, the plants will tell you what they need, when they need it. And all you have to do is pay attention, open your eyes, open all of your being and receive the information that's coming in.

Etha and I invited Peter Burchard, who was writing a biography of George Washington Carver, to deliver the keynote address at the USC Carver event. As part of his research, he was interviewing everyone alive who personally knew Carver. He asked me to visit the UCLA historical film library in Hollywood to find audio recordings of Carver. There were only four. I discovered that Carver had the voice of a six-year-old child.

I asked Peter, "Since you intend your book to be the most

definitive study of Carver's life and work, are you going to discuss his being a eunuch in the book?" He was undecided at the time. My attitude was that he had a responsibility to weigh in on this debate. It is not clear if Carver was castrated prior to going to University as a requirement for entry, or if he was castrated as a youth by one of his slave owners. Regardless, not including this historical controversy would be an act of whitewashing history and dismissing a potentially huge crime committed against this major icon of America.

Leimert Park was a small neighborhood bordered by Crenshaw Boulevard, not far from the Food Association office. Four jazz clubs, one Blues bar, two museums and three theaters, including the one founded by actress Marla Gibbs, were all located in one square block of the expanse. The World Stage, created by legendary jazz percussionist, Billy Higgins, anchored this creative enclave. I had loads of fun listening to the music, talking with artists and just hanging out. At every opportunity, I availed myself of the opportunity to listen to the healing force of the universe, music.

After 18 months, which included three months in Sacramento, I felt much better. My blood sugar had leveled out. My mind was clearer. My spirit was brighter. I had walked all over West Los Angeles and my physical fitness improved. I renewed old high school acquaintances and made new ones. I spent considerable time with Diane, one of my oldest friends, and her family. In the summer of 2004, I got the call that signaled a new world on the horizon.

Fools learn from their mistakes.
I'd rather learn from other people's mistakes.

Bismarck

Chapter 20

Ghana

One day in spring 2004, I received a surprise call from Dave Miller. This is the same man who conducted the Miller report I commissioned while working at the USDA. Dave developed his agribusiness experience at Miller Farms, a 160-year-old family farm located near the town of Arlington, in Early County, Georgia. This experience positioned him to be asked by the government of Ghana to purchase the Ghana Cotton Company. He formed a company named GhanAmer Farms LLC, based in Atlanta, and asked me to assist him in managing the Ghana Cotton Company after he completed the acquisition. I saw this as a great opportunity. I traveled to Atlanta to begin the project. After several weeks of preparation, I departed to Accra, the capital of Ghana.

GhanAmer was 95% owned by GhanAmer Farms LLC and 5% owned by the Agricultural Development Bank of Ghana and other former Ghana Cotton Company Ltd. shareholders. The Ghana Cotton Company was a leading national company, with fifteen facilities, over 370 employees and control of approximately sixty percent (60%) of Ghana's cotton processing market.

Miller sought financing to acquire the assets and liabilities of the Ghana Cotton Company. GhanAmer Farms LLC, through its subsidiary, GhanAmer Farms Ltd., had a goal to acquire, process and sell two (2) million bales of cotton in Ghana. The strategy was to replicate the model used to grow cotton in the state of Georgia, United States of America.

GhanAmer planned to provide products and services at all stages of the cotton production, processing and marketing chain, including:

- Organization of cotton producer groups
- Mechanized land preparation services
- Input supply services
- Transportation services
- Crop financing services
- Extension services
- Seed cotton ginning
- Logistics management

As the owner, GhanAmer would continue the responsibilities that the Ghana Cotton Company (GCC) had traditionally assumed. GCC had been financing grower costs, including land preparation, seed, fertilizer, chemicals and hauling cotton after harvest. GCC processed seed cotton into cotton lint and cottonseed at five facilities located in northern Ghana. Farmers grew the crop, and the company collected the raw lint, ginned and marketed the bales of cotton on the international market, and paid the farmers for their services.

When I arrived in Accra, I continued the research that I had begun on the Ghanaian Cotton Company. We needed to learn the full scope of their operations, detailed processes and key relationships. Certain aspects of the real conditions on the ground simply could not be gleaned from overseas. Among other things, I needed to look at internal documents, meet managers, visit facilities and get acquainted with the farmers. I had been there for three weeks when misunderstandings that had been brewing came to a head.

In response to Miller's optimism that the sale would be successful, GCC had relinquished many of its responsibilities to the farmers. They had not been paid for the cotton they produced. All parties had come to consider GhanAmer the new owner of the Ghana Cotton Company Ltd., even though the purchase had not yet closed. Miller was still seeking adequate financing for the purchase.

The delay in capitalization of GhanAmer created tremendous distress in Northern Ghana. The local economies were totally dependent on an economic system that had been extant since the colonial era. The farmers endured many weeks being unpaid by either GCC or GhanAmer. They had no other resources to pay their ongoing expenses, including fuel, school fees, groceries, etc. The local economies in Northern Ghana were shut down because of this failure.

Upset by the disruption of their lives and lack of action from GhanAmer, a delegation from the North descended on the airport residential area where the office was located. The men were very distraught, believing the lack of payments and crop processing were the sole fault of the Americans, who made promises that were not kept. I called Miller, who was still in Atlanta, and told him of the problem. Miller called the company's Washington lobbyist, who happened to be on Air Force One with President George W. Bush. A call from the plane was made to the American Embassy in Accra. Just before the angry employees cut the phone and electricity, I received a call to my mobile phone from the Marine Guards at the Embassy saying, "We heard there is a hostage situation at this address. Do you need us to send over some Marines to rescue you?"

Oowee! I could not believe what I was hearing and broke out laughing.

The Ghanaians must have thought I was crazy. Here they were confronting me in a very serious situation, and I was laughing.

They could not have known that I was laughing at myself. The humor was in realizing the United States government and the U.S. Marines were honestly volunteering to rescue me from a potentially hostile situation. I would never have imagined that reality. I spent all my adult life feeling a level of detachment from America because of the obvious racial oppression experienced by Black people. Here I was in a situation where the government was clearly ready to defend me as an American citizen. As it turned out, I was able to talk reasonably with the farmers without the assistance of the Marines. The situation de-escalated. However, the irony of the culture shock remains.

The conversation that ensued between the farmers and me did not resolve the issues at hand. I was, however, able to sufficiently lower the temperature of the conversation and, by God's Grace, did not get physically hurt. Negotiations to finance and manage the Ghana Cotton Company eventually fell apart because Miller could not raise the necessary capital. GhanAmer eventually evaporated as an organization. The Ghana Cotton Company was taken over and managed by the Agriculture Development Bank of Ghana.

Although I undertook this adventure with my usual fervor and enthusiasm, I sensed the project was wrought with tragic potential from the beginning. There were issues that I would ultimately be forced to oppose directly. One of GhanAmer's partners was the Agriculture Department at Tuskegee University. Tuskegee was heavily funded by Monsanto and promoted the Monsanto product, Bt cotton. Miller intended to have the Ghanaian farmers plant Bt cotton. I knew at some point Miller and I would have collided on the issue, but I thought there was a small possibility I could persuade him differently. In all honesty, the collapse of the transaction, while disappointing, was somewhat of a relief. The biggest lesson learned was to never promise what you cannot deliver.

I was in no hurry to return to the States and chose to stay in Ghana for 19 months. Years before, during my time in Nigeria, I had learned African macro culture. Ghana provided the forum for learning African microculture. Renee Neblett, founding Director of the Kokrobitey Institute, introduced me to many upper-crust Ghanaians. I observed their manners and etiquette.

On one occasion, Miller and I were attending a meeting of government officials and bank officers to discuss the proposed investment by GhanAmer. The setting looked like a school classroom with chairs arranged neatly in rows facing forward. As we entered the front of the room, I started shaking hands with the men in line immediately on my left. A distinguished-looking gentleman across the room loudly shouted, "No! Start here." He was Chairman of the Board of the Agricultural Bank. The Chairman was the senior person in the room. I thought the protocol breached was not greeting him first.

The Chairman was kind enough to explain that when greeting people in a reception line, you never wanted to start on the left end. Approaching from the left end of the line meant I was extending the back of my hand to the back of the official's hand, which is considered rude in Ghana. I was unknowingly being impolite by starting on the left side of the receiving line. The polite and correct manner of handshaking in a receiving line is to begin on the right side of the line, while moving along the line to the left. In this way you will shake hands with folk, open palm to open palm, which is considered most respectful. This is one example of Ghanaian microculture.

I worked on various projects during the remainder of my stay in the country. I did desk research for Ghana's Millennium Challenge Account, the organization that applied for aid to the United States on behalf of the Republic of Ghana. The Millennium Challenge Corporation is a United States foreign aid agency, independent of the State Department and other aid agencies. Countries are eligible to apply for support based on an evaluation of "good governance" according to MCC standards. The MCC website states:

"Created by the U.S. Congress in January 2004 with strong bipartisan support, MCC has changed the conversation on how best to deliver smart U.S. foreign assistance by focusing on good policies, country ownership, and results. MCC provides time-limited grants promoting economic growth, reducing poverty, and strengthening institutions. These investments not only support stability and prosperity in partner countries but also enhance American interests."

In order to be accepted for MCC finance, Ghana had to demonstrate behavior acceptable to the U.S. Government. I am sure Kwame Nkrumah would have eschewed the MCC as a contemporary example of American neo-colonialism.

The research work I performed was part of the application process for Ghana to receive a Millennium Challenge Account. My area was Smallholder Extension Outreach. I was contracted to create a plan to:

1. Identify existing institutions by carrying out research and development in horticultural products;
2. Assess their current capacities and delivery mechanisms to industry;
3. Propose a program that would build their capacities and efficiencies in dissemination;
4. Propose models preferable for delivering extension needs and training for farmers;
5. Estimate their needs and how they could be supported under the MCA program; and
6. Assess the impact of the various models on smallholders.

The extension model was to be implemented through the farmer outreach programs of existing agribusiness firms. We wanted to:

1. Learn how they implemented services to the farmers;
2. Get their economic models and financials;
3. Ask how Millennium Challenge Account Ghana could assist in extending the reach of their companies to growers;
4. Determine how they would use monies; and
5. Determine what outcomes and sustainability factors

would be enhanced by Millennium Challenge Account assistance.

Ghana received a Millennium Challenge Account. However, the concepts I presented were not included in the final submission.

I also worked for some time with Ron and Andre Jewell of Jewell Industries, Inc. Andre, the son, lived in Ghana, and his father Ron lived in Virginia. The Jewells built a spice processing facility in the tax-free export zone located in Tema, near the port. Ron obtained credit from the Small Business Association to purchase state-of-the-art equipment. What they lacked were sources to originate raw materials to feed the plant.

They were clear on which products they wanted to process. They also had relationships with major spice companies in the States. I did field research to determine the availability of an upstream supply chain. My conclusion was that there was insufficient feedstock available to supply the plant. A great deal of extension work was necessary to develop a supply chain. Much like the cotton business, the Jewells would have to contract with individual farmers and supply seed and other inputs to get the raw material required to manage the business.

The father and son were continually in conflict with each other, in sometimes very animated disagreement. Their dynamic, combined with the fact that they did not understand the work I was putting in, made my tenure short lived. They brought in a replacement for me, who realized the extensive homework I had completed, and came to the same conclusions I had drawn. I understand Ron Jewell lost everything at the end of the day.

For entertainment, I posted up at a place called Jazz Tone, a restaurant and music venue based in a house located in the airport residential area. Toni Manieson, an expatriate jazz singer from Los Angeles, owned the club. I always loved to read books and listen to live music. Tony's place was perfect for both. Sometimes I would scat and play drums with local musicians. Hugh Masekela was married to a local Ghanaian woman. He came into the club one night and joined us on stage, scatting to *Ornithology*, a Charlie Parker tune written on the changes of *How High the Moon*. The club was a fun place to be.

One day, three women from Atlanta came through Jazz Tone, and we began to talk. Mary Casey Bey was a music teacher, Zina Stuckey an IT specialist and Alma Jean Billingsley Brown a university professor. They wanted to be "Gentle Lady Farmers," and they asked me to look at some materials and analyze their farm concept. I said, "Well, I'd like to tell you what I want to do." This was the first time that I was promoting my own idea, rather than someone else's. The timing was spot on. They decided to help me get started.

Part VIII

SERVICE

―――❦―――

Everything that happened in my life, which preceded these final three chapters, was preparation for the creation of the Truly Living Well Center for Natural Urban Agriculture (TLW). Truly Living Well represents the culmination of my lifetime endeavors in the agricultural realm. Fifty years of living and learning informed and primed the work undertaken over thirteen years in Atlanta.

These chapters are not a prescription. They are not offered as a blueprint for anything. I am a cheerleader and advocate for urban agriculture and development of local food economies. I think it important that everyone be given time and space to learn from their own mistakes. Or, you can save time, and learn from mine.

I have outlined, in a very specific manner, the process undertaken to grow Truly Living Well from its humble beginnings to the successful model it became. Many times, I have been asked to replicate TLW in other cities. The answer has consistently been "NO." Each city must develop its own unique local food economy, based on the actual conditions found at the individual location. The difference in the new revolutionary paradigm is local control, local imagination and innovation, local power. I am willing to share my experience. It is essential for me to be of service. These chapters and this book are part of my attempt to do so. I salute the many food revolutionaries out there, who are creating higher ground with their daily work of growing food, growing people and growing communities.

Revolutions are brought about by men,
by men who think as men of action
and act as men of thought.

Kwame Nkrumah

Chapter 21

Truly Living Well 1.0

Ghana was still my residence in early 2006. I wrote an email to my big brother, Ernest Dunkley, telling him what I wanted to do when I returned to the States. We first met in Nigeria, and after all these years, we are still friends. Looking at that email, it was really nice to see that, in general, we have actually achieved most of the actions proposed. In part, the email read:

> I will be coming back to the States on 16 February and will settle in Atlanta. Done just about all I can here within the constraints presented me. Besides, it is time to work for myself rather than helping other people put together their dreams. I have a slew of concepts to develop that will create work for all of us.
>
> Nuri Management Group will create a bouquet of enterprises around food and health called Truly Living

Well (TLW). One of the first projects will be consumer supported agriculture (CSA), where we grow food in the city at TLW Urban Organic Farms and home deliver boxes of organic produce on a weekly basis to subscribers who pay in advance for the service. Sassafras Institute will teach health and nutrition for a fee. TLW Good Food will prepare salads, smoothies, other goodies, as well as offer fresh produce to customers. TLW Foundation will solicit grants and materials to support these projects, work with young people and obtain foodstuffs donated by big corps for distribution to less advantaged folk in the community.

I am excited. Already working on it. Check out the link. When I was in California, I looked at managing that 100-acre organic CSA farm featured, but the woman who interviewed me for the position decided to run it herself. Probably a good idea, because NOW I can do it in my own image. Explore the site; I would like to know what you think about doing it in Atlanta.

I am the Founder and former Chief Executive Officer of the Truly Living Well Center for Natural Urban Agriculture. All the activities that I've been involved with over the years inform the work that I do. Agriculture has taken me around the world, helped me see local food economies and understand the role that food plays in civilization and culture. There *is no* culture without agriculture.

Civilization began when man settled in one place and began to grow food. In order to have a doctor to take care of people, there had to be somebody to grow food for the doctor. And, if you wanted to have a teacher for the children, someone had to provide food for the teacher. That's not to negate the value or the culture of hunter-gatherers. They did have culture. They did have civilization, but it was of a different type than what we've seen in modern incarnations.

We started Truly Living Well by planting in the backyard of a residence in Riverdale, Georgia on 17 February 2006. Mary

Casey Bey owned the property. She was one of the three sisters I met in Ghana who agreed to invest in my new venture. The yard was dark from lack of sunlight. We really couldn't grow much because of the shade, but we started anyway. Ernest and I set out to find where the agricultural resources were in Atlanta. We were planting seeds, literally and figuratively.

Mjumbe Ashe generously offered us site number two, on Harbin Road, right off of Campbellton Road. Mjumbe's only condition was that we grow everything organically, without any chemicals. Site number three, on Washington Road, was made available to us by Melinda Williams, a longtime community businesswoman. Mary was getting beauty work done in Melinda's salon and told her of our endeavor. She offered us the Washington Road site. I visited the location and immediately availed myself of the opportunity. The office of Truly Living Well remains at that location. We just started doing the work—just doing it.

Early spring of 2006, I asked Eugene Cooke, with whom I worked in Los Angeles, to join us in developing the sites. Without hesitation, Eugene packed up his van and moved to Atlanta. The investment provided by Mary, Zina and Jean gave us the working capital we needed to begin production. Bobby Wilson, who worked for the University of Georgia Extension Service, gave us tremendous support.

More than anything, the story of my gardening is the story of my relationships. An intimate reminder of this came in a moment of solitary non-defensiveness. I was preparing to go and pay a visit to a friend, recently hospitalized with a particularly fast-moving and virulent terminal cancer. I asked myself whom I would want to see if I were facing a near and certain death. My answer surprised me, and attests to the profound impact of relationships that are rooted in the garden. The authentic answer was Eugene, the young man with whom I have had one of my most challenging friendships.

A friend of mine, Julie Rainbow, wrote one of the better guides to relationships that I have read. In her book, <u>Standing</u>

the Test of Time: Building Relationships that Endure, Julie recounts stories from elder African American couples whose marriages endured 30 years or more. Julie shares the wisdom of these elders in the context of gardening, from "preparing the soil" to "smelling the roses." The processes within each of the ten steps that she describes go from personal introspection to unity. If ever there were a manual for healthy garden relationships, this is it.

When Eugene and I worked together, our combined talents grew astonishing things. There was also a fundamental tension between us that was equally powerful. Perhaps it's age, worldview, communication styles, or all of the above, plus some. Whatever the source of the tension, the combined talent and tension grew healthy, nutritious foods. And that's our abiding point of agreement.

Eugene is one of the most talented agriculturalists that I know. We met in a circle of California innovators who all shared a calling for urban agriculture. We were all determined to provide a means for the community to feed itself, to employ natural agricultural techniques and to create beautiful spaces. Several years later, when I asked Eugene to work with me to initiate an urban farm in Atlanta, he agreed immediately.

For the foreseeable future, urban areas will be the natural venues for agriculture. Forecasts for the next century envision 70% of the world's population becoming urban by 2050, growing from 52 percent urban in 2011. Right now, 82 percent of Americans live in urban areas. It stands to reason that food production will follow the people.

When we started TLW, there were several very difficult years. I lived in a shotgun house in Peoples Town, near Turner Field. The house belonged to Dr. Thomas Simmons, a pharmacist who permitted me to live there for three years and did not allow me to pay rent. I spent a year and a half in that house before I was allowed to pay utilities. When I took over the utility payments, there were days that I went without hot water—no electricity or heat. Had I been forced or required to get a job to pay my rent,

I never could have built Truly Living Well. So, Tom Simmons is an angel as far as I'm concerned; he provided opportunity and support that was critical in the early days.

The first business plan was dated 26 February 2006. We incorporated as a limited liability company named Truly Living Well Urban Organic Farm. Truly was the name of Mary Casey Bey's uncle. She used his name for her personal care home. When I heard it, I thought the name perfect for what we proposed to do, and she gave permission for us to use Truly Living Well for our business.

It was not long, however, before I got a call from a man who challenged our use of the term "organic," because we were not USDA certified. I tried to explain that our work was beyond organic, but he was not having it and informed the Georgia State Department of Agriculture. An official called and told me we could only use the term if our gross receipts were less than $5000. More than that and we would have to obtain permission and purchase the right from USDA. I planned on earning more than $5000. We eventually became Truly Living Well Natural Urban Farms.

Truly Living Well Natural Urban Farms (TLW) launched with a mission to combine elements of health, nutrition, food production, community work and social service to develop a model of community supported sustainable agriculture. Our initial goals were to:

- Serve people who want to eat healthy, nutritious food;
- Provide the local community with fresh, chemical-free fruit and vegetables;
- Reconnect consumers with the sources and growers of their food;
- Expand operations to 40 acres in metro Atlanta; and
- Develop processing facilities.

We envisioned Truly Living Well making urban land available for food production to provide affordable locally-grown produce. We began to create green spaces to beautify the urban setting, cool the concrete environment and re-connect urban dwellers to the sources of their food. Our work brought together communities in the act of growing food. Advocacy for local food production to be included in community zoning decisions began on Day 1. Updating zoning regulations provides one way for local governments to assist community-driven efforts to bring the benefits of urban farming to urban communities.

The average American consumes food that is transported an average 1500 miles before it reaches the home dinner table. This transport adds to nutritional loss in the food and further distances the farmer and consumer, in ways that make food consumption much less a holistic process than in the past. For most of mankind's history, food was produced within walking distance of where it was consumed. There was a direct connection between man, land and his food. The urbanization of America has made this now a remote possibility, as well as a distant memory for most Americans.

Urban agriculture topples the myth that food production has to occur in wide-open spaces on large tracts of land. Local food economies create enterprises that grow, handle, process and sell locally produced food. This results in local food production that minimizes costs while maximizing the freshness and vitality of food that is consumed.

Most people are aware that organically grown food is free from exposure to harmful chemicals, but that is only one small part of what the organic movement is about. A larger part of organic agriculture involves the health of the soil and of the ecosystems in which crops and livestock are raised. Organic agriculture is born from the idea that a healthy environment significantly benefits crops and the health of those consuming them. In addition, organic practices are viable in the long term because they are efficient in their use of resources. Organic practices do not damage the environment of local communities like large-scale chemical agriculture does.

Everywhere we turn these days people are talking about organic food, whether in the news media, through advertisements or in conversations with neighbors. Eating organically used to be something only hippies and other counter-culture people expressed interest in doing. The organic food market has grown at an extraordinary rate and now exceeds hundreds of US$billions as an industry.

What is organic food? How is it grown? What are the benefits? Does organic food taste better?

In the simplest terms, any food grown without chemical fertilizers or pesticides can be termed organic. People who do not understand the organic food movement often argue that there is no significant difference between organic and so-called conventional food. There is, however, a lot more to the argument than meets the eye.

For most of agricultural history, food crops were grown utilizing natural fertilizers such as animal manures, dung and decomposed plant materials, otherwise called compost. Creating good soil was the focus. Crops took nutrients from the soil, and all crop refuse was returned to replenish the nutrients removed. Adding these natural elements back to the Earth feeds not only the plants, but also the micro-flora and micro-fauna that provide micronutrients for the soil, which are subsequently extracted from the soil by the plants.

Composting is the transformation of plant matter, through decomposition, into a soil-like material called humus or compost. Insects, earthworms, bacteria and fungi help transform the material into compost. Composting is a natural form of recycling, which continually occurs in Nature. An ancient agrarian product and Nature's fertilizer, compost is the fundamental soil enhancer, essential for maintaining fertile and productive agricultural land. All food and animal wastes should be composted before being added to the soil.

Today there are several different reasons why composting remains an invaluable practice. Compost added to gardens improves soil structure, texture, aeration and water retention. When mixed with compost, clay soils are lightened, and sandy soils better retain water. Mixing compost with soil also decreases erosion and increases soil fertility, proper pH balance and healthy root development in plants. The practice also minimizes waste material sent to landfills.

The success with which the organic substances are composted depends on the organic material. Some organic materials are broken down more easily than others. The most rapid composting occurs in matter containing 25 to 30 times more carbon than nitrogen by dry chemical weight. Grass clippings have an average carbon-to-nitrogen ratio of 19 to 1, and dry autumn leaves about 55 to 1. Mixing equal parts by volume approximates the ideal range. Different decomposers thrive on different materials, as well as at different temperature ranges. Some microbes require oxygen, and others do not; those that require oxygen are preferable for composting.

Decomposition occurs naturally anywhere plants grow. When a plant dies, microorganisms and invertebrates in the soil attack the remains, and it is decomposed to humus. This is how nutrients are recycled in an ecosystem. Creating ideal conditions can encourage this natural decomposition. The microorganisms and invertebrates fundamental to the composting process require oxygen and water to successfully decompose the material. The end product of the process is soil-enriching compost.

Predators attack the weak and ill-formed. Pesticides are not necessary when sufficient humus or compost is present. Plants grown in soil that is complete with all the nutrients that Nature provides grow strong, healthy and disease resistant. Plants grown with chemicals are themselves weak, and must be protected against attack from insects, funguses and other pests by the application of synthetic chemical insecticides and other toxic poisons. These poisons get into the food and cannot be removed. The toxins then enter our bodies through ingestion of the food and may lead to other health problems.

Food grown by conventional methods conforms to specific standards, designed to meet a consumer demand, subliminally created through intensive advertising and standardized merchandising. Much of it is genetically modified or hybridized.

All of the food looks the same. Fruits and vegetables are often picked unripe to aid storage and ease shipping. Produce is often gassed with more chemicals to ripen it before presenting it to buyers. The food is unblemished in appearance but bland and tasteless. The nutrient content of conventionally grown food is limited and must be supplemented by vitamin and mineral tablets in order to maintain consumer health.

Natural processes produce food that is better tasting, with higher nutritional content. In the past, organic food was not as pretty to look at as the "steroid food" found in the local grocery store. However, to clearly know the difference, just eat some food grown locally and organically. The absolute, unequivocal proof that naturally grown food is superior to conventional food is simple. The proof is in the tasting!

My first impression of successful urban agriculture was Wilson Farm. The farm land has been in the Wilson family for four generations. Established in 1884, it is a 33-acre farm located in the center of Lexington, Massachusetts, where the Revolutionary war began. I discovered Wilson Farm in 1967 because my wife Lauren's family lived in a house that bordered one of the fields. Produce is grown in the middle of this upper-income family community. The entire community can see its food growing, and the food is marketed right on the farm site.

Wilson Farm sells fresh fruits and vegetables. They supplement what is not grown in Lexington from larger acreage owned in nearby New Hampshire, as well as imports of some specialty items. They have a greenhouse that sells cut and potted flowers, along with garden supplies. Inside, where there is now more store than farm stand, customers are offered nuts, cheeses, fresh apple cider, juices, jams, jellies and whatever is in season, such as pumpkins for Halloween and trees for Christmas. What cannot be grown on the farm, or not produced locally, is purchased by the company and resold to its legion of loyal customers. Unfortunately, Wilson Farm is not committed to organic growing principles. Otherwise, it was a perfect model for TLW development.

To the extent possible, TLW Natural Urban Farm intended to replicate this model in the Atlanta region. A 33-acre site was not necessary, as long as some land was available at our retail outlet that enabled customers to see organic food growing. An urban farm can be as small as ¼ acre, although 2-5 acres would be ideal. The original thought for Truly Living Well was to include a larger plot, within an hour of Atlanta, where primary production could take place for community supported agriculture (CSA) customers, wholesale customers and distribution through a retail outlet.

The TLW CSA program distributed fruit and vegetables produced by TLW Natural Urban Farm. From the beginning, we offered year-round service to our customers. CSA members paid in advance for fresh organic fruits and vegetables to be picked up from our farm stand or delivered to their homes on a regularly scheduled basis.

Community supported agriculture is a relatively new idea in farming, one that has been gaining momentum since its introduction to the United States from Europe in the mid-1980s. The CSA concept originated in the 1960s in Switzerland and Japan, where consumers interested in safe food and farmers seeking stable markets for their crops joined in economic partnerships.

In basic terms, a CSA consists of a community of individuals who pledge support to a farm operation so that the farmland becomes, either legally or spiritually, the community's farm. The growers and consumers provide mutual support and share the risks and benefits of food production. Typically, members or "shareholders" of the farm or garden, pledge in advance to cover the anticipated costs of the farm operation and farmer's salary.

In return, they receive shares in the farm's bounty throughout the growing season, as well as satisfaction gained from reconnecting to the land and participating directly in food production. Members also share in the risks of farming, including poor harvests due to unfavorable weather or pests.

By direct sales to community members, who have provided the farmer with working capital in advance, growers receive better prices for their crops, gain some financial security and are relieved of much of the burden of marketing.

Most CSAs offer a diversity of vegetables, fruits and herbs in season; some provide a full array of farm produce, including shares in eggs, meat, milk, baked goods and even firewood. Some farms offer a single commodity, or team up with others so that members receive quality food on a nearly year-round basis.

Truly Living Well only plants heirloom, open pollinated varieties of seed. Hybrid food is unnatural. Historically, farmers planted a crop and, at harvest, retained a portion of the seed for the next years' crop. The concept of tithing comes from the principle of saving one-tenth of the crop for planting the next season. When you plant seed that you have saved from the previous year, you expect to produce a crop quite similar to what you produced the year before. Hybrid seed, however, cannot be replanted. You are forced to go back to the seed company, like Monsanto, to purchase additional seed. If you plant seed collected from a hybrid crop, the plants produced would bear only a slight resemblance to what grew previously. Hybrid seed is unnatural and should be scrupulously avoided.

GMOs, however, are exponentially more bizarre and environmentally damaging. Seed companies like Cargill, Syngenta and Monsanto, and their supporters, strenuously work to control the germ plasma and the hybridization process. In response to the widespread unleashing of GMOs into the ecosystem, the Gates Foundation has funded the collection of as many seed types as possible. The Foundation is storing them in a frozen Norwegian underground cave to maintain germplasm of all heirloom and open-pollinated varieties.

What are the differences between seed types? Seed Savers Exchange describes their organization as one that "aims to conserve and promote America's culturally diverse but endangered garden and food crop heritage for future generations by collecting, growing, and sharing heirloom seeds and plants." On their website, Seed Savers Exchange gives clear explanations of seed types:

- *Open-pollination* is when pollination occurs by insect, bird, wind, humans or other natural mechanisms.

  o Because there are no restrictions on the flow of pollen between individuals, open-pollinated plants are more genetically diverse. This can cause a greater amount of variation within plant populations, which allows plants to slowly adapt to local growing conditions and climate year-to-year. As long as pollen is not shared between different varieties within the same species, then the seed produced will remain true-to-type year after year.

- An *heirloom* variety is a plant variety that has a history of being passed down within a family or community, similar to the generational sharing of heirloom jewelry or furniture.

  o *An heirloom variety must be open-pollinated, but not all open-pollinated plants are heirlooms.* While some companies create heirloom labels based on dates (such as a variety that is more than 50 years old), Seed Savers Exchange identifies heirlooms by verifying and documenting the generational history of preserving and passing on the seed.

- *Hybridization* is a controlled method of pollination in which the pollen of two different species or varieties is crossed by human intervention.

  o Hybridization can occur naturally through random crosses, but commercially available hybridized seed, often labeled as F1, is deliberately created to breed a desired trait. The first generation of a hybridized plant cross also tends to grow better and produce higher yields than their parent varieties, due to a phenomenon called 'hybrid vigor.' *However, any seed produced by F1 plants is genetically unstable and cannot be saved for use in following years.* Not only will the plants not be true-to-type, but they will also be considerably less vigorous. Gardeners who use hybrid plant varieties must purchase new seed every year. Hybrid seeds can be stabilized, becoming open-pollinated varieties, by growing, selecting and saving the seed over many years.

Seed Savers does not define the most lethal and insidious type of seed. GMOs, genetically modified organisms, are living organisms whose genetic material has been artificially manipulated in a laboratory through genetic engineering. This creates combinations of plant, animal, bacteria and virus genes that do not occur in Nature or through traditional crossbreeding methods. The scientists seem to be saying, "<u>G</u>od <u>M</u>ove <u>O</u>ver. We can do this better than you."

Dr. Norman Borlaug won a Nobel Prize in 1970 for creating the so-called Green Revolution, utilizing hybrid seed. A review of diabetes, obesity and COPD, among other chronic illnesses facing the West, shows that they have proliferated since the widespread introduction of hybridization. We can track and correlate the increase in use of hybrid seed with the increase of these ailments. For tens of thousands of years, humans have eaten bread made from grain. Why is it that, in the past fifteen years, people have begun to require gluten free foods? Why are our bodies allergic to and rejecting the same food we have eaten for millennia? It is because hybrid and GMO foods are unnatural.

Foods produced from heirloom, open pollinated varieties of seed are best for our health. You will probably be surprised to learn that even food labeled organic may have originated from hybrid seed. To the extent possible, buy and consume food grown locally, from growers you know. Your life may depend upon it.

TLW growing practices emulate Nature. Why try to reinvent the wheel? God has provided all of this bounty and beauty for us. I think my work is to try to emulate Nature as much as possible. Outside of my window, there is a small forest of beautiful, old growth trees. There is no one doing soil tests, no one is putting fertilizer on the trees, there are no chemicals being applied to grow those trees. The trees grow leaves. The leaves drop down to the ground, break down and feed the soil. All the microorganisms in the soil create the web of health that's in the soil. All of these elements are interdependent and interconnected with one another and create those beautiful trees.

My mantra from the inception of TLW was "Compost, Compost, Compost!" Building the soil is the essence of my agricultural philosophy. Most of the farmers in metro Atlanta were not using compost when we started TLW, were not even thinking about it. We introduced the importance of feeding the soil. The local food community immediately gravitated to the concept. Now everybody is making and using compost. I'm pleased to say that many of the people who are involved in urban agriculture in Atlanta came through Truly Living Well at one time or another.

Atlanta is such a magnificent place. It is a giant forest, with houses dropped in the middle. We can grow all year round. It's really lovely. So, it makes it easy just to emulate what we see in Nature. That is what we do in the garden; that is how we grow food. Compost, compost, compost—that is still my mantra.

Commercial agriculture tries to dominate Nature, but that paradigm is broken. Commercial farmers dominate because they provide most of the food to feed the people. They're serving garbage, based on all the chemicals that are dumped on the food. Their goal is to produce food that's uniform in its color, uniform in its size, and that's not how Nature works. Big Ag companies aim to have tomatoes that all ripen at the same time and have harder skins, so they won't break on the way to the processing facility, or to the market.

Supermarkets and grocery stores want to have bananas that all ripen at the same time in the store. In Nature, a bunch of bananas starts to ripen as you pull them off and eat them; the next ones get riper and riper as you move down through the bunch, which stays on the tree. Avocados don't even begin to ripen until you take them off the tree. Many of these fruits are gassed, often with ethylene, to make them ripen at the same time.

Large-scale production, storage and transport of food involves techniques designed to make fruits, vegetables and meats conform to the industrial matrix that is here in front of us. It is much to the detriment of the food and the consumer. Much of the nutrition is gone out of your food, in order to create the conformity that works for large-scale commercial and industrial food companies. Fruits and vegetables are designed for harvesting by machines, with a minimum of damage to the plants and the fruits. That's *not* how Nature works. At TLW, we instituted just the opposite, growing food to make it as healthy and nutritious as we possibly could.

I can remember when Eugene and I first began selling our food, standing out in front of Goodwill in the West End of Atlanta. I'd invite people over to the truck to look at the produce. They would say, "Well, I don't want to buy anything."

I'd tell them, "I am not asking you to spend any money. I just want you to look at the food." The food sold itself. It looked good and tasted good.

Just give people a sample, and they say, "Oh wow! I haven't had a tomato like this in x-amount of time." All that cardboard-tasting steroid food that you get in the stores has no flavor to it at all. We don't have to sell the food. The food sells itself.

This is a lesson I learned from my experiences of the 60s: revolution is not blowing up buildings and killing people. That's rebellion. Revolution is creating institutions to replace that which is destroyed. What I am doing is creating institutions that can carry us into the next stage of civilization. Transitioning to the next stage is bumpy at times. Making it through the rough terrain requires endurance and adaptability. A whole lot of folks do not have survival skills. We're working to teach people, help people to obtain these much-needed skills for transformation.

Science and politics have been consistently present in my life. I've learned the science of agriculture, but I've also learned the science of politics. I also understand the dynamics that bring people together, as well as those that cause them to cleave, to stay apart from one another. We have to change the dynamics of human interaction that keep people apart and create disunity. The only way I know to bring about the change that I want to see is by what I do.

Initially, most of TLW's food was sold at the market we held each Wednesday behind the house on Washington Road. Waketa Marshall, Billy Mitchell and William Brown were consistent volunteers. I used to say, "It would not be Wednesday without William." The building was not yet used as an office. We were there rain or shine, snow or heat. We made tables to display our produce using doors supported by sawhorses, set underneath a large longleaf pine tree in the center of the yard. Whatever produce we harvested from our several sites was displayed in half-bushel peach baskets. Most CSA programs pack a box or bag for customers. We decided to let people choose what they wanted. I felt this would help minimize loss, because some people like broccoli, for example, and some don't. It would be a waste to give people food they would not eat.

Our CSA program was available 52 weeks a year, from the start. A full share 13-week subscription would feed a family of 4-6 people, or they could purchase a half share for 2-4 people. Each customer was allowed to take as much food as they needed to last him or her a week. We asked our people not to can or freeze our produce and, most of all, not to waste food. Only once did we have a problem with people taking too much produce. That was when three families wanted to share one subscription. We also had a handful of customers, like Drunetta Smith, to whom we delivered food every Friday. Sight unseen, Drue invested money with TLW and bought two full-share CSAs at the very beginning of our work. She trusted us so much; it was three years before she ever visited the farm. Because of her confidence in our work, Drunetta received food for ten years, even when she could not afford to pay for it.

Each customer was given a 4x6 index card indicating the type of subscription. The card had 13 stars printed, and a star was punched each time the customer came for a pickup. I had a cashbook in which I noted every transaction. I managed the business with this book. I wrote down the date of every CSA pick-up and the total cash sales each week.

Our collard greens, broccoli, tomatoes and okra were highly prized. We had special sales for holidays. I recall three or four occasions when the weather was so cold that water droplets on the collard leaves froze as I was washing them in preparation for the market. I was insistent that quality produce and customer service were paramount. Excellence in all our work brought its own rewards.

It was wonderful to feel community building under that tree. People would come to our market, not only to get food but also to establish camaraderie with others who supported our work. Our customers came from all walks of life. We had welfare mothers, lawyers, professors, educators and blue-collar workers, all joining each other in a common purpose: quality food! Conversation was wide-ranging, on all imaginable topics. They all knew the food they carried home from TLW was grown without the use of chemical fertilizers, pesticides or herbicides. Our customers knew who grew their food, where the food was grown and the quality of the food: horticultural literacy at its best.

Producing the food and getting it to market was very much a community effort. TLW benefitted from thousands of hours of work from volunteers, ranging from individuals doing community service, school groups on learning tours and regulars wanting to learn by helping. I took every opportunity to lecture and teach at any venue that would have me. During this period, I was appointed Artist in Residence at Woodward Academy, an elite private school in College Park, near our office site.

Financial resources were a problem throughout the history of Truly Living Well. I went to several banks and asked for money and was flatly turned down. They would ask what we wanted to do. We had a business plan to submit. Long ago, I learned that the purpose of the business plan was to show supporters that: 1) you are a student of your business; 2) you have thought through what you want to do and 3) the dollars make sense. Most often, if the front of the proposal is substantive in content, they will smell it, but generally just turn to the back and study the financials.

The next question I was asked is, who else is doing this work of urban agriculture? We were pioneers. Few others were engaged in the business. Since there was no precedent for our work, I was turned down on numerous occasions. I talked with banks and private investors. Twice I was told that we could get money if we wanted to open a Burger King or a McDonalds, but not for urban agriculture.

I soon made a determination that the limited liability company business model was not an appropriate vehicle to raise private investment capital. It was not going to work for Truly Living Well. There was insufficient knowledge about the value and worth of our enterprise. So, we established a 501c3 nonprofit to attract foundation and corporate funds. A nonprofit can also accept tax-deductible contributions from individuals.

It took 18 months for the Internal Revenue Service to approve our application in February 2009, but it was backdated to a June 2007 effective date. From that point forward, dialing for dollars and fundraising began to take up much more of my time. Acquiring nonprofit status also meant I had to find and recruit competent people to assist with the heavy lifting of building Truly Living Well.

Individual commitment to a group effort—that is what makes a team work, a company work, a society work, a civilization work.

Vince Lombardi

Chapter 22

Truly Living Well 2.0

My eldest son moved to Georgia in 2009. Kamal left a banking career in New York and chose to work unpaid with Truly Living Well for the next two and a half years. It was during his tenure that TLW evolved to the next level. We realized that the organization was actually an educational institute, predicated upon urban agricultural production as its base. We were teaching people how to grow food; we were reconnecting people back to the land. We were helping people understand more about their food, reacquainting them with their food in ways previously unimagined. Our real work was building community, with food production as the foundation of our work.

The work needed continuing financial support. Sevananda provided the very first grant that we received, $5000. Sevananda is the largest customer-owned food cooperative in Metro Atlanta. The Environmental Protection Agency gave us $10,000, and later, $75,000. I was so happy and proud that I unwittingly made a grave error, by announcing the amount of the awards in our newsletter. I immediately started getting phone calls and emails asking for jobs, gifts and contracts. For an individual, a gift of $75,000 is a lot of money. However, for a fledgling organization like TLW, the money was a drop in the bucket in relation to the work we had to do. From that point until his departure, Kamal assumed responsibility for financial development and successfully wrote a number of grants on behalf of TLW that proved critical to our growth.

I took advantage of every opportunity to speak at meetings and before groups. I taught at public libraries and to children at schools. We conducted classes and educational tours, primarily at our East Point location. A six-weekend series was the most thorough training we conducted, until we formed a partnership with Historic Westside Gardens and Fulton Atlanta Community Action Authority to implement a training grant. That collaboration enabled us to conduct a hands-on training program, five days a week for 10 consecutive weeks. Trainees were recruited from the Vine City/English Avenue neighborhoods. The first cohort was comprised of 10 students.

The success of the collaboration and the burgeoning interest in urban agriculture, agricultural education and farm-to-school programs led us to revise and upgrade our business plans. Americans were expressing concerns about the health risks of pesticides, hormones, antibiotics and other chemicals used in food production. Consumers also felt that small-scale family farms were more likely to care about food safety than large-scale industrial farms. It became important to people to know whether their food was grown or produced locally or regionally.

Trends in the tourist industry showed an increasing demand for experiential, hands-on tourism activities. As the U.S. population grows and continues to rapidly urbanize, consumers who travel increasingly favor experiences over traditional goods and services. They want more than just a trip or a hotel stay—they want a living, breathing experience. We wanted to provide people with that experience.

Agritourism was one of the fastest growing segments. This

segment focuses on travel that is low-impact and empowering to local communities, socially and economically. Parents wanted their children to know how food is grown and that milk actually comes from a cow—not a carton—and that peanuts do not grow on trees.

At this point, it became clear that TLW needed a larger venue to implement our plans. I used a shotgun approach, looking at every possibility shown to us, in attempting to find a new home for our work. After an exhaustive search, in 2009 Truly Living Well explored developing a farm on the site of the former Wheat Street Gardens Apartments.

For 52 years, the Reverend William Holmes Borders served as Pastor of Wheat Street Baptist Church in Atlanta. He campaigned for civil rights and distinguished himself as a leader and spokesman for the city›s poor, Black and dispossessed. Borders was instrumental in the hiring of Atlanta›s first Black police officers in the 1940s. He led the campaign to desegregate the city›s public transportation in the 1950s and established the nation›s first federally subsidized, church-operated rental housing project in the 1960s.

By the time we came along, Wheat Street Gardens apartment complex had come into significant disrepair. All the former tenants were dispersed far and wide. The Wheat Street Charitable Foundation technically owned the housing complex. Its demolition left an 11-acre open area in the middle of the Old Fourth Ward, near downtown Atlanta. As soon as I saw the site, I was determined to make it our premier location and demonstration farm, right in the shadows of the downtown skyscrapers.

Charles Whatley, of the Atlanta Development Authority, brought us to the table with the Wheat Street Charitable Foundation. He was waiting on Congressional re-approval of Empowerment Zone funding to finance the project. Whatley introduced us to a group that grew potted plants on several large farms in Florida that was also interested in the site. We visited their operation and had lengthy discussions about possible

261

collaboration. There were multiple problems with the potential deal. Foremost was that their operation was not organic. Second, and most important, the dollars in their proposal did not make sense. They essentially wanted TLW to provide labor for their endeavor. We turned it down.

During this time, we put together our own coalition, avidly interested in making the project a reality. This group included Atlanta City Councilman Kwanza Hall, GA Tech, the Georgia Department of Health and several large foundations. We realized it was incumbent upon us to raise private funds to launch the project, rather than continue waiting for action from the Atlanta Development Authority.

Our home site in East Point was a great meeting point for a wide cross section of Atlanta society. On market day, doctors, lawyers, civil servants, teachers, people of varied nationalities, young and old, began to meet, share stories and recipes and generally learn about people with whom they would not otherwise socialize. We believed the centrality of the Old Fourth Ward, the proximity of Wheat Street and Ebenezer Baptist Churches, the neighborhood's relatively stable population of older citizens and the existing Auburn Avenue/Wheat Street business districts would provide a complementary template for community-building. We wanted to demonstrate that urban farming could exist side-by-side with skyscrapers, community businesses and inner-city neighborhoods. The farm would enhance the health and lives of everyone who visited or lived nearby.

Forming a collaborative partnership with the Wheat Street Charitable Foundation was the essence of our pitch and negotiation. Project benefits for the collaboration included:

- Transforming an area affected by urban blight into a unique city amenity
- Job creation
- Educational opportunities and enhancement of community health
- Increased supply of quality food

- Positive environmental impact and significant waste disposal savings by using green waste for compost
- Increased traffic to support area businesses
- Development of a unique social/recreational gathering place
- Convenient, accessible market focused on local products and
- Participation in growing Atlanta's agro and experiential tourism industries.

The Wheat Street Charitable Foundation insisted that their charter was to develop new housing on the site. We had to convince them of the benefits that the farm would bring to the Foundation. Rather than having an open and empty 11-acre space, the creation of an urban farm would significantly improve the neighborhood. Leasing the land to TLW would increase cash flow for the Foundation and improve the property. The Wheat Street Garden Farm was an opportunity for the Foundation to leverage the social, educational, and environmental aspects of the project to support other programs. The farm would be a model for healthy, sustainable communities.

After almost a year of negotiation, we broke ground at Wheat Street on 5 December 2010, a very cold day in Atlanta. About 250 people attended the dedication. The Arthur M. Blank Foundation gave us a (literally) big check for $50,000 as part of the program. We had also received $100,000 from the Cox Foundation. This was our working capital.

The farm design was conceived one rainy night, while I stood alone on the site under a full moon. Demolition of the apartment complex had left concrete slabs that were the footprints of the old Wheat Street Garden housing complex. Rather than removing the slabs, I decided to install raised beds. By doing this, we were able to demonstrate the efficacy of raised bed growing, which allows greater control of the soil and weeds. It is also easier for seniors, because it requires less effort in bed preparation. We did remove one parking lot and had other land onsite designated for in-ground growing. Other design elements included a greenhouse, aquaponics, community garden space, a composting facility, a market and event pavilion and, of course, space for flower, herb, vegetable and fruit production.

Eugene Cooke returned from varying enterprises to again work with TLW as Farm Operations Director and was responsible for implementing the vision. A visual artist by training, Eugene's aesthetic added immeasurably to the overall design.

I always tell people the first thing they should do in creating and building a garden or farmscape is to plant fruit trees. Trees are easy to maintain and generate long-term income. By March of 2011, we had planted over 100 fruit trees at the Wheat Street Farm, including apples, pears, plums, peaches and persimmons. Blackberry and raspberry vines sprouted. Collard greens, mustard greens and broccoli were being harvested from the fields and sold at our new on-farm market. This gave us the opportunity to sell at our downtown location, in addition to the continued sales in East Point. We collected compostable materials from local markets, restaurants and coffee shops. Neighbors brought kitchen scraps to add to the ever-increasing compost pile. Community residents bought starter plants from the greenhouse, and we created a community garden for seniors. It was a good start.

Truly Living Well became the largest urban farm in the metropolitan area. The terms of our agreement with Wheat Street Charitable Foundation were quite steep. We paid about $50,000 per year in lease payments. No farmer in his right mind would pay what we agreed to pay. But I thought it would be a great investment in the future of urban agriculture in Atlanta. We could be an example of the efficacy of growing food in the city. We could be seen from the highway, in the shadow of the downtown skyscrapers. I loved being able to say that. More importantly, I knew that our success would benefit the entire local food movement. Truly Living Well demonstrated proof of concept for urban agriculture in Atlanta.

Although TLW was the largest urban farm in Metro Atlanta,

it was our education and outreach programs for youth and adults that distinguished us from other urban agricultural organizations in the area. My son, Kamal, wrote the Urban Oasis Beginner Farmer Training, Internship and Incubation Program for submission to the USDA, which was funded in 2011 at nearly $1 million, spread over three years. To this day, it remains the largest single grant ever received by TLW. He was assisted in drafting the proposal through collaboration with EcoVentures International, a Washington, D.C. based firm. The prototype for the program was the work we did in the ten-week program Kamal administered with Historic Westside Gardens in 2009.

The development and management of the Urban Oasis Program provided the framework for the expansion of a sustainable infrastructure that provided employment through the production of affordable, locally grown foods. The internship experience and Urban Oasis Incubation Program provided the hands-on learning, mentoring and business skills acquisition needed to launch successful urban farming enterprises.

Ras Kofi Kwayana was hired to be our master trainer. His background was teaching. He had a wonderful facility in relating to the students. There were twenty-five trainees in each 6-month cohort. They learned urban agriculture and technical business skills from a curriculum initially created by HABESHA, Inc. and further developed by TLW. Practical implementation of the classroom work took place on Truly Living Well sites in East Point and Southwest Atlanta. As part of their education, trainees received nutritional information and healthy lunches, made primarily from vegetables grown at the farm. Trainees gained hands-on experience in agricultural production, ultimately enabling them to plan and develop their own gardens.

In addition to an in-depth agricultural education, students learned the importance of planning, execution, business math, economics, budgeting, marketing, basic cost-benefit analysis, time management, plan presentation, negotiation and many other transferable skills. The students demonstrated their skills in a final project that involved writing a business plan for a plot of land, executing the plan and selling their products at market. The trainees also initiated personal and/or business plans, whether it was for starting a small garden market or preparing for the job of their choice.

Truly Living Well's long-term goals for the Urban Oasis Beginner Farmer Enterprise Training, Internship and Incubation program were to:

1. Increase economic prosperity for low-income communities through viable self-employment and employment opportunities in urban farming;
2. Increase access to and consumption of healthy, local food for all income levels in Metro Atlanta;
3. Implement a comprehensive beginning urban farmer training program and support network that results in increased production of healthy food without the use of petrochemicals;
4. Develop and use accessible business models and tools for beginner urban farmers; and
5. Increase food literacy, particularly awareness of how food and food choices impact health.

The first cohort of students from the Urban Growers Training Program graduated In October 2012. Eighty-one percent of the 31 graduates were subsequently employed, either as self-employed farmers or as employees of TLW and other farming or environmental organizations, including Atlanta Food & Farm, Captain Planet Foundation, East Lake Farmers Market, Global Growers Network and Southeastern Horticulture Society.

Aside from being one of the few professional agricultural training programs in the metro area, the Urban Growers Training Program was distinct, in that it offered students the opportunity to see the practical application of natural materials and farming techniques in a variety of urban settings. Another distinction was the curriculum's modular content, which made the program adaptable for different audiences. In this way, TLW was able to collaborate with community organizations serving a variety of constituents, including homeless veterans, juvenile offenders and high-school dropouts. Our collaborations provided tangible job skills training, as well as important life skills.

In 2011-2012, for example, TLW:

1. Trained a group of homeless individuals in how to create and maintain a large roof garden at the Peachtree and Pine shelter where they were living;
2. Worked with teens from Tri-Cities High School, Blackstone Academy Charter School and Benjamin E. Mays High School to introduce them to alternative careers in agriculture; and
3. Provided instruction and practical on-site farming experience to nearly a dozen teens identified by their counselors as being in danger of dropping out of school and losing their way in life.

Through these experiences, TLW has seen firsthand how working with the soil and learning valuable life skills can lift individuals' self-esteem, reconnect them with their community and set them on a positive path for the future.

TLW initiated its Growing Families Project in 2016. The W.K. Kellogg Foundation funded the project in the amount of $500,000 over 3 years. Growing Families used urban agriculture as a transformational tool to improve economic and health outcomes for women and children. Adults learned fundamental practices in urban agriculture through participation in a 12-week training program. The mothers spent four hours in an interactive classroom setting to learn the science and principles of natural agriculture, and eight hours in experiential learning at the TLW farm sites. Children learned age-appropriate gardening techniques to support family interaction in producing food.

Families learned to make better food choices that improved their health outcomes. A registered dietitian incorporated nutrition education and food prep training around plant-based diets into the curriculum for women and children. During the program, families received two additional servings of fresh produce a day, to promote healthy food consumption and address food insecurity.

Amakiasu Howze directed the Summer Camp. She is a remarkable educator, who has great empathy with children. Her genuine respect for children instills a sense of equality and confidence in their own capacities. Under Amakiasu's tutelage, the children were fully engaged in the learning process. Using elements of organic farming, environmental stewardship, health, wellness and self-discovery, Amakiasu created a transformative experience for children at the Wheat Street Gardens Summer Camp.

Campers demonstrated improved self-discipline, while engaging in critical thinking and team building. Fun activities reinforced their use of math, science and creativity. The children gained measurable health outcomes from the physical activity of gardening, swimming and creative movement, combined with eating healthy food and learning to make healthy food choices.

Food production became the platform or the plate upon which the programs were served. TLW became a plug-n-play organization. I could design a program for just about anybody around whatever his or her interests were and plug it into the new paradigm of urban agriculture. The menu included after-school programs, food coops, summer camps, the Urban Growers and Young Growers Programs, Boot Camps, agritourism and edutourism. Children attended farm trips with school groups and participated in farm activities. We shared the importance of agriculture from a very practical point of view with everyone we could reach. The gardens were a unifying force within the community. We grew food. We grew people. We grew community.

It was incredibly gratifying to look around and see that we were actually DOING THE WORK that had been at the heart of my earlier studies. I had absorbed the spirit and practice of men and women who built the post-colonial world. After studying the work of those revolutionaries, I had the opportunity to see many of the countries that had gained their independence and witness firsthand some of the successes and failures of both colonialism and independence.

We were engaged in building a nation. By growing people, we were helping people reach new dimensions. We were introducing people to a greater variety of fresh foods. Having fresh food, grown in the community, to put on people's tables, is a wonderful thing. The 360-degree process of urban agriculture improves nutrition and health, beautifies the community, raises the property values, creates green spaces that clean the air, provides a meeting place for people and creates jobs. Through growing food, people are learning new skills that are transferrable to other professions and other areas of their lives.

We had folk who loved coming out to the garden, just to see it and feel it. They talked about the peaceful energy of the garden space. In this society and in most societies, holidays are always associated with food. This is when people come together, and they come together around food. Halloween is primarily candy—they should forget that stuff. But Thanksgiving, Chanukah, Christmas, Kwanza, New Year's, Easter, Memorial Day and the Fourth of July—you name a holiday or any time when people come together—there is always food associated with the occasion. And I think that's important. It's tradition, it's history, and TLW positioned itself to play a part in maintaining those traditions. We provided a place for people to come together. At a minimum, one or two times a month, there were food-centered events at the farm.

Market day at the farm was Friday afternoon. I would set up chairs under a tree across the parking lot from the market pavilion. People knew I would be there and frequently would come over to talk with me. It was an opportunity to talk about urban agriculture and any other subject folks wanted to raise. It was a good way to introduce and welcome people to the urban ag community. The discussions covered the gamut of community issues, program problems and personal concerns. This was time

I set aside as community outreach, and I thoroughly enjoyed the engagement.

In 2005, a group of interested citizens and organizations began a dialogue to create a more sustainable food system for Metro Atlanta, resulting in the creation of the Atlanta Local Food Initiative (ALFI). Three women led the effort. Peggy Barlett is an Emory University Professor, and a very early proponent of environmental sustainability in academia. Barbara Petit was a local chef and a major food activist. She was President of Georgia Organics and the first Executive Director of the Atlanta Local Food Initiative. Alice Rolls was and is the Executive Director of Georgia Organics.

The Atlanta Local Food Initiative envisioned a transformed food system, in which every citizen of Atlanta would have access to safe, nutritious and affordable food, grown by a thriving network of sustainable farms and gardens. A greener Metro Atlanta that embraced a sustainable, local food system would enhance human health, promote environmental renewal, foster local economies and link rural and urban communities.

I began working with ALFI in late 2006. It was a very reachable group, yet I was the only Black person at the table. We decided to produce a manifesto on urban agriculture that expressed the collected wisdom of the group. One of the definitive lessons of that experience was the difficulty of attempting to have a group of 25-30 rotating people wordsmith a document. Finally, we appointed a steering committee to draft the 17-page document entitled, *A Plan for Atlanta's Sustainable Food Future*, that was edited by the entire group.

After two years of work, the manuscript was finally published in 2008. Although it took considerable time to produce, the plan was strong and has stood the test of time. The eight goals in the plan are well thought through. Truly Living Well has been instrumental in implementation of the goals through its own organizational commitments.

ALFI Goals

Supply

1. Increase sustainable farms, farmers and food production in Metro Atlanta.
2. Expand the number of community gardens.
3. Encourage backyard gardens, edible landscaping and urban orchards.

Consumption

1. Launch Farm-to-School programs (gardens, cafeteria food and curricula).
2. Promote consumers' cooking skills for simple dishes made from fresh, locally grown foods.
3. Develop local purchasing guidelines and incentives for governments, hospitals, and Atlanta institutions.

Access

1. Increase local, fresh food availability in underserved neighborhoods.
2. Increase and promote local food in grocery stores, farmers' markets, restaurants, and other food outlets.

The next phase in ALFI's work was to educate policy makers and community leaders to integrate the visioning and goals into sustainability plans and initiatives. One of our greatest successes was having the ALFI plan used as a guideline for the food component of Mayor Kasim Reed's sustainability initiative.

ALFI worked with the Emory Turner Environmental Law Clinic to draft and propose an urban agriculture ordinance for Atlanta. The Clinic provides important pro bono legal representation to individuals, community groups and nonprofit organizations that seek to protect and restore the natural environment for the benefit of the public. Through its work, the clinic offers Emory students an intense, hands-on introduction to environmental law and trains the next generation of environmental attorneys. Led by Mindy Goldstein, the Clinic drafted a potential urban agriculture ordinance for Atlanta.

The problem was that the City of Atlanta had no inner city zoning ordinances that addressed growing food. Technically, farming in the city was illegal. We live in a system that requires citizens to get permission to do just about everything. This allows the government to collect fees. Although unlikely, if your neighbor objected to bees pollinating the vegetable garden in your yard, the neighbor could call code enforcement and have them write you a ticket because gardens are not in the zoning ordinance. Absurd, I know!

The draft ordinance prepared by the Emory Turner Environmental Law Clinic was presented to ALFI at one of the monthly meetings. I strenuously objected to the process, because farmers had not been included or consulted in the course of drafting the legislation. At that time, a majority of the inner city farmers were Black. ALFI's membership was primarily White. Therefore, my objections were received and perceived as a racial issue. The discussion became quite heated, until Susan Pavlin, a tall White woman with blond hair and blue eyes, stood up and boldly declared: "Rashid is right. You cannot put together anything about farms and farming without including farmers in the process." I will forever respect her for that proclamation.

Subsequently the issues were resolved, farmer input was included, and the result was the most progressive zoning ordinance in the country at that time. Farming was permitted in every sector of the city, with the caveat that former industrial zones would require soil tests for toxins and pollutants before farming could commence. A similar community exercise helped resolve issues around location and rules for farmers' markets.

Georgia Organics also helped to make significant inroads in building Atlanta's local food economy. Georgia Organics is a statewide nonprofit that supports the efforts of organic and natural farmers and educates the public about organics and nutrition. Alice Rolls, one of ALFI's founders, is the Executive Director. I served on the Board of Directors of Georgia Organics from 2008-2014 and as chair from 2012-2013. My leadership marked a clear delineation in the organization's becoming more racially diverse and inclusive in its strategic direction and outreach. The Georgia Organics Annual Conference now has a very racially diverse mix of attendees, possibly more than any statewide sustainable agriculture conference in the country. I was proud to be honored for my work and leadership as the recipient of the Georgia Organics 2017 Land Stewardship Award.

In 2010, I started appearing on a radio program on the Atlanta-based independent community radio station - WRFG, Radio Free Georgia – that also affiliates with the national progressive Pacifica Network. Heather Gray is a researcher, journalist and producer of the "Just Peace" program on WRFG. Once a month, we explored virtually all aspects of agriculture and its history, with a focus on organic production. This included information about techniques and strategies for healthy gardening, without the use of chemicals, which destroy the soil and human health.

Beyond techniques for gardening, we also explored agriculture, politics and history from a worldwide cultural perspective. Along that line, we also discussed food politics and how food can be used to control people, and how the lack of food can and does lead to war. Our discussions included the efforts by US corporate interests to control food production, distribution and exchange, and the concerted efforts to suppress the historic independence of small farmers and their communities throughout the world.

On the monthly radio show, people called in and joined the conversation. They would ask insightful questions about gardening techniques, as well as food politics. 'Just Peace' and my monthly interviews continue to be inspirational for me. Program producers and listeners express they are also inspired by the topics covered in the interviews.

In the summer of 2011, I made one of the better decisions of my career. Truly Living Well had established proof of concept.

We had demonstrated that Atlanta could support an urban farm in the middle of the city. It had not been done before, and despite the critics and cynics, we had assembled the physical infrastructure and created an admiral showcase that many farmers and organizations emulated. The organization had grown. Truly Living Well had created 35 livable wage (seasonal and permanent) jobs in urban agriculture. In addition, entrepreneurs in our grower training program developed agri-businesses in the Atlanta area. We bought locally and circulated dollars within the metropolitan economy. It was time to consolidate and formalize our administrative infrastructure.

A mutual friend introduced me to Carol Hunter, suggesting she could help organize the administrative work that TLW required. I contracted with Carol for her to conduct an evaluation and suggest a course of action. She accomplished the study with great aplomb. After reading her report, I congratulated her on the good work and asked her to implement the content. That was a great decision.

Carol became the Chief Administrative Officer (CAO). She managed all activities associated with human resources. She supported fundraising efforts by writing proposals and led the grant writing team. She created the Personnel and Board Manuals. She kept minutes and records from all Board meetings. Carol headed up all of our educational efforts, both creating and managing programs. As the CAO, Carol interfaced with all stakeholders to promote and develop an environment of continual improvement in every aspect of TLW's products and services.

By 2012, we had made tremendous progress with implementing our business plan. It was time to present a vision for the future of Truly Living Well. I was suffering blank page writer's block trying to figure out what to put on paper. One day I was riding Amtrak's Surfliner from San Diego to Los Angeles, after having visited my sisters. On the train ride to L.A., I came to the realization that I did not need to come up with anything new. Rather than writing about what we were _**going**_ to do at

Truly Living Well, I realized the story to share is what we *were* doing. Thus, the title of a twenty-page document:

Doing the Work of Urban Agriculture

The Truly Living Well Center: A Model for Sustainable Local Food Systems

After six years of practical experience, we were able to codify and articulate what we were doing and achieving through our work. We envisioned ourselves as a national leader in natural urban agriculture. We demonstrated sustainable and economically viable solutions for helping people to eat and live better. We recognized that our work transformed both people and places.

The transformative power of the work that we did at Truly Living Well confirmed the potential of a renewed paradigm— the local food economy. Our mission was to grow better communities by connecting people with their food and the land through education, training and demonstration of economic success in natural urban agriculture. Much of the following text comes straight from the pages of *Doing the Work*, which aptly described what TLW was and is all about:

> Eating well is a right for all, not a privilege for the few. Sustainable local food systems establish perpetual cycles of productivity. They make healthy food accessible to all, enhance the natural environment and create employment. The TLW model of natural urban agriculture combines the economic vitality of city life with the benefits of being close to nature and creating communities that are truly living well.
>
> Truly Living Well thrives because we understand that natural urban agriculture is about more than growing food in small spaces. Connecting people with the land builds positive personal relationships and establishes an ethic of community and environmental stewardship.

Our guiding **principles** encourage vibrant and manageable growth:

- We emulate nature
- We educate
- We prioritize partners' interests and input

We keep our **values** central and simple:
- Superior quality
- Integrity and honesty
- Diversity and teamwork
- Creativity and imagination

A positive response from the community, fellow nonprofits, educational institutions, philanthropic organizations and others help to fuel the growth of Truly Living Well. Widespread support affirms our approach and guiding principles. The strength of this foundation assures progress toward the goals and objectives for the next three to five years.

Goal 1. Solidify our base to achieve economic self-sufficiency
Objectives:

A. Purchase and develop a 15 to 25-acre permanent home base and training facility for the Truly Living Well Center for Natural Urban Agriculture
B. Strengthen our human capacity to manage and support growth
C. Expand and diversify our revenue base
D. Create an effective method to measure and evaluate progress

Goal 2. Strengthen the social and political foundation for urban agriculture
Objectives:

A. Strengthen public, private and nonprofit alliances
B. Improve the regulatory and legal environment for urban agriculture
C. Increase resource availability for urban agriculture
D. Increase consumer awareness of the local food system

Goal 3. Increase access to natural, locally grown food
Objectives:

A. Expand Truly Living Well Center as a food hub Increase production, distribution and exchange of local food
B. Expand and diversify our revenue base
C. Educate and train a multitude of urban agricultural entrepreneurs
D. Increase urban agriculture-based employment
E. Sustain and expand community outreach services

Goal 4: Raise $5,000,000 in investment over the next three to five years to accomplish these goals:
Objectives:

A. Develop fundraising and capital campaign initiatives
B. Identify financial benefactors
C. Expand relations with foundations

We worked hard to achieve these goals. We expanded as opportunity arose, following nature's example of expansion only when and where growth is sustainable. Patience was essential! We started small and mastered one thing before beginning another. Although pushing boundaries, we understood that taking on too much at once would likely lead to being overwhelmed and unproductive.

Our Board of Directors took on these goals as part of our

strategic plans. Board development was the one area of our work that I found most difficult, and in which I was least successful. When we disbanded the LLC and incorporated the nonprofit, it meant that control and governance of TLW would be handed over to an "external" board of directors. I understood this reality. Throughout my tenure, I had the latitude to recruit and invite men and women to join the board that I thought would help our efforts. I was recruiting people to help run TLW, and these same people could potentially fire me. It was, however, necessary and important.

I was taught there are two types of boards, each requiring different skills and expertise. The first is a working board, whose members raise money, develop contacts for the organization and act as ambassadors to the community. The second type is a governing board. The governance role involves protecting the public interest, being a fiduciary, selecting the executive director and assessing his or her performance, ensuring compliance with legal and tax requirements and evaluating the organization's work. Nonprofit organizations are accountable to the donors, funders, volunteers, program recipients and the public.

Financing a nonprofit organization is the principal challenge of the CEO and the board, particularly one with a mission that people don't completely understand. I had personal financial challenges in building TLW, like the times I had no heat, water or electricity. I always had food, because I was growing it. Nothing is more dispiriting than cash flow issues that lead to missing payroll, which means being unable to pay employees for their hard work, done in good faith. There were times when missing payroll resulted from cash flow issues, such as the unpredictable timing of grant allocations.

I had Board members who quit because they thought it was unconscionable to not pay employees in a timely manner. I took a deep breath there, because I got very angry. As a Board member, their job was to help me raise money, so I would not have to face that situation. I thought it was unconscionable for a Board member to stand back and basically tell me to shut down the business because of cash flow issues. My answer was no. I was not going to shut down.

Nonprofit finances were a particularly great problem for urban agricultural organizations. I had to bring to people the understanding that all agriculture in this country, at every single level, is subsidized. People visit a farmer's market and think they are paying more out of pocket than they do at Kroger or Publix. The difference is that food at Publix has been subsidized. California is the richest agricultural region in the history of the world, and feeds not only other states, but other countries as well. Data from the USDA Economic Research Service show that California's plant-based agricultural exports grew from 16% to 20% of American agricultural exports between 2000 and 2017.

The history of California is the history of water. Have you ever seen the movie *China Town*? Fundamentally a true story, *China Town* is the history of California's water. It is water that has been paid for by the taxpayers of America. If those farmers had to pay for the water out of their own pockets, there never would have been any agriculture in California. Agriculture at every level is supported.

Education is the same way. It is subsidized and supported. There are no schools that can run on the tuition they charge. Many students pay their tuition with state and federal grants and loans. Post-secondary institutions seek grantors and donors. Professors write grants to support their research; they have to go out and get their own money. Alumni donate money to their alma maters. The very best schools in this country have the largest endowments, which they are able to draw upon to manage the institutions.

My work was both agriculture and education. We needed support. We were able to increase our earned income to 25-30% of total revenues. My goal was to get income earned from programs and sales up to 50-60%. The rest of the operating capital had to come from donations and grants to support our education and training programs.

The early TLW Boards were comprised of friends and

individuals who supported me. Not everyone understood the zeal with which I approached the work of urban agriculture. Over time, as folk saw the progress and success that we achieved, many became believers, and certainly champions. As we moved forward, the board participated in developing strategic plans that further reflected and detailed the goals and objectives. I was eventually able to recruit men and women, Black and White, rich and poor, who were committed to Truly Living Well. The following individuals sat on the TLW Board of Directors as of August 2018. All of these members enthusiastically and dutifully supported the mission, vision and goals of the organization. I am grateful to have had the opportunity to work with them.

CHAIRMAN: Mr. Chuck Meadows, JIM ADAMS FARMS
VICE CHAIRMAN: Mr. Quinton Watson, Urban Construction, LLC
SECRETARY: Ms. Allison Duncan, AIC PRINCIPAL Planner, Atlanta Regional Commission
TREASURER: Imam Plemon T. El-Amin, Imam Emeritus, Atlanta Masjid of Al-Islam

DIRECTORS:
Ms. Jessica Collett, MS, RD, LD, Professor, Georgia State University
Mr. Art Frazier, Director of Facilities Management & Services, Spelman College
Mr. James Harris, E.D., HJ Russell Center for Innovation and Entrepreneurship
Mr. Kevin Jackson, Principal & Managing Partner, KloudTools, LLC
Mr. Kelly Jordan, Founder, Point Center Corporation
Ms. Mary Reilly, President, RFP Fund
Mr. Scott Satterwhite, Managing Director, Artisan Partners
Mr. Charles Whatley, Managing Director, UrbanIS USA

Even after all this time
The Sun never says to the Earth,
'You owe me.'
Look what happens with a love like that.
It lights the whole sky.

Hafiz

Chapter 23

Truly Living Well 3.0

In the spring of 2015, I received a call from the Board President of the Wheat Street Charitable Foundation, inviting me to meet with her and the Board. Over the years, we often met to give updates, negotiate terms of engagement or to request amendments to our agreements. Carol Hunter, our Chief Administrative Officer, and Imam Plemon El-Amin, the TLW Board Treasurer, accompanied me. In addition to the usual Wheat Street representatives, two people attended the meeting, representing The Integral Group LLC.

Integral, founded by Egbert Perry, had a solid reputation for bringing innovative community, housing and infrastructure solutions to strengthen and revitalize urban communities. They developed Centennial Place, the nation's first holistic community revitalization project. Centennial integrated mixed-income rental housing and home ownership, including an early childhood development center, a K-12 STEAM public school, a family recreation center, and health & wellness YMCA, along with family support services.

The lease we had for Wheat Street Gardens was only for three years, and we also had the ability to renew the lease on an annual basis. In the spring of 2015, we had used the site for four and a half years. At the June meeting, we were told that the lease would not be renewed, and we were given one year to vacate the space. The Foundation Directors were ready to return to their original charter to build housing. The plan was for Integral Group to develop housing on the site. An urban farm was not part of that plan. Knowing how important the farm site was to Truly Living Well, the folk from Integral brought with them a plot map of a potential site to which TLW could move if it proved satisfactory. I was impressed and grateful that Integral and Wheat Street Charitable Foundation had taken steps to prevent a loss of the community benefits of urban agriculture and Truly Living Well.

I immediately sensed something special was about to happen. The site being offered was in the West End area of Southwest Atlanta, on the land where Harris Homes Apartments had previously stood. The projects had been torn down in preparation for the Olympics in 1996. On the Harris Homes site, Integral had developed a mixed-income neighborhood, similar to Centennial Place, called Collegetown, directly across Lowery Blvd from the Morehouse Stadium. At the far western edge of the site, there were approximately ten acres of land yet undeveloped, likely because of the topography. The Atlanta Housing Authority owned all of the land, and Integral maintained development rights.

When I went to view the property, I was exhilarated by the possibilities. Before us was an opportunity to own our own land, in the middle of the rapidly gentrifying Black community. They offered us three plus acres of flatland at the bottom of a hill, which we would initially lease, but eventually would own, at a very reasonable price. We negotiated a lease for another three-plus acres of hillside we that we could use but would not own. Complicating the transaction were the tripartite political machinations between Integral, the City of Atlanta and the Atlanta Housing Authority.

In September 2015, I wrote a letter to Trish O'Connell, Vice President of Real Estate Development for the Atlanta Housing Authority. In it, I said that TLW welcomed an opportunity to collaborate with Integral and the Atlanta Housing Authority to establish an urban farming oasis in Collegetown. TLW sought to establish a permanent base for its operations. We were interested in the 3-acre Collegetown property and would like to first obtain an access agreement and subsequently purchase the property, currently owned by the Atlanta Housing Authority.

We also requested a letter from Integral stating they agreed with our proposal and supported the project. Integral signed off on that portion of the deal. This letter of support was submitted to the Atlanta Housing Authority (AHA). It enabled TLW to continue the approval process with the AHA for the Collegetown Urban Agriculture Education and Training Center.

The Collegetown location was ideal for Truly Living Well. The area around the farm site is designated by the U.S. Department of Agriculture as a "food desert," meaning an area with limited or little access to fresh food. In addition, the area is within walking distance from the Atlanta Beltline and home to our core constituency and ideal partners, including:

- Atlanta University Center – Morehouse, Spelman and Clark
- Senior housing and services
- Mixed income housing
- Boys and Girls Club
- YMCA
- M. Agnes Jones Elementary School
- Atlanta Public Schools Instructional Center
- Multiple Churches

Loss of land access and land ownership is one of the major issues facing Black people in America. The amount of land owned and controlled by Black people has continued to decrease from its height of 18 million acres, reached in 1910. The problem in the inner city is heightened because landowners and developers are looking for the highest paying and best use of land. Urban agriculture is not considered the best use. TLW was presented with an historic opportunity, but the issue was how to finance the transaction.

By 2014, most of my time was engaged in fundraising—dialing for dollars. My to-do list on any given day was much the same as it was on any other day. Emails. Meetings. Phone calls. Where to find money to cover payroll! Those were the fields that I plowed.

I cultivated relationships through emails and meetings. I would travel up and down the rows of emails, turn them over, test the quality of the soil, examine them for telltale signs of life: earthworms, roly-polies, lizards. I inhaled the aromas, hoping for the full, rich fragrance of nutritious humus, food for my crops. I would toss out hundreds of communications that amounted to chemical additives—pesticides, herbicides and fertilizers—before I chanced upon the rare real deal. Good quality, natural, soil-enriching compost was exceptionally hard to find in my mailbox. Meetings were the same: the perpetual probe for the right combination of ideas, words and people that would propel us beyond the day-to-day search for sustenance.

I asked myself, if I'm a farmer, why do I feel so much like a hunter-gatherer? Isn't agriculture supposed to make food provision easier? It shouldn't be this hard to find money to feed people. Everybody eats. Many folks want to help poor folks eat, and they do so. My perpetual task was to find those folks with whom I could create synergy among the emails and meetings.

A typical work day would go something like this: After breakfast (which, by the way, does not originate on our farm), I'm off to one of our sites. A visit to the fields is redemptive. The plants grow on, dependably oblivious to the politics that surrounds their existence. Similarly, a delightful gaggle of children is dismounting from a yellow school bus as I approach. Eager to escape the firm reins of their keepers, the children are ready to mingle their innocence with that of the plants and flowers in the field.

They dutifully make their best imitation of a straight line and march up to the person who greets them, to begin their tour. All bets are off. Some form a circular swarm around her, while a few go off on self-guided adventures—touching, smelling, running back to ask burning questions about what they have experienced. They deliver smiles all around, to the crew, to the neighbor visiting the farm for the first time after a friend shared some of our greens with him. And they pay me a visit. Their excitement reminds me of why I do this work.

The children, the plants, the neighbors...I'm inspired just to see the looks on the children's faces when they ask their questions or taste some of the food. Some of them say, "Well, I don't eat vegetables," but then when they taste food freshly plucked from the vine, they say, "Whoa! That's good!" And even when they say they don't eat a particular thing, they still don't hesitate to try. Children give their curiosity full reign. We adults can learn so much from the children. When I see young people learning and know they are growing from the experiences on the farm—I know how right and necessary all this work really is.

In 2014, John Bare of the Blank Foundation introduced me to Ann Curry, Dan Priester and Lindsay Caldwell of Coxe Curry & Associates. Coxe Curry provides professional counsel to help greater Atlanta nonprofit organizations attract resources, accomplish their missions and serve the community. They have participated in many of the major fundraising efforts in greater Atlanta.

Truly Living Well began its work with Coxe Curry in February of 2014. With support from the Arthur M. Blank Family Foundation, TLW engaged the firm to provide strategic guidance and assistance with growing our base of funding from the philanthropic community. The financial model that we used combined earned revenue—from market, restaurant and community supported agriculture (CSA) sales—with philanthropic contributions.

Over a period of five months, Coxe Curry developed a case for support that properly told the story of Truly Living Well. The case statement provided an historical overview of the organization. It explained to the philanthropic community the work being done by TLW and how we served as a valuable resource in the food movement. It went on to describe how we played a key role in urban agriculture in the City of Atlanta. The documents confirmed TLW's need for a greater level of support from a broader network of donors to effectively and successfully continue these critical efforts.

Coxe Curry recognized that TLW's priority funding needs were to provide for the day-to-day operations of the organization. They conducted research to identify potential institutional and individual donors who might be interested in and willing to support the work. Additionally, as part of the engagement, Coxe Curry worked with us to enhance the strength and capacity of our Board of Directors. They helped identify potential members and established a plan for their recruitment. TLW leadership was provided with a plan that guided the organization's efforts to establish and maintain ongoing relationships with prospective donors. In addition, Coxe Curry offered strategies that aided in successfully securing funding from the donors that we approached. I received an advanced degree in how to raise money. The primary lesson was to continually, incessantly knock on doors.

In October 2015, we returned to Coxe Curry & Associates for a subsequent engagement to support urgent organizational needs. From October 2015 through October 2016, Coxe Curry worked with Truly Living Well to provide advice and guide our strategy for the $2 million "Growing into the Future" campaign. This campaign was intended to raise funds for the transition to a new home and provide for operational infrastructure at the Collegetown site.

Over the course of 12 months, Coxe Curry helped us develop a compelling case for support that articulated the campaign purpose, strategic plan and immediate, as well as future, philanthropic investment funding needs. Interest from the philanthropic community was assessed through key conversations with high-potential institutional donors. We developed a plan for the launch of the campaign.

Coxe Curry guided our leadership team through strategic conversations with valued partners and potential early supporters of the effort. Once the campaign was underway, Coxe Curry offered ongoing input on the campaign plan. They facilitated discussions with key funders and assisted with crafting requests for financial support. At the end of this engagement, nearly $500,000 had been raised towards the $2 million goal.

Over the years, Truly Living Well raised over $6,000,000 from revenue generation, philanthropic investment and grants. Many individuals and organizations supported us. Some of our major donors included:

Chick Fil-A Foundation	MailChimp
Community Foundation of Greater Atlanta	Target Foundation
Clorox Foundation	Wells Fargo
Home Depot Foundation	William Josef Foundation
W. F. Kellogg Foundation	Glenn Family Foundation
PNC Bank	The Rich Foundation
Food Well Alliance	Kendeda Fund
Robert Curry	Scott Satterwhite
Whole Foods	RFP Fund

Our partnerships with local food movement organizations, government entities and educational institutions moved our work forward exponentially. Our partners included:

Atlanta Housing Authority

Atlanta Public Schools – M. Agnes
Jones Elementary

Boys and Girls Club of Metro Atlanta

Certified Naturally Grown

City of Atlanta, Mayor's Office

Corporation for National and
Community Service

Georgia Institute of Technology

Georgia Micro Enterprise Network

Georgia Organics

Grady Health Systems

Hands On Atlanta

Morehouse School of Medicine
Atlanta University Center

Urban Oasis/Atlanta Community
Food Bank

YO Boulevard! Initiative

Wholesome Wave Georgia

Raising money became a way of life—as much a part of nonprofit urban farming as planting and teaching. I was often asked, "When are you going to start making a profit?" I have to repeat the important historical lesson, that education and agriculture have always been and still are, heavily subsidized. And I am smack-dab in the middle of both.

Our role is to prepare entrepreneurs, who can then go out and create profit-making enterprises. I see urban agriculture as a middle-income profession. The focus is on enriching whole communities, not creating run-away profits for individual people or companies. However, we never know when the next social innovator(s) will come along, who will envision an economic organization capable of building significant wealth for both communities and individuals.

In full expectation that these innovators will emerge, I regularly dialogue with politicians, churches and philanthropists to supplement the agricultural education of hundreds of future entrepreneurs. In addition to the future business people, there are the future backyard gardeners, whose collective contributions to urban ecosystems are invaluable.

The Food Well Alliance, chaired by Bill Bolling, is an important community organization that is an outgrowth of the collective work done around the mission of urban agriculture in

Atlanta. It is a collaborative network of local leaders working to build thriving farms and gardens that enhance the health, vitality and resilience of communities across Metro Atlanta. One of its significant contributions is their 2017 Baseline Report, that quantified the size and impact of the local food economy. The report outlined an incredible amount of growth and participation.

- 52 urban farms
- 300 community gardens
- 110 locally produced food products
- 5 commercial shared kitchens
- 2 locally-sourced food hubs
- 63 farmers' markets
- 40 food hubs launched
- 524 farm-to-school programs
- 4 locally owned food waste recovery companies

These are some of the critical local food system assets Metro Atlanta has today. With projected urban population growth and the advantages of our environmental and economic climate, we have the need and opportunity to expand our local food system. When TLW began its work in 2006, there were very few farms in the metro area. It was difficult to locate a farmer's market. Now you can find a market any day of the week.

Truthfully, I've met some really great people at networking sessions. Am I still schmoozing? Probably. It *is* a way of life, as I said. Nothing would delight me more than for a great philanthropist to read this book and decide to invest in America's sustainable future. As a social enterprise with a high and wide-ranging return on investment, urban agricultural ventures are some of the best places to put your money: where your nutritious food, beautiful, safe spaces and breathable air are to be found.

There's another level of schmoozing or networking that is just as important, if not more so. It is among regular folk. It is their aggregate investment (spending) that keeps endowment interest accounts growing, that keeps the American economy the largest in the world and that keeps business humming globally. These are my toughest investment analysts.

Regular folk are looking for results. They're looking for reliability and responsible leadership. They're looking for differences in health outcomes and prospects for their children's futures. And they're looking for great-tasting food. They are my bosses, the people that I serve. With this set, you come right or not at all. All-in: body, mind, soul and pocketbook.

What I would come to miss the most about my daily work with Truly Living Well is getting to talk with people every week, at our Farmer's Market, with tour groups, and random visitors to the garden. Then there are the volunteers who pull weeds and shovel compost; the self-appointed publicists who take it upon themselves to spread the word about our work; and the CSA members who faithfully purchase their baskets and come regularly to have them filled.

It's also the incredible staff, who worked through times when we did not make payroll, because they share the vision, they see the future and they make the sacrifice. In no uncertain terms, these folks kept me going, they keep urban agriculture going and they keep our collective evolution going. They let me know that, together, we can become a truly inclusive, ethical and environmentally balanced society.

The Truly Living Well Center for Natural Urban Agriculture Collegetown Farm and Education Center is the largest urban ag site in Metro Atlanta. It was designed to be a premier urban agriculture destination. We wanted to recreate TLW's natural and organic demonstration farm site and create an aesthetic, biodiverse environment that would serve as a model of urban agriculture. TLW 3.0 @ Collegetown made a commitment to the following developments:

Community Engagement

- Spaces for children's learning garden, a veteran's garden and community garden for local residents

- Children's summer camp program on site
- Internship and other urban agricultural education opportunities
- Capacity for local residents to use food stamps to purchase produce
- STEM related educational programming in the garden for local children, offered through local elementary, middle and high schools
- Tours and volunteerism, engaging an anticipated 4000 people
- ADA accessible pathways throughout the garden

Farm Operations

- Utilize organic and permaculture farming methods that do not use any synthetic pesticides, herbicides or GMOs onsite.
- Meet Certified Naturally Grown and USDA Certified Organic standards.
- Utilize 4x36 foot raised beds in the flat bottom area of the farm.
- Tap into city utility and water lines and utilize water conservation (rainwater collection) to support irrigation and water needs.
- Run below-ground irrigation lines throughout the property.
- Construct a small chicken coop to house up to 25 chickens.
- Erect poly or glass greenhouses or hoop-houses onsite, including an aquaponics facility.
- Create compost with natural waste materials.
- Grow vine crops and fruit tree orchards in-ground on the sloped portion of the properties.
- Plant perennials for aesthetic purposes.
- Establish beehives on the property.

Education Center/Pavilions

- Education center and open-air pavilions to be installed,

as a community gathering space and headquarters for tours, volunteers, farm operations, and administrative functions

- Roofs of the pavilions may include solar power

We had attained control of the land. We had a design plan for the site. Now began the arduous task of actually moving the Wheat Street Farm to the new location. We had built and fed the soil at Wheat Street for five and a half years. I had been teaching the importance of soil building all my adult life. There was no way I was going to leave this soil to be bulldozed by potential new construction at the old site.

What we proposed to do was unprecedented. Many people have built farms, but very few have moved a farm the size of TLW. We obtained a grant that allowed me to hire Frank Burdette to assist with the logistics of making the move. Frank inventoried and tagged each and every one of the 125 fruit trees we chose to move. Each of these trees was dug up and moved one at a time and transported 3½ miles from the old site to be replanted at the new site.

We dismantled approximately 100 raised beds at Wheat Street, each measuring 4x24 feet, and loaded this quality soil onto dump trucks that we then took to the new farm in the West End. Our compost operation had about 250 tons of finished compost, which we transported to the new site. There were two large fields at Wheat Street where we planted crops in-ground. We scraped those fields and removed the topsoil.

One day I was sitting under a tree at Collegetown and caught myself saying: "Whoever came up with the idea to move all this dirt and trees was stark raving mad." I resemble that remark!!

It took over a year, from the summer of 2016 until the fall of 2017, to get the major portions of the infrastructure built at Collegetown. It cost $750,000 to make the move. Very little of the money I raised was specifically designated for the move. Part of my considerable stress was due to the continual need to obtain general operating funds and meet payroll. At the end of each year, TLW generally broke even or achieved a small profit. The problem was always cash flow, receiving the money in a timely manner.

By the end of 2017, I was tired—and I guess I deserved to be tired. I knew it was time to turn over leadership of TLW to somebody else, someone much younger, with more energy. It was time for me to sit back and start recounting and reflecting on the paths that I have crossed in my life. I wrote a letter to the Board of Directors announcing my resignation.

10 January 2018

To the Board of Directors:

Today, I am happy to announce my advancement to another level of service to Truly Living Well. I will step into the role of Elder and Advisor to the organization, helping to select and mentor the Board's next appointee to the position of Chief Executive Officer.

On my 70th birthday, August 31, 2018, I will pass the torch to another generation of leadership to manage daily operations.

For more than a decade, Truly Living Well has stood as a center for urban agricultural education. Dedicated Board members, staff, volunteers, partners and funders have joined forces to make an impressive impact on urban agriculture. From a foundation of intensive food production, we have created jobs, entrepreneurial opportunities and connections with our food and the land. We are feeding hundreds of families, we have pioneered the urban agricultural movement in Atlanta, and we have inspired a new generation of environmental stewards. And there is much more work to be done.

Thank you for your contributions to this work over the years. I ask that you offer the new leadership even more of your wisdom and talents, as Truly Living Well opens new vistas of innovation, food security and healthy communities.

Thank you for your time and consideration.

Sincerely,

K. Rashid Nuri

My resignation energized the Board. They became quite active implementing a succession plan. Several sub-committees were formed. We officially began to solicit candidates to apply for the position of Executive Director/CEO of Truly Living Well. Twenty-six applications were received. Several rounds of interviews were conducted. An executive recruiting firm donated an assessment test, which we administered to the final four candidates. After this exhaustive process, Carol Hunter was appointed my successor and assumed the role of Executive Director on 1 August 2018. Carol had worked with me for seven years. This made the transition easy, because Carol played a major role in creating the organization that Truly Living Well had become.

My last day was 31 August 2018. The community gave me a wonderful sendoff. At least 350 people attended the Rashid Nuri Day Celebration. I received a proclamation from the Atlanta City Council for my work and testimonials from many distinguished leaders in the urban agricultural community. My siblings, nephews, children, grandchildren, friends, colleagues and many well-wishers were all in attendance. It was a grand affair.

Working in agriculture has brought me close to nature. And it is by looking at nature and understanding how great God is that I have been able to improve myself as a human being. From the beginning of my life to the end of my days, I would like my epigraph to read, "he lived a good life; he made a contribution."

My work does not define me as a person. It is my person, my values, and my character that define my work. The distinction is important to make. My person is defined by the spiritual values that I have been able to attain and the spiritual understandings that I have acquired through the course of my travels.

My work all of these years has been God-inspired, stemming from the "burning bush" experience I had as a young man. The question I had to ask was: is my assignment complete? Have I done what was I instructed to do? I am satisfied that I have done my job. The moment at hand is the proper time to accept new work at another level. To paraphrase Hunter S. Thompson:

"My life has not been a journey to the grave with the intention of arriving safely in a pretty and well-preserved body, but rather to skid in broadside in a cloud of smoke, thoroughly used up, totally worn out, and loudly proclaiming: "Wow! What a Ride!"

I am at peace!

52373766R00176

Made in the USA
Middletown, DE
10 July 2019